Exploring British Cities

D1151510

To my mother, Margaret Masterman-Braithwaite.

Exploring British Cities

Lewis Braithwaite

A & C Black · London

First published 1986
A & C Black (Publishers) Ltd
35 Bedford Row, London WC1R 4JH

ISBN 0–7136–2748–4

British Library Cataloguing in Publication Data

Braithwaite, Lewis
  Exploring British cities.
  1. Cities and towns—Great Britain—
  Guide-books   2. Great Britain—
  Description and travel—1971- —
  Guide-books
  I. Title
  914.1′04858   DA650

  ISBN 0–7136–2748–4

Printed in Great Britain
by Butler & Tanner Ltd
Frome and London

Contents

Ordnance Survey 1" and 6" maps are reproduced by kind permission of the Syndics of the Cambridge University Library and with the help of the Library's Map Room and Photography Department.

The drawing on page 118 is by John M. Harrison for the cover of *Liverpool Conservation Areas* and is reproduced by kind permission of the Liverpool City Planning Officer; the drawing 'in antis' on page 17 is by Zette Braithwaite.

Introduction

This book is an attempt to guide readers to the historic buildings, Conservation Areas and best townscape of British cities, using Victorian Ordnance Survey maps (mainly first edition 6″, published between 1848 and 1890) which show the historic street patterns on which the cities developed and which can be compared with what exists now.

The word city is used in the modern sense, meaning the largest and most important towns in the country, rather than the older British legal sense of a town which is the seat of a bishop. (This definition will be discussed later.) Many 'cities' in that older sense were described in *The Historic Towns of Britain* (A & C Black 1981), to which this is a companion. The cities described here range in size from Glasgow and Birmingham, both with populations once exceeding a million but now rather less, through major provincial centres such as Manchester and Bristol, and the capital cities of Edinburgh and Cardiff, to the 'cathedral cities' of York and Norwich, the university cities of Oxford and Cambridge, and down to Georgian Bath with a 1981 population of only 80,000.

Other guides, and particularly the *Blue Guides*, cover cathedrals, churches, museums and castles, so these aspects are not dealt with here. This is the only one-volume guide which takes one round the best streets and buildings – usually Victorian, like the maps. It is particularly necessary to be guided to the best parts, since large areas of all these city centres were devastated both in the war and even more in the redevelopment boom of the 1960s and early 1970s, and should be avoided.

To attempt a general book about British Cities, all of which deserve, and in fact almost all of which now have, their own complete architectural guide full of photographs and plans, is obviously to try to get a gallon into a pint pot. But I feel it is still worth extending the approach of *Historic Towns* to the historic areas of the big cities – to try to counter the anti-urban prejudices of the Anglo-Saxon and to show that, despite their image and local postcards of the nastiest modern developments, there are good things to be found in Birmingham – yes, Birmingham – and in Manchester.

The definitions of a city The earlier legal definition of a city is an incorporated town that is or has been (before approximately 1834) the seat of a bishop. Most of these cities are today small towns. The only towns which in 1834 were called 'city' by 'prescriptive right' and are today big towns – in other words which are cities by both definitions – are, in England, London (a city both through its bishopric and by virtue of being the capital), Bristol and Coventry; and in Scotland, Edinburgh and Glasgow.

In Scotland, Edinburgh had no medieval bishop but was a city because it was the capital; Glasgow has the best medieval cathedral in Scotland; and the term 'city' which applied originally to Old Aberdeen with its medieval cathedral became mysteriously applied also to New Aberdeen in the eighteenth century, though the two were not merged until 1891.

Because the title of 'city' was a coveted badge of status, the up-and-coming manufacturing and industrial towns, after acquiring municipal status and local government corporations ('incorporation') for the first time in the late 1830s, then strove to acquire the title of 'city' by Royal Charter whether they had cathedrals or not, and succeeded roughly in the order of their then population size and importance; and they have continued to do so right up to the present day.

Manchester, incorporated in 1838, acquired a bishopric in 1847 and city status in 1853; Liverpool, a bishopric and city status together in 1880; Newcastle-upon-Tyne jumped the gun by getting both in 1882, as did the much smaller town of Wakefield in 1888, helped by being the county town of Yorkshire West Riding. Towns then started acquiring city status without getting (or having had) bishoprics: Birmingham and Dundee in 1889; Leeds and Sheffield in 1893; Bradford, Kingston-upon-Hull and Nottingham in 1897.

Then we come into the twentieth century with Cardiff (1905), Leicester (1919), Stoke-on-Trent (1925), Portsmouth and Salford (1926), Plymouth (1928), Lancaster (1937 – a coronation gesture by King George VI because he was Duke of Lancaster), Cambridge (1951), Southampton (1964), the City of Westminster (1965), Swansea (1969), and most recently Derby in 1977.

A hierarchy of British cities Modern population figures give a misleading picture of the order of size and importance among the cities, because some are the centre of continuous conurbations and some have adjacent 'dormitory' local authorities. The official census figures represent only the central authority.

As a rough guide here is my personal 'hierarchy':

Category	Cities in order of size
1,000,000	Glasgow, Birmingham
750,000	Manchester (inc. Salford), Liverpool
500,000	Leeds, Sheffield, Edinburgh, Bristol
300,000	Cardiff, Newcastle-upon-Tyne, Bradford, Nottingham, Kingston-upon-Hull, Coventry, Leicester
250,000	Brighton & Hove, Plymouth
200,000	Portsmouth, Southampton, Dundee, Aberdeen, Derby, Swansea
100,000+	Birkenhead (linked with Liverpool), Salford (linked with Manchester)
100,000	Norwich, Bath, Oxford, Cambridge, York
60,000	Wakefield

The choice of cities included in this book As is shown by the examples of Lancaster, Wakefield and Cambridge (which only got city status because Oxford already had it) it is somewhat arbitrary whether British towns in the middle range have acquired city status or not. So I do include several towns, technically not 'cities', that would be called 'cities' anywhere else – the thoroughly metropolitan 'London-by-the-Sea' of Brighton and Hove, a quarter of a million in population, and Birkenhead, which I've treated together with Liverpool. There is not enough space for certain large British towns with city functions that *feel* like cities to me, and which I had originally hoped to include: Sunderland, Middlesbrough (included by Asa Briggs in *Victorian Cities*), Huddersfield, Halifax with its amazing eighteenth-century Piece Hall, Preston with its Georgian quarter and Roman Catholic churches, and Wolverhampton; nor, in Scotland, Greenock and Paisley. And had space permitted I should have liked to pick up some 'large historic towns' not in my previous book – Northampton, Reading, Ipswich and Cheltenham.

I do cover all the cities so far mentioned except Lancaster (covered in *Historic Towns*), London and Westminster (which are too vast an undertaking and need their own volume) and Stoke-on-Trent, which has no overall coherence or urban focus. Of the 'Five Towns' (really six) with a 1981 population of a quarter of a million, Hanley is the shopping centre, Burslem the only town centre of any architectural merit, and Stoke itself has really only the railway station with a fine 1847 Jacobean-style forecourt.

The idea of the city Whatever its legal and administrative definition in this country, the idea of a city, said Asa Briggs in *Victorian Cities* (1963):

> had deeper and more universal undertones. It was enriched by
> the knowledge that there had been great cities in the past and the

belief that there could be even greater cities in the future.... Religion and history came into the picture at many points. The King James Bible spoke usually of 'cities' not of 'towns'. It could be used to point to the need both for civic obligations and social reform. The experience of both the Greek *polis* and the Renaissance city-state was held up for study and emulation.

I personally hope that after a disastrous suburban anti-urban reaction, with the inanities of the New Towns movement, this late Victorian attitude will prevail again a century later – that we can learn to live in and enjoy living in our big cities, can restore and preserve the best of the old and create new housing schemes on a human scale – facing perhaps one of my beloved urban canals, learning perhaps to lessen our dependence on the motor car but to use instead a much improved public city transport system and inter-city rail services – in a world that, despite occasional gluts of oil, still has an energy crisis.

This book does not describe the famous personalities who formed the 'civic gospel' that often accompanied the growth of the great Victorian cities; but this growth found physical expression in a number of fine public buildings that are a major part of their architectural character. Foremost was the vigorous competition to build bigger and better town halls. Sometimes these are public halls, sometimes municipal offices. Birmingham started off the town hall competition with its Roman temple in the 1830s, stimulating the greatest of them all, at Leeds in the 1850s. Both of these were public halls, as were also the St George's Halls in Liverpool and Bradford. The later Victorian Town Halls at Manchester and Sheffield (and City Chambers in Glasgow) were built to house the mayors and local government staff, as also were the 1870s Council House in Birmingham and Municipal Buildings in Leeds.

New buildings were required as the cities acquired new functions. In Birmingham, for example, the fine Ruskinian Gothic School Board Office built in 1876 in Edmund Street (after the Education Act of 1872) was designed by the architect J. H. Chamberlain who went on, with his partner William Martin, to build fine Gothic 'Board Schools' all over the city, and also the superb nearby 1880s College of Arts and Crafts. At the end of Joseph Chamberlain's new Corporation Street (Joseph was no relation to J. H.), which was modelled on Haussmann's Paris boulevards, though unfortunately with no trees, are Aston Webb's lavish redbrick and terracotta 1887-91 Victoria Law Courts, 'the granting of an assize to the town being dependent on the provision of suitable courts' (Pevsner).

The greatest change came when these cities were given all the functions of a county. The English and Welsh ones were made 'County Boroughs' in 1888 (Oxford 1890), Plymouth and Devonport being made separately; and the Scottish ones a 'County of a City' in 1894 (Aberdeen 1900). But Wakefield was only made a County Borough in 1915 and Cambridge and Hove were never made County Boroughs at all.

The 'civic gospel', whereby cities wished to expand their powers and responsibilities and obtain County Borough status, was less important to those cities which had already been important as medieval towns. They tended to regard these newcomers as upstarts. Long before 1888, the most important medieval towns had freed themselves from county control by acquiring, in their charters from the king, the ultimate status of being 'counties corporate', with the power to appoint sheriffs of their own. London acquired this status in the 1190s; Bristol in 1373, followed by York in 1396, Newcastle-upon-Tyne in 1400, Norwich 1404, Lincoln (not in this book) 1409, Kingston-upon-Hull 1440, Southampton 1447, Nottingham 1449. Coventry acquired it in 1451, lost it to Warwickshire in 1842, and in a sense got it back again when it became a County Borough in 1888.

These medieval towns also displayed their importance by having stone townwalls, as had also Bath, Leicester, Oxford, Sutton (the original nucleus of Plymouth), Cardiff and Swansea; but Derby, a Danish stronghold, was not refortified after the Norman Conquest, and Cambridge only had an earthwork to the East as a defence, besides its river. Edinburgh had its own sheriffs after 1482, but only flung up its hasty 'Flodden Wall' in 1513. Scottish towns tended to be less defended: Glasgow, Dundee and Aberdeen relied on the combination of a continuous street frontage with gates.

The Victorian Ordnance Survey maps For the cities that have a medieval core, the Victorian maps have an intrinsic interest as historical evidence, as explained in more detail in *Historic Towns*. One can find in them elements of their Saxon and medieval plans, such as market places (often 'infilled' later), the line of the walls and/or gates even where no physical remains of either survive, and the characteristic long thin 'burgage plots' (again often later 'infilled' with insalubrious industrial 'courts'), which can be most clearly seen in the medieval core of Wakefield and the original seventeenth-century nucleus of Leeds.

It might be thought that, even allowing for all the nineteenth- and twentieth-century pressures of growth and redevelopment in all British cities, those with a well-defined line of walls would have kept their street pattern and historic buildings preserved as an 'Old

Town', as has happened on the Continent, with modern shops and offices sited extramurally near the railway station. Surprisingly this is not what happened, even in the cathedral cities of Norwich and York which have large areas completely redeveloped within their walls. Whereas when I used the First Edition Victorian 6″ maps in *Historic Towns*, they were basically usable as plans of the towns today, this is not true for the cities in this book. Their centres have undergone considerable changes since the Victorian maps, from additional railways and road 'improvements' in late Victorian times to the Inner Ring Roads and new shopping centres of the second half of the twentieth century.

Nonetheless the First Edition 6″ maps are of such outstanding visual quality and historical interest to study at home that they are still used in this book. There are still extensive historic areas, where the maps do show what can be seen today, and where the reader can imagine himself or herself as an ant walking round the map and experiencing the varied spaces between the frontages that are the essence of good 'townscape', and which are rarely experienced in post-war developments. Parts of the maps not picked out or given numbers are almost certainly changed out of all recognition now; and throughout, the reader should note carefully the *dates* of the maps and the dates of the buildings and streets referred to in the text, as many good buildings and streets are later than the maps and the text does not always indicate this. Historic buildings also frequently change their uses and the text often refers to the use for which a building was designed rather than its present function.

To show how the maps can be used, let us look at the map of Nottingham on pages 8 and 9. This is the First Edition 6″, published 1885, surveyed 1880-1. Nottingham, a city in the middle of my hierarchy, has: medieval elements; an attractive Victorian industrial area (the Lace Market); a remarkable leafy Victorian residential area (the Park) near the centre; and the twentieth-century developments of a destructive Inner Ring Road and two new shopping centres. As a regional capital, Nottingham serves over a million people.

Find the market place. To the SE the street plan round St Mary's shows the original pre-Conquest Anglian hill-town, now the Lace Market area. This was later captured and developed as a *burh* by the Danes, so streets tend to be named '–gate', and gates 'bars', as in York. The defences lay outside the curve of High Pavement, but within the curve of the next ring – Carlton Street, Goose Gate, etc.

In more peaceful late Saxon times, the present market place of Snotingaham developed *outside* the defences. The Normans dropped the 's' to call it Notingham. They established the castle on the rock and a Norman borough beneath it, which grew towards the market place. The later medieval town wall included all three – the burh, the market place and the borough. No trace remains, but the line is clearly shown by the streets on the map: from the castle N round Standard Hill to the site of Chapel Bar, E along Upper Parliament Street past the site of Cow Bar to St John's Bar, curving SE to pick up the burh defences (next to the graveyard). The river Leen formed the southern defences and is now a fascinating piece of urban canal.

The map shows the two contrasting nineteenth-century developments – the notorious high density 'courts' infilling the burgage plots north of Market Place, and the spacious layout of The Park, west of the castle, with trees and huge villas.

Developments since this 1885 map include the Great Central Railway driven north across the centre, with a tunnel from outside the SW corner of the burh to Victoria Station (across Milton Street from the church, north of Cow Bar and now a shopping centre); a second shopping centre at Broad Marsh, south of the tunnel entrance, with new roads; and an Inner Ring Road (Maid Marian Way!) driven through the Norman borough, 'opening up' St Nicholas (marked *b*), splitting Castle Gate and demolishing the 1709 courtyard of Collin's almshouses.

As this description has shown, it is difficult to guide you verbally to particular points, so on subsequent maps we have inserted numbers to help the perambulations. These are sometimes near, rather than on, the point indicated, to avoid obscuring interesting detail on the map. The small page size (to fit in a pocket) also means that the 6″ map rarely covers the whole historic town centre, as it did for the smaller historic towns. This matters less than might be expected, since the cities are too big to be explored in one walk, and therefore have to be broken down into 'sectors' in any case.

To give the general layout of the biggest cities, we have sometimes used First Edition 1″ maps, doubled in scale. These date from the same survey as the 6″ in the case of the Scottish and Northern English cities, but in the case of Birmingham, Bristol and Cardiff the 1″ was surveyed fifty years earlier than the 6″, making interesting comparisons.

Using this book As far as possible, the book has been designed with as much text as possible opposite or close to the map to which it refers. Sometimes this need has determined the order in which the cities are presented or, within a city, whether the text starts off with the city centre or, as for Sheffield, with its early nineteenth-century 'West End'. So the cities are *not* presented in any order of merit or of size, only in the vaguest geographical groupings.

As with *Historic Towns,* there is surprisingly little overlap with the Blue Guides (*England, Scotland, Wales* and *Cathedrals & Abbeys of England and Wales*) which are recommended for their accounts of the cathedrals, castles, museums and historical associations not covered in this book. The *AA Book of British Towns* presents city centre plans of today without comment other than on the cathedral or museum – which are useful for finding car parks and loos, but which are in no sense a guide to the architecture, historic streets or historic buildings.

Parking a car is of course a problem in city centres; for someone exploring a big city centre for the first time the best approach is to arrive at the main central railway station (often a fine Victorian cast-iron trainshed plus station hotel in its own right), slap in the city centre, with no worries of feeding two-hour parking meters. Then use the excellent suburban electric railway services and/or metro systems in the larger city regions. So the best entry to Manchester is from Piccadilly Station; to Birmingham from New Street; from Central or Queen Street stations bang into Glasgow's metropolitan city centre; from Waverley Station into Princes Street, Edinburgh; or, most dramatically of all, through the deep Piranesian rocky cutting into Liverpool Lime Street, to emerge on the terrace with the best view of St George's Hall (the excellent Merseyrail metro making it easy to incorporate Birkenhead in the visit as well).

My visits to all these British Cities were based on discovering in advance which areas have been designated Conservation Areas and which buildings were now Historic Buildings – and in particular which were picked out and graded as I and II* (above the normal Grade II); so my comments, and the areas which I have chosen to explore, are not just personal quirks, but embody a synthesis of the opinions of city planners and other 'conservationists' as well.

City architecture For most of these British cities the 'historic' buildings and streets which are explored are Victorian and/or Edwardian, that is, they were built between 1837 and 1914. The value of this period is only now belatedly being recognised with statutory protection for its 'listed' historic buildings. The list was recently extended to include some buildings built before 1939. In fact the most notable change between my 'surveys' of historic towns in the late 1970s and of British cities in the early 1980s has been the recognition, largely due to the efforts of the Victorian Society, of the value of Victorian commercial architecture, emphasised by the low quality of much that has been built since. The phrase 'Victorian historic town' is less a contradiction in terms than it was. Indeed, transatlantic or Australian visitors will probably feel more at home in the Victorian cities of this book, than amongst the Georgian and timberframe buildings of the Historic Towns; by contrast with the over-antiquarian British, they feel little difficulty in accepting the late nineteenth century as 'historic'. There are, after all, many analogies and similarities to be found between the splendours of Victorian Liverpool or Glasgow and developments of a similar date in Boston, Chicago, New York, Melbourne or Sydney – the last was made a 'city' by Queen Victoria in 1852 – even before Manchester.

Like Asa Briggs, I strongly disagree with Mumford's blanket anti-urban dismissal of Victorian cities as 'insensate' and as being all like one another. In fact, the bigger the British city, the more likely it is to have developed an individuality of its own and be 'unique'. So, apart from tackling the confusing question of cities and cathedrals, this book will have no more general introduction, using the space instead to attempt to deal more adequately with each individual city.

Though I am describing the visual pleasures of walking round the streets and looking at the buildings, this book deliberately excludes photographs. For even if there were the space to include the many photographs which each city richly deserves, photographs of streets always look 'crowded' if full of people and vehicles, and 'dead' if not; and they can never convey the essential sense of 'enclosure' given by being in the space between the fronts of the buildings on one side of the street and those on the other side of the street. One never knows whether to try to photograph the complete street showing both sides, or to concentrate on showing adequately (if one can get sufficiently far back) buildings on one side only. If you want a picture guidebook, get one of the individual architectural guides to each city that can now be bought locally.

Inevitably I use a number of architectural terms. Many of these were illustrated in *Historic Towns* and they can be found illustrated in any dictionary of architecture or in the Pevsner guides. One term

'In antis'

does need an illustration and that is 'in antis'. This is usually applied to a portico or pedimented facade to describe whether the classical columns in it project from the face of the building (the normal situation) or are set back, 'receding into' the building, to line up with the face of the front wall on either side. I've tended to call this 'recessed' in the past, or 'in a recess'; but columns 'in antis', picked out by the deep shadows of the recesses, are very different visually from, say, a groundfloor window all of which is set within a recessed frame.

A comprehensive architectural glossary of Victorian buildings would be impossible to provide in any case, as the Victorians imitated any previous style in a burst of historicism, from ancient Egyptian, through classical Greek and Roman, to medieval Romanesque, Gothic, Renaissance and Baroque, frequently combining styles inventively within one building; you may consider the results *ugly* (though they always contribute greatly to the liveliness and variety of the street-scene as a whole) but they are never *dull*. Only with Art Nouveau in the 1890s and 1900s do styles begin to be developed that owe little to the past, and which start to show the implications of the new materials of cast iron and later steel and concrete. But these buildings are still rare before 1939; before then 'historicism rules OK'.

It is assumed that the reader will explore at least the city centres on foot, and will look at buildings above groundfloor shopfront fascia level (where they are usually wrecked), crossing where necessary from one side, to the middle, to the other. Try not to be run over by the city traffic; increasingly, traffic-free pedestrian streets are being created in British cities, but rarely in the streets of greatest architectural interest.

Whilst this book provides maps and comment as a starting point towards an appreciation and enjoyment of the historic urban environment – the physical appearance of the city – it is also hoped that the reader will enjoy other facets: street names, references to famous people, historical associations, museums, art galleries, open air and covered street markets, specialist shops, jazz or folk singing at pubs. Enjoy and savour the diversity not just of the architecture, but of the activities of each city; and while you look at their past, think also of their future.

A drawing of the Great Hall of the University of Birmingham by its
architect, Aston Webb. Exhibited at the Royal Academy in 1907.

Notes on the maps

Maps are numbered I, II, III . . . and up to VII and VIII for Edinburgh, Glasgow and Bristol. Because of the layout problems caused by the need to present double-page maps on double-page spreads where they did not have to be cut down the middle, the cities are not presented alphabetically but on a regional basis.

With the exception of the twelve double-page maps, basic map information is given in a caption at the foot of the page opposite the map. In the case of the double-page maps, the caption is at the foot of the page immediately preceding or following the map.

All the captions contain the name of the city, whether 1″ or 6″, the degree of magnification and the date of publication of the map sheet reproduced. All maps are first edition Ordnance Survey (OS): thirteen are one inch to the mile (1″), the rest are six inches to the mile (6″). All the 1″ maps are doubled in size (×2), and about half the 6″; three 6″ maps (York, Bath and Brighton) are quadrupled in size (×4). Without any mention of magnification, the maps are reproduced at their original 6″ scale. Where two or four OS sheets had to be used for one map, two or four dates of publication are given to indicate this (even if the dates are the same), with the dates printed in positions to show whether sheets are above each other, side by side, or both!

Dates of first edition OS 1″ and 6″ maps

The 34.03 series is used for England and Wales (later than the original 34.01 series), with early railways added (and, in Birmingham, some late canals). No dates are given for the preliminary surveys. They were presumably three or four years before the date of publication. It is too complicated to summarise the dates of the many detailed additions on the 34.03 sheets (read the comments on the facsimile reproductions published by David and Charles), so dates are given here – and in the text – as 'plus' (+).

In Scotland, the first edition 1″ series came much later and included early railways, so the first publication series has been used. This comes from the same survey as the 6″.

Leeds 1″ 1858 and 6″ 1852 are similarly based on the same survey information. For other northern English cities the 1″ and 6″, though close in date, do not contain the same information – but probably embody some of the same survey material. These maps are: Manchester and Salford 1″ 1843+, 6″ 1848; Sheffield 1″ 1840+, 6″ 1855; Liverpool 1″ 1840+, 6″ 1851, 1850. Contrast them with: Birmingham 1″ 1834+, 6″ 1889, 1890; Bristol 1″ 1830+, 6″ 1887, 1889; Cardiff 1″ 1833+, 6″ 1885, 1886; Portsmouth 1″ 1810+, 6″ 1857; Plymouth 1″ 1809+, 6″ 1867.

For technical reasons, the 6″ sheets are not always those from the first year of publication – sometimes a year or two later. But they are based on the same surveys – of which the dates are given on the map sheets – which were in some cases carried out more than ten years before publication. For more details see pp. 249–51.

Where more than one OS sheet is needed for a map, areas have been trimmed and 'matched' as well as possible. Occasionally, however, the joins are visually unacceptable, hence the white 'corridor' across the double-page map Oxford II and the unusual split of Bristol VII and VIII into two smaller maps on facing pages. The early OS sheets in the Cambridge University Library were cut for mounting. This caused 'corridors' which have to be omitted in reproduction, but these joins can be effected satisfactorily.

Despite all the problems (sheet joins, deletion of Cambridge University Library 'corridors', half-tone reproduction in order to pick up sufficient detail, and the insertion of numbers), it is hoped that any reader obsessed by old maps, as I am, will enjoy the maps included in this book and admire the standards of cartography of the nineteenth-century Ordnance Survey!

WALES

Swansea

Swansea originated in an English town round a Norman castle, which acquired walls (murage grants 1317 and 1337) at the time the castle was replaced by a fortified manor; no remains of town defences – their line (1) (2) (3) on the map – but tower and battlements/arcade of 'castle' survive today. Swansea then developed industrially as the outlet of several valleys (becoming by 1700 the largest port in Wales) – initially coal, then copper and other metals in c19, reaching its peak about the time of the map, which shows intensive works down the valley, plus the Swansea Canal (4) with its outlet (5) to the river Tawe (little left of either today).

After extensive bombing in the Second World War, Swansea was rebuilt, like Coventry and Plymouth, largely to a new plan as a regional shopping centre; its historic Wind/Castle/High Streets are still worth exploring on foot, plus the Maritime Quarter – with the unexpected early c19 streets of a seaside resort, 'The Burrows', which changed into a late Victorian/Edwardian commercial port area (reminiscent of Bute Town, Cardiff) after the construction of South Dock in 1859.

Three directions half a mile off the map offer interesting phases in Swansea's development: N up the valley beyond (6) to Vivian Street and Vivian's Town, developed in mid C19 by the Vivian family for workers in their copper works and using brown stone with copper slag in the 2-storey terraces; W beyond (7) along Walter Road, towards Gower, into a late Victorian suburb with trees and large villas; and W beyond the jail (8) to the 1934 Guildhall (of Portland stone, like those in Cardiff and Newport). Its slender tower, together with University College, founded in 1920, a mile W, the new Leisure Centre – N of (10), and new West Glamorgan County Hall (9) show the C20 emphasis on the superb bay round the coast to Mumbles.

Start at the Industrial Museum (10) – in warehouse since map. 1840s stucco terrace with every other bay advanced, round Gibbs doorways (11); past 1900s Baroque to pedimented and pilastered 1835 Royal Institution (12), museum; Assembly Rooms (columned and rusticated ground floor) and redbrick Cambrian Place (13), built 1812-25 to face Burrows Square (later, as map shows, timber yard), which has delightful 1st-floor tripartite windows with cast-iron balconies and canopies; to grand stone classical facade (14), and mixed stucco and redbrick Georgian row (15) with recesses.

Across the traffic into historic Wind Street: at first C19 Italianate and gabled; nasty mid C20 horizontal, 1890s old GPO with cupola opposite Georgian group on curve – 1807 redbrick with stucco pilasters, stucco pilastered with recess, with stucco down street to rebuilt C16 Cross Keys and spacious St Mary's (1897, rebuilt after bombing). Then the 'castle', now cleared of C19 additions, long 1920s block with large groundfloor arches (16), to High Street (stucco inns), which becomes rundown towards station; good C19 chapels at (17) and (18) – beyond 1900s Palace Theatre. From station Alexandra Road runs SW, with 1900s redbrick and stone Baroque police station with tower (corner of Orchard Street), Art Gallery (19), and Central Library (good facade).

Cardiff

From Norman castle and small medieval walled town, with the construction of the Glamorganshire canal and docks, Cardiff boomed during C19 as outlet for the mineral and industrial wealth of 'the Valleys' to become the largest coal exporting port in the world. When this declined, Cardiff changed in C20 to become largely an administrative and professional town, made 'capital' of Wales in 1955.

North Lodge Lodge (N? 49) BM 46 Lodge

11

Remains of
Francis's Convent
or Grey Friars 1280
Lodge

Castle
Gardens

B.M. 39

CASTLE
GREEN

Draw Bridge
remains of
CAMP

St Luas Sch

12

Cardiff North Gate
Castle (Site of)
Well

2

Queen St

10

99.4

CROCK

ANGEL ST

Hotel

Hotel

DUKE ST

5

3

HIGH ST

4

St John the
Baptists Church
(Vicarage)

FREDERICK ST

Market

9

Town
Hall

Police Station

1

Court House
Rocket Court
Fire Engine Station

LITTLE PARK

6

Circus

TEMPERANCE

B.M. 29.2

TOWN

Hotel

Sch

27

PARK STREET

WOOD STR.

SCOTT'S STR

GOUGH STR

TAYLOR ST

School
(Boys & Girls)

Sch! Theatre

Tabernacle
Chapel

8

Heads

WHARF

CAROLINE ST

7

South
Gate
(Site of)
Customho.
Bridge

27.1

Gt West? Sta?

Ward

BY

Hope

BRIGHTON

EAST 32?

WHARF

F.P.

F.W.

Cambrian Cillegg
Hotel

Box 43.4

Und.

S.B.

City centre (Map I)

The map shows the canal (closed by 1900) which defined the Eastern line of the walled town; Little Park has now disappeared under the Arms Park Rugby Football grounds; Westgate Street marks 'extramural' line of the river quay, (1) being the site of a gate, (2) of North Gate, (10) East Gate, and (7) South Gate.

Start from superb tower of c15 St John's (3). N towards (2), W along wall (island gone since map) of the castle (largely remodelled as a Victorian extravaganza with fantastic interiors in 1860s by Burges) to late Victorian Corner (4); fine view of castle towers from park. Back to Regency stucco facade (Venetian window, recesses), through the first – round (5) – of the late Victorian covered arcades that are such a feature of the city centre, to explore main medieval High/St Mary Street to S, from two fine stone buildings – 1892 giant Corinthian pilasters opposite 1835 pediment and Ionic columns.

The best buildings are late Victorian (about time of map). E side: second arcade ('three-legged' this time), view to St John's tower, into spacious covered market. W side: bank palazzo, site of old Town Hall, stuccoed corner next to redbrick and terracotta; down Galate to former shoreline and elaborate GPO and County Court (6); good Victorian banks, fine frontage with 1878 theatre; to neo-Gothic gabled curve (7), stone classical (Venetian windows), looking across site of South Gate to 1840s classical Custom House, built next to canal.

Returning N: past pilastered pub, zigzag along three arcades – E down Wyndhams, past Italianate chapel (8), W down Royal to emerge under varied Venetian windows, E down Morgan to emerge at green with statue and neo-Renaissance yellowbrick library (9). From (3) through dull c20 arcade to another Venetian facade, once canal offices, at site of East Gate (10).

Queen Street is pedestrian and dull, except for classical 1919 bank and 1885 Park Hotel (on site of Theatre Royal) with 'chateau' roofs. To N, 1893 Institute (11) and 1905 stucco theatre. Church loop S from (12) – down Charles Street, back N along dual carriageway, to St David's RC cathedral and four good chapels – two classical but two surprisingly Gothic. W of (12), N into attractive tree-lined Windsor Place: stucco (splayed 'Egyptian' 1st-floor windows), opening out into 1860s redbrick terraces with elaborate window surrounds, round doorways, cast-ironwork; across disruptive new road, brown stone villas round church; left to three villas – neo-Tudor, neo-Gothic 1874 by Burges, stucco pedimented – facing gardens, just off map N of (11).

Cardiff I (city centre)   OS 6" × 2   1886

Top map labels:

157

3

Plas turton

T.P. Castle

Canton

1

2

Nursery

T.G. Longcross

Up Splot

169

Station

Gaol

Penarth

CARDIFF

5

Station

Card iff

West Moors

Mill

C a r d i f f

E a s t   M o o r s

Bridge

Leckwith

The Grange

4

Docks

Sea Bank

M o o r s

Bottom map labels:

T

Draw Br

Ship's

S

BUTETOWN

Draw Br

Graving Dock

Buoy

Under Chapel

DOCK

Cronne Iron

B.M. 30

O

Floor Br

U

Iron Laundry

B.M. 31·7

S

Bute Iron Works

West Y Vale MX

9

B.M. 30

Boring

B.M. 29

School

11

10

Lock

30

Offices

B.M. 31

8

Lock Church

7

N

Dumballs Marsh

Port

B.M. 26·4

12

W

Salt Marsh

River Hospital Hotel

Dogs H

BUTE WEST DOCK BASIN

Lock

6

B.M. 31·2

7

ROATH

B.M. 29·7

Swing Br.

Pontoon &r Landing Stage Steps &c

Dolphin

B.M. 31·7

madryad Hospital Ship

Swing

Iron Works

Graving Dock

Saw Mill

Rock

B.M. 31·8

Swing Br

Ragstaff

Posts

WINDSOR R

Acres

1892

Buoy

including

912

Centre and Bute Town (Map II)

To NW (use the upper map) lie the amazing early C20 white Portland stone public buildings of Cathays Park (1). Cross in front of the neo-Baroque dome of fine 1900s City Hall; then N between its superb tower and the cupolas of 1901-4 Law Courts, both by Lanchester (plans), Stewart (died 1904, role uncertain) and Rickards (detailing). Notice varied neo-classical details: plain Doric columns (Law Courts); small Ionic; coupled fluted Corinthian (County Hall), plain columns (College of Technology 1916), square columns of 1937 Temple of Peace and Health; 4-storey US-style pilasters of 1938 (chunky new concrete block with modern colonnade behind) – facing war memorial at centre in garden. Return S past 1900s University College with courtyard, redbrick and stone for a change, to end at the rotunda of the National Museum (1910-27).

E of Queen Street, over new roads and under railway, past neo-Gothic 1918 university tower and portal, is an attractive Victorian residential area (2) – of trees, and stucco and brown stone villas.

West of bridge, Cathedral Road leads (3) past Victorian Gothic villas 2½ miles to the 'village green' of *Llandaff*, originally quite separate, as was Old Aberdeen: ruined bishop's palace gateway; ruined belltower and cross; impressive medieval cathedral, seeming larger than it really is because encountered, like St David's, from above, at tower level.

1½ miles S of General Station is the strange decayed area of *Bute Town* (4), memorial of Cardiff's late C19/early C20 pre-eminence as a great coal port. One dock has been filled in, but Bute East Dock (since 1″ map) just survives in water, with fine warehouses at its N end (5). Explore, using lower map, from crisp new Maritime Museum (6), looking onto the handsome terracotta 1896 Dock Offices with tower (7): elaborate stucco terrace, 1880s offices with huge classical porch (8), into an area of 1880-1920 commercial buildings denser than most of present 'downtown Cardiff'. To former 1840s station (9); back to huge Ionic columns of 1920s bank (10); and into Mount Stuart Square – originally stucco houses with Venetian windows (shells), some replaced by late C19 offices, at its centre the huge yellowbrick neo-Renaissance 1886 Coal Exchange (11), adapted for possible use by a Welsh National Assembly. Return to (6) via 1880s corner office palazzo (12).

Mains of
Scotstown
Roadside
Cairnfold
Bankhead
Danestone
Westfield
Buckie
Bellfield
Balgownie
Foulpeel
18
Damhead
nestone Ho.
47
Balgownie
Lodge
oodside
Grandholm
Works
odside
Mills
Hayton
Seaton Ho.
17
Church
33
16
Smithfield
OLD
ABERDEEN
Old Town
or
Kings Lin
r Middlefield
Dowis Ho.
Kings College
Hilton Ho.
15
Lady Mill
118
nitehill
Rosehill
pperfield
Militia
Depot
14
St Nicholas
Poorhouse
Cornhill
Ho.
13
Burnside
5
Raeden
Ho.
ABERDEEN
6
4
12
awden
Ho.
11
7
TORRY
10
9
3
8
Rubislaw
Works
Torry
Farm
1
113
2
66
Wellington
Suspension
Forbesfield
Louisville
Little
282
194
94

NORTH SCOTLAND

Aberdeen

Map I
Thriving 'capital' of Northern Scotland and the North Sea offshore oil industry – whose strange supply ships mingle with fishing boats in its harbour (excitingly 'downtown'; extended since map, in 1872, s to include former river Dee), Aberdeen today includes two medieval towns – New Aberdeen (the older, present city centre and harbour) and Old Aberdeen (medieval cathedral church), merged in 1891; each had its own university, Old with King's College, founded 1494, and New with Marischal College, 1593, merged in 1860. Dee bridges: 1881 Victoria; 1829-31 Wellington (plus 1983); 1939; 1520-7 7-arched Bridge of Dee.

Architecturally Aberdeen is the 'Granite City', with fine Georgian and early c19 residential areas, after 1800 built of granite, well-proportioned classical details simplified to suit the stone (as in Cornwall) by the outstanding local architect, Archibald Simpson, plus amazingly extensive late c19 granite suburbs since maps – such as Ferryhill (1), Great Western Road (2) and, most spectacularly, out to (3), extending N to wilful 1880s 62-96 Hamilton Place (4). By contrast, where seafront beyond (5) and harbour beyond (6) meet, are textural 1808-9 'fishertown' cottages of Footdee ('Fittie').

Early nineteenth-century granite suburbs From Western end of main Union Street: 1907 GPO (7) opposite 1910 Prudential; then 2-storey early c19 residential down, and up, behind trees, to Simpson's sophisticated Marine Terrace (8) – begun 1837, railings 1838, finished 1877. Returning N: left along Springbank Terrace behind gardens; right to Simpson's post-1823 Bon Accord Street, left (Old Mill Road) along Crescent (9), through Square; to sculptural 1908-9 telephone exchange (groundfloor arches).

W out along Union Street (twin-pilastered 474-84 built as 1830 water cistern). Between neo-Gothic for a change (1850 with tower, 1887 single-storey) into gardens and trees of Albyn Place (10): left, nicely varied classical and Italianate villas plus Simpson's superb 1839 school; right 1860 Victoria Street, terraces – 1852 Rubislaw (crowsfoot gables, now with 2-storey bay windows), Albyn ('Baronial' ends, rounded dormers), to chunky ('wilful' side doorway) 1879 church (11); beyond, nearly at (3), original and wilful 1886 Gothic 50 Queen's Road. Back to (10), in along Union Street. N side: in Huntly Street, 1860 RC cathedral, 1877 spire (12), Georgian houses; Simpson's 1820 Ionic Music Hall portico; late c19 Scots Baronial, Renaissance offices; to Union Gardens and Bridge.

City centre (Map II)

Medieval New Aberdeen (no walls but gates, 'ports', none left) extended to Gallowgate Port by technical college (**Map I**, 13), but rest was rough extent of **Map II** (to sw, up to railway valley).

Start at (1): c18 houses (Castle Inn archway, eared windows); 1896 Balmoral Salvation Army (castle site Infantry Barracks on map, now tower flats); lavish 1686 Mercat Cross; Georgian (surrounds) next to 1763 corner; fine 1801 corner bank (pilastered windows, triglyph frieze).

From Simpson's Ionic Atheneum (1706 wellhead, moved) stretches magnificent classical Union Street, laid out 1800. N side, from 1868-74 'Flemish medieval' Town House (overawing 1615 Tolbooth, 1627 tower) superb curve: Simpson's 1839 Corinthian corner (good bank interior), Doric columns, pilasters, Ionic portico, classical church with round tower – up contemporary King Street (with 'characteristic' round groundfloor openings), worth exploring past (2), Simpson's 1817 Gothic Episcopal cathedral (white gilded interior). Beyond (3) to Old Aberdeen: no. 151, former 1894 County Hotel (roundels); 1863 Baronial barracks.

Down 1767-89 Marischal Street (surrounds), over bridge (doubled 1984), to 1902 classical corner facing harbour; E to 1771 mansion (eared windows, Gibbs doorway), exuberant 1898 Baroque (temple top, curved first floor), 1760s Venetian windows (4). W: Ionic pilastered pubfront; 1883 harbour offices with clocktower (5). Up Shiprow (6), 1710, 1593 Provost Ross's houses (carved dormers, museum). Back along harbour, to late c19 Guild Street: Baronial; 1872 stripy Gothic; to bizarre 1892 elliptical arch facing station.

Up Market Street, E side: 1875 classical corner; 1858-9 palazzo bank; Simpson 1845 (large pilastered windows), former GPO. Opposite, past palazzo corner, into medieval street pattern, late c19 Gothic Imperial Hotel (7) and the Green (original market place). Union Street again: 1830 Ionic screen to St Nicholas, largest medieval burgh kirk in Scotland, c14 East crypt, Aberdonian James Gibbs' 1752 West church, huge 196ft 1874 steeple (carillon). Left, 1846 Tudor Trinity Hall. Right, explore beyond quoined Georgian mansion (8), massive 1840 Doric portico to right. Over 1802-5 Union Bridge (railway later) to 1810-21 Golden Square (9).

Walk now becomes mainly exuberant late Victorian and Edwardian. Union Terrace: superb 1885 corner; early c19, harled late c18; to 1896 Renaissance offices, similar library. (Off map beyond (10), up early c19 Skene Terrace, to delightful 1815-25 Skene Place; behind, 1810 Dutch gables, fanlights, quoins.) Behind library, Simpson's 1833-44 Infirmary (pedimented pilastered facades; green dome). Past 1892 domed St Mark's, 1904-6 theatre

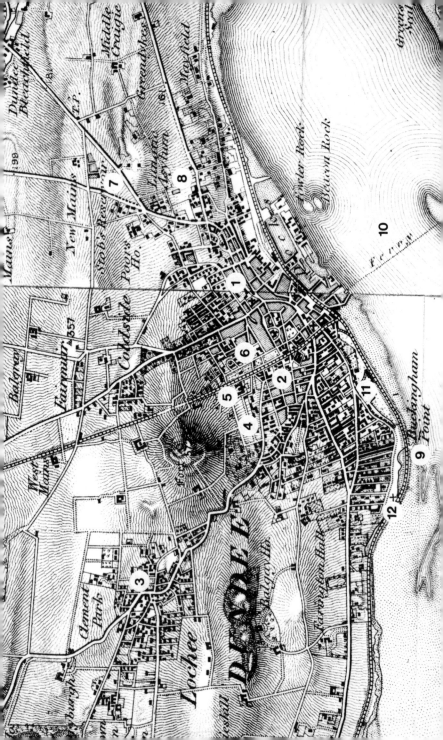

(refurbished) – since map, as road layout. To 1923-5 quadrant corner, 1883-5 Art Gallery and symmetrical facade to Gordon's College: 1830s wings (pedimented, laurels) to William Adam's 1732 centre (11) with Venetian window, little spire. Opposite: Simpson's fine 1844 Marburg-like *redbrick* spire; Georgian house (museum).

Finally along Upper Kirkgate (12): late C18; C17 rendered gable; 1694 corbelled skews (sundials); 1899 (1680 dormer). Find, opposite, C16-17 Provost Skene's house (interiors, museum). To emerge under new office block at climax (13) of amazing filigree granite 1903-6 Marischal College/Greyfriars facade (1837-41 Simpson courtyard, superb 1893-7 top of 233ft tower). (Off map, N up Gallowgate: huge C18 rusticated pend archway; opposite, delightful redtiled 1898 church).

Old Aberdeen (Map I)

Georgian houses, built of huge blocks of granite, a strange-textured place with an atmosphere of medieval and Jacobite grandeur about it, a place that really makes you feel you are in the Northernmost seat of learning, so remote, so windswept and of such a solid, grey strangeness.   (Betjeman)

Good houses up Spital at (14), later cobbles. Good walk from University Road (15): turreted 'oriental' 1834 gateway, detached Georgian houses; superb King's College (1500s chapel with crown spire, 1658 tower in courtyard, 1926 monument in front); Georgian mansions – right 3-storey bow windows, left pedimented behind gatepiers; right along Grant's Place (1732 lintel), back past astrolabe memorial; 1623 'end-on'. High Street funnels attractively to 1788 Town House with cupola (16).

Across new road to fine houses (another pedimented) of the Chanonrie, 1801 almshouse courtyard (belltower), C15 cathedral church (1520s spires); (17) re-erected 1616 tower. SE from cathedral: 1519 crowsfoot gable; delightful cobbled redtiled Don Street (through arch, corbelled tower, 1676 plaque) curving back to (16). Delightful houses (1655, C17-18) lead to 1286-1320 Brig o' Balgownie (18), oldest bridge in Scotland.

Dundee

Map I

Dundee has a fine largely late C19 central area (reminiscent of Glasgow) plus an unexpected Regency area to SW. Famous for its jute industry, Dundee still has many C19 mill buildings, with an impressive group at (1), a fine facade along Lochee Road (2) – opposite mid C19 court buildings (Doric portico) – and at Lochee itself, (3) having 1865 182ft campanile/chimney; between is C17 Dudhope Castle (4). N of C19 Royal Infirmary are 1840s classical

villas (5) on slopes of Dundee Law, which mark start of an attractive c19 suburb, as does also winding Constitution Hill (6).

The maps are earlier than fine late c19 streets and buildings, lavish French Gothic 1866 Morgan Academy (7), 1863 Renaissance loggia in Baxter Park (8), old and rebuilt Tay railway bridge (9), new foreshore on reclaimed land, and 1966 Tay road bridge (10).

City centre (Map II)

Start at splendid c15 steeple (1). Down fine classical Union Street (laid out 1828) to 1890s Whitehall Crescent, Street (2). Along former waterfront, behind civic Caird Hall (1914-23), past classical corner facing good 1828 block (3), past (4) to 1840s Custom House with Ionic centre (by John Taylor who designed similar one in Glasgow), 1822 HMS Unicorn in Victoria Dock. Back to (3); up Castle Street – pedimented facade (bust of Shakespeare, 1808 former theatre). Then up classical Reform Street, laid out to 1834 Doric High School portico (5), in Euclid Crescent!

Along burial ground (interesting monuments), to (6); huge 1890s GPO, 1869 warehouse (round arches), 1911 library (Baroque tower). Up Constitution Road past 1830s Gothic chapel to classical corner (7). Further N, off map, delightful Regency villas of Constitution Hill. E to late Victorian curve (8). S to *Gothic* revival for a change – corner 1853 Flemish Royal Exchange (on map) facing Gilbert Scott's 1867 Albert Institute (9) plus statues (since map).

Finally E past new Wellgate shopping centre (10), to superb c18 church with steeple and octagonal chapel (11), opposite nice terrace; in Cowgate behind, c16 'Wishart's Port' (12), arched town gateway. Back to (10); down Murraygate – bank palazzo (rotunda inside); across late c19 Commercial Street, cut through from (4) to (9); to sculptural island bank, Gilbert Scott's 1850s Gothic Episcopal cathedral (13) – on site of castle.

South-West to Georgian/Regency area (Map II) Along Nethergate; under new road; to strange 1780s terrace (recesses, Gibbs doorways, windows), 1835 RC cathedral (14); NW to good houses of Tay Square, South Tay Street (classical porches, little cast-iron balconies); beyond (14), fine 1790s house, flamboyant French Gothic 1878 Queens Hotel, opposite c18 tower with bowfront.

Map I: Georgian houses (several now University); Airlie Place – rusticated ground floor (like Edinburgh) and cast ironwork; to (11); along Perth Road, similar 1828 Springfield (Doric porches in pairs). Back past (11), down to delightful early c19 Magdalen Yard Road area – stone walls, narrow cobbled streets, trees – with fine houses culminating in amazing 1836 neo-Greek villa (inclined windows, saucer dome). Along former shore to paired Doric doorways of 1830s Windsor Place (12); to N, later Italianate (balconies).

Edinburgh

One of Europe's most scenic cities, Scotland's capital since c15 but having no medieval bishopric, the original Edinburgh was along the ridge between the castle and Holyrood Abbey/House (the Royal Mile), lined by tall tenements, with numerous 'wynds' (lanes) and courts off. In 1760s Edinburgh expanded with bridges – South over Cowgate to George Square, North past Nor' Loch (drained in 1816, now Waverley railway station) to the extensive planned New Town. **Map I** (double page) shows contrast between medieval Old Town and Georgian grid streets, squares, etc. to N. Most guidebooks emphasise Edinburgh's historical associations, but an excellent illustrated Architectural Guide appeared in 1982, which I quote occasionally.

New Town (Map I)

Start at city centre: 1852 Wellington statue in front of Robert Adam's elegant 1770s Register House with 'country house' corner pavilions and cupolas, 1895 North British Hotel (1) and 1860s Renaissance GPO giving, by contrast, a big-city scale, continued over the huge 1896 iron arches of rebuilt North Bridge to cliff-like 1898 Carlton Hotel and 'the Scotsman'; explore over (view of extraordinary skyline of Calton Hill) to Tron Church (2), on Royal Mile (to be seen later).

Now explore first phase of New Town – to grid plan of 1766, George Street as axis between squares, Princes and Queen Streets facing outwards to gardens. Original houses are simple stone Georgian, often with slated round dormers – in rows rather than the formal architectural terraces found in later phases.

Princes Street is famous less for its architecture than shops, fine public buildings in gardens, and spectacular views across to the Old Town, probably the most famous backdrop/skyline in Europe – from Tron spire and crown of St Giles, back of City Chambers (11 storeys high), 1860s Baroque bank (forward) with domes, square New College towers, Tolbooth St John's spire, Outlook Tower, strange red and white 1890s gables of Ramsay Garden (brainchild of Patrick Geddes), culminating in the castle, capped by Lorimer's luxuriant 1920s Gothic War Memorial. The frontage is mixed – Georgian houses (often masked by shops), exuberantly ornate late Victorian/Edwardian stores, faceless 1930s and 1950s, and results of 1967 Princes Street Policy of 'first floor walkway, two projecting upper storeys, groundfloor shops', rightly now abandoned.

w from (1) to another huge railway hotel (5). Three corners: early c20 Baroque and steel frame (3) with roof caryatids and globe; 1883 hotel opposite opulent 1894 Jenners (3-storey 'arcade' inside), well seen from intricate 1840s Gothic stonework and statues of 200ft Scott monument – lined up with street, as are, with Princes Street, Calton Hill monuments and three spires of St Mary's Cathedral. Then c20 horizontals, narrow 1888 Renaissance gable (like Glasgow); to 1830s Academy, facing Hanover Street, surmounted by Victoria, its superb triglyph frieze, Egyptian sphinxes, fluted Doric columns contrasting with more feminine 1845 Ionic twin portico of National Gallery (walk round both) – on the Mound (of spoil from New Town). Then PSP, Georgian, 1880s French roofs, 1882 classical plus glass, 1869 turreted (4) – 3-storey 'arcade' inside. Pilasters, PSP, 1890s pilastered bow window; 1890s corner and gable; another 1880s classical plus glass (5), facing step-gabled red 1902 Caledonian Hotel. In gardens 1816 Gothic St Johns (fan-vaulted interior) and 1894 Baroque St Cuthbert's with apse towers, grafted onto 1779 steeple.

Past 1790s twin bowfront into Charlotte Square (6) with monumental terraces: N side (Robert Adam 1791) has lady sphinxes at ends, Grecian pilasters (square at ends, round in centre) plus pediment and frieze (No 7 'Georgian house' open to public); W side 1811 St George's (tall green dome) between terraces with Ionic pilasters (square and round), huge central 'Adam' window; S like N side, but no sphinxes!

Now George Street – traffic, treeless, bad mid c20 offices, fine c19 banks (good interiors). N side – No 127 Georgian restored, 1860s 3-bay palazzo, early c20 with round granite arcade, 1790 pilastered with frieze. Six Castle Street houses have 3-bay centres between 3-storey bows, (7) pilastered and pedimented. Nasty 1950s corners; N side – 1884 palazzo bank between two Georgian, 1830s Regency (round windows, cast-iron columns), 1903 gable, 1908 Baroque corner dome (next to sculptural gables); S side – inventive 1912 classical Freemason's Hall, Ionic tripartite doorway 'in antis', 1903 Baroque (now bank) with 'early modern facade facing lane at rear' – near new pedestrian shopping street.

N side – 1905 French Renaissance bank, 1860s palazzo, several Georgian with even quoins, Ionic colonnade with Corinthian porch; S side – 1870s Italianate bank, 1780s-1843 Assembly Rooms/Music Hall (bow window over pavement). In Hanover Street, 1939 US-style Ionic portico, 1860s Italianate (8) – columned 2-storey bay windows, shell windowtops. N side – 1841 corner bank with Corinthian pilasters and columns – as in George Hotel (plus Corinthian attic storey); 1780s St Andrew's with thin steeple, oval interior; 1898 Renaissance gable; good infill, late c19 classical re-using pediment dated 1825. S side – 1908 corner dome; 1840s Doric porches, triglyph over (and across building), pedimented and columned windows; tall 1890 Renaissance; 1847 Corinthian bank portico to balance church.

St Andrew Square with 1821 column (9): W side nasty early C20 left, better 1969 infill right – behind, unexpected 1760s houses facing garden, oldest in New Town; S side good 1961 infill, 5-bay 1920s back of (3), 1897 Prudential – by Waterhouse in red sandstone rather than brick and terracotta. E side chunky offices masking bus station; pilastered Ionic wings with urns to set back 1770s Dundas mansion remodelled as bank in 1857 (superb iron 'star light' dome); sculptural 1850s bank with columns capped by statues; 1920s US-style. Follow dense zigzag, past 1862 Café Royal (1890s interior), 1864 Venetian Gothic warehouse, 1860 Register House palazzo (5-storey iron-galleried interior) to (1). Finally round red sandstone 1886 'Doge's palace' portrait gallery (10), along Queen Street to Grecian 1845 facade with statues.

Across gardens (11) to more attractive later post-1800 phases of New Town – on slope down to Water of Leith, trees and gardens, with the rusticated ground floor I call 'New Town' (often ironwork above), and a formal and inventive treatment of terraces, crescents, circuses, their centres and ends picked out, usually with pilasters. Abercromby Place curve (ends higher); Heriot Row – first terrace with pedimented centre/ends (scroll balustraded windows above round openings), but second centre confused (not as designed). Down 1819 India Street – 1980s courtyard infill (12), down steps (13); original shopfronts, columned market gateway (3-storey row behind) to (14); past bow ends – left 1876 Gothic school (end recesses) to 1823 church, through Saxe Coburg Place (Ionic pilastered centre/ends) down to 1861 'Colonies' (15) – not houses but flats with access from two sides; pedimented villa wings, earlier Georgian quoined house (16); to (17), with new housing facing and over bridge.

Past Doune Terrace (pilasters in twos or fours) into superb 1820s Moray Place (18): 1+2+3+2+1 pedimented 'mansion chunks' with Doric columns, linked to splayed 3+4 (pilastered ends); central 'mansion' short sides but two 'mansions' long sides, linked by splayed 23 bays (3+5+3 pilastered and columned centre). Out S past rounded/square corners to terraces – simple advanced centre/ends contrasting with 'mansion' centre, to pair, varied tripartite doorways (19).

N past sloping 5+6+9+6+5 Wemyss Place to paired Ionic pilasters (tripartite windows between), on approaches to Royal Circus (20) – pilastered centre/ends, to (21), 1827 St Stephen's (overscaled with splays, tall tower as focus of street). Then grand Great King Street – Ionic pilasters, lunettes, pedimented and balustraded windows, into similar Drummond Place (22). N, more domestic Cumberland Street, to 1980 ziggurat computer centre (23); 5-bay advanced on curve (24). Past Ionic porches, terrace (alternating end windowtops) to 1830s Academy portico, pedimented mansion (25). Via (14), (21), from (26) down Northumberland Street (domestic but s side treated as terrace), back to (22). Left at Doric corner (27), to sloping Bellevue Crescent (Ionic pilasters again) round St Mary's. N to (28) – crescent semis, doorways simple recesses. Then (27), 1876 Norman church, rounded buttresses (29), to chapels – pedimented Ionic, 'square cut' with round windows, niches; behind, to Albany Street Grecian pair (laurels, roundels). Around (30): E to pedimented centre, N to another, church portico, (29). Up to (31) and early c19 Gothic churches – 'college chapel', RC cathedral (later additions). Back down York Place, finished 1800 – two 3-bay houses with central pedimented windows.

Finally E from (1). Between porticos, pilastered terraces of 1815 Waterloo Place, over Regent bridge (Ionic screens), past Old Burial Ground (Hume monument, etc.), to (32), opposite massive 1934-9 offices (site of jail). Nice late c18 houses (left), up Calton Hill (33): view, 1816 Nelson monument/telescope; classical 1822 National Monument (Parthenon), monuments, 1818 observatory (little dome) contrasting with picturesque 1776 castellated. Splendid Doric temples of 1829 High School (34), for the 'Athens of the North'; Corinthian rotunda Burns monument. Round amazing development started in 1819 (not finished on map): houses with Doric porches, ironwork (key motif); scroll doorways on sharp curve; to greatest terrace of all (35), 118 bays, broken up by 5 and 6-bay columned blocks (fluted, unfluted, Corinthian, Ionic); down to pilastered single storey (tenements below), 3-storey (36). Out along gardens: round corners with Doric columns 'in antis', then Ionic (37) – up street continuous balconies, Doric doorways; colonnade (38) to tenements (39) with pedimented Doric columned doorways between pilastered. Returning, pilasters and pediment (40); worth avoiding bulky new St James' Centre (41). (42)-(44) covered en route to Leith later.

Link, up to castle, from (5) Into 1830s Rutland Square (45) with Ionic porches, pilastered ends – as also 1830 chapel (46). 1910 Baroque Usher Hall (47) plus 1883 Lyceum Theatre, to Castle Terrace: unusual 1835 St Mark's facade; sophisticated 1867 gabled block (48); over 1827 King's Bridge (obelisks), past 1872 barracks, up steps (49) to Castle Esplanade.

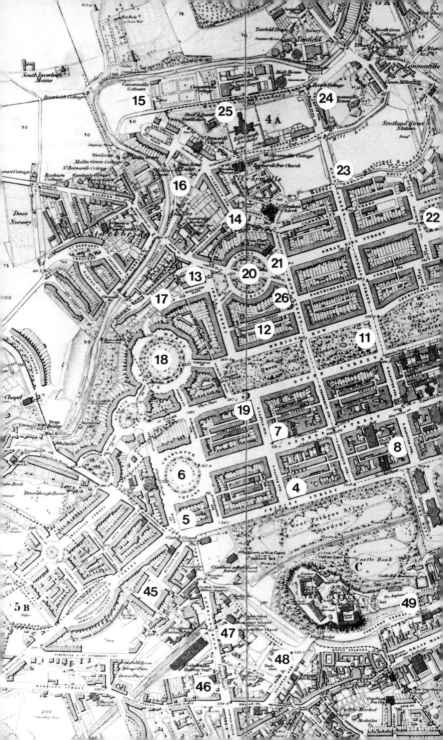

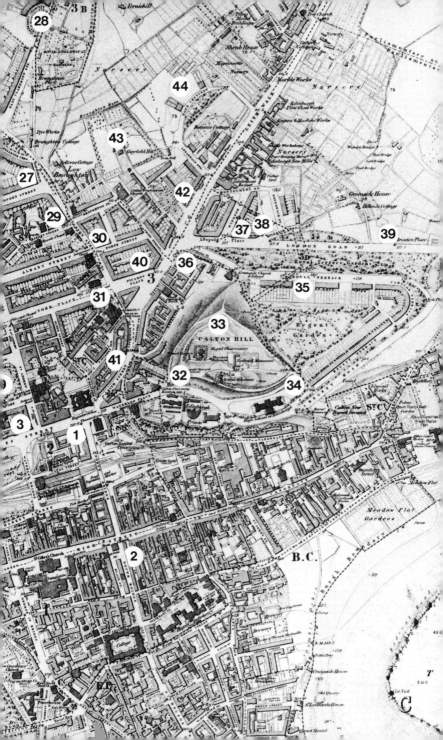

Edinburgh Old Town

The spine is the Royal Mile (Castle Hill, Lawnmarket, High Street, Canongate), whose amazing 6 or 7-storey tenement blocks give a feel of medieval high density, more like the older parts of Paris than anywhere else in Britain. There, too, were the mansions of the aristocracy, but 'by the 19th century, the Quality had removed to the New Town, leaving the old to squalor'; in 1847 'poverty and misery seem to peep out of the open hatches which normally serve as windows'. The population of the Old Town was over 20,000 in 1801, nearly 40,000 in 1861 (St Mary's Wynd had 1,504 persons per acre), leading to 'Improvement Acts', and more spacious late c19 Scottish Baronial tenements; the 1971 population was 4,000. Patrick Geddes in 1890s tried to get professional people back to the Old Town, and recent years have seen much-needed restoration projects and infill housing, trying to keep the 'grain', scale, sense of enclosure, marvellous textures and materials.

The Old Town should not be hurried (it may take several days), as nearly all the wynds and closes are worth exploring (exhausting, as downhill either side); there are numerous historical plaques and names to be noticed, as well as c18 water supply 'well heads' in the streets, and characteristic carved and initialled lintels, dormer tops, etc. (many from older buildings). Not only the Royal Mile is included (its N side already seen from Princes Street), but sallies off – interesting and heightening an appreciation of the Royal Mile.

Royal Mile: Castle End (Map II) Start from the castle (1742 3+5+3 Governor's House with rusticated pilasters) and the Esplanade (1): to E, step-gabled house (1630 initialled dormer, stone guides for timber shutters, cannon ball in W gable); varied 1890s Ramsay Garden courtyard (incorporating Allan Ramsay's octagonal 1740s lodge plus his father's simple c18 house). Castle Hill: c17 Outlook Tower with 1853 castellated top (camera obscura) opposite c17 Boswell's (pedimented dormers, moulded doorway in court); 1840s Tolbooth St John's with fine spire. N frontage of Lawnmarket: back of Assembly Hall; 1690s Milne's Court (moulded doorway, octagonal staircase tower in court); 1720s James Court; contrasting gables, external staircase, ground floor arcade of 1617 Gladstone's Land, 1893 timberframe with oriel windows (interconnected backs), plus 1622 Lady Stair's house (literary museum, 1890s 'medieval' interiors like Cardiff Castle).

Loop, round late c17 corner (wallhead gable), past 1930s classical courthouses, 1870 Baroque bank (2), down to 1860 Jacobean incorporating N frontage of James Court, into 1850s Tudor courtyard (Assembly Rooms at end); up superb townscape sequence of Milne's Court back to Lawnmarket. Now S side: Upper

Bow to emerge (between 1860s Gothic churches) on walkway above Victoria Street; 16-bay 6-storey c18 frontage (part library) with 6 curved gables – elaborate arch into c17 Riddle's Close (1726 staircase tower), further court with late c16 house (crude door pilasters, fine ceilings); c17 gabled Brodie's Court with dormers (in close, hall with 1646 ceiling).

Loop South to Grassmarket (Map II) Past obtrusive 1970 offices (3) – better 1900s Baroque opposite; down 1840s Victoria Street (1864 India Buildings) to c17/18 West Bow/corner of Grassmarket (4): N side new infill, c18 White Hart. W of (5) – site of West Port – 1900s Baronial housing; up steps past 1830s Brown's Place, to pick up 1513 Flodden town wall (tower) up to (6); its line is clear on map – E to (16), N past (17). W past 1810s tenement terrace (rusticated ground floor) to 1977 stone facade (in courtyard behind, 1910 Art College portico, on site of cattlemarket), 1898 fire station, opposite 1860s Italianate hospital. Back E into courtyard (tops of 200 windows reputedly different) of 1628-93 Heriot's Hospital (7) – 'Scotland's finest early Renaissance building, with plentiful, rich stone carving and tracery'; out S, noting churchyard strip to E (Covenanters' prison), back down Flodden Wall, past (6), (5) to (4).

Along Cowgate – in 1550 'where the nobility and chief men of the city reside' but relegated 'below stairs' by late c18 bridges, in 1840 'the poorest district in the metropolis': Magdalen Chapel with 1621 tower (panelled interior, mid c16 stained glass); under bridge; to door and window lintels (8) in brewery courtyard (remains of 1621 Tailor's Hall), 1889 lawyers' Gothic library poised above. Back to (4), up delightful Candlemaker Row: c18 harled on street under bridge, 1722 guildhall (9), backing onto churchyard (fine monuments) of Greyfriars church (E end 1620, W end 1722) with Covenanters' prison. Over George IV bridge, past 1861 church 'free Romanesque with a wedding-cake steeple', 1887 French Renaissance Public Library (hipped roof, cupola), 1837 Jacobean corner (huge 1st-floor windows), back to (3).

Royal Mile: High Street (Map II) S side fine public buildings round Parliament Square: early c19 facade with Ionic centre (magnificent Signet Library interiors) and, round 1685 Charles II statue (as Roman emperor on horseback!), rusticated arcaded ground floor, Ionic portico, lady sphinxes on top (inside 1640s Parliament Hall with 49-ft wide hammerbeam roof); balanced, beyond Mercat Cross, by rusticated arcade between Venetian windows (Gibbs windows above) across courtyard of 1750s City Chambers (built as Royal Exchange); at centre is huge cruciform High Kirk of St Giles, capped by 1500 crown spire, only pre-Reformation parish church within city walls, (medieval

vaulted choir, luxuriant 1910 Thistle chapel by Lorimer).

N side: opposite St Giles, under C17 rubble facade, down Advocate's Close to thin C17 house facing N (apse capped by heraldic windows), emerging at Information Office (10); to E, Art Gallery in 1899 warehouse (giant arcade). Up curved 1860s Baronial Cockburn Street (since map) to early C18 7-storey tenement (corner wallhead gable). S side: Gothick doorshafts (Mary's Chapel); pedimented Ionic doorway to 1813 Doric bank (11), Wax Museum; 1633 Tron Kirk (hammerbeam roof) with 1829 steeple.

Beyond North Bridge, N side: gable/chimney to Paisley Close (boy's head commemorates its predecessor's collapse in 1861); C18 with painted surrounds, to picturesque C15/16 group into street (12) – 'forestairs', overhanging timber gables and galleries (as once on much of C16 High Street), Renaissance window (little urns) on John Knox's house; beyond, site of city gate, Netherbow, removed 1764. Opposite, court to C16-18 Tweeddale House (near church on map).

Loops North and South (Map II) N down Carrubber's Close to spacious 1883 church; under new offices (13); back up Chalmer's Close to re-erected C15 Trinity College Church choir (museum store) with richly vaulted apse. S down Blackfriars Street: W side late C16 'carved ogival doorhead, tympanum'; E side 1870s, early C18 (set back) with moulded doorway, 1981 patterned infill (14). Up past C17 tenements (15), into former Royal Infirmary (now university): 1777 Old High School Doric portico; under arcade to courtyard with C18 house, 1690s old Surgeon's Hall (eared doorway); out to 1850s pedimented, behind re-erected 1738 Baroque gateposts (urns) – on line of Flodden Wall, which follow round surviving corner (16) to (17). W down Cowgate: 1771 church with steeple, re-orientated since map; (15); oval 1763 St Cecilia's Hall; under South Bridge (1786 pediments above). Past (11), up to good houses facing Tron church: pediment, pilasters, triglyph frieze; pedimented corner; 4 fluted Grecian pilasters, tall round windows; 7-bay pedimented.

Royal Mile: Canongate (Map III) Canongate was an independent burgh (founded by Holyrood Abbey) until 1856, and became the favoured area (more space since outside Flodden Wall) for the mansions of the aristocracy; Defoe described Moray and Queensberry Houses in 1720s as 'very magnificent, large and princely buildings, all of Free-stone, large in front, with good gardens behind them'. In 1707 the Treaty of Union was signed (in a garden pavilion of Moray House), the Court moved to London, and the area declined; after further decay and sporadic rehabilitation in the '30s (such as Acheson House and Huntly House) the City initiated a post-war policy of restoration and rebuilding – of the 'lands' (tenement housing blocks).

1867 tenement corner; left, on 4 arches, rebuilt c17/18 Morocco Land (effigy of Moor); right, under new arcade to mid c18 chimney/pediments of Chessel's Court – (1), Gibbs round doorways, windows. s side: c17 staircase tower in Old Playhouse Close, c17/18 Masonic Lodge behind (stepped gables, round tower); superb 1628 Moray House (corbelled balcony, Renaissance 'conical' plaster ceilings, rear alternate pedimented windows), through obelisk gatepiers to 1913 Renaissance education quadrangle (2) – famous garden pavilion in yard/carpark to E. N side: Shoemakers' Land dated 1725; 1958 arch; c17 red stucco, pantiled, panel; Bible Land 2+2, 1677 staircase tower (round ogee top), 5-bay gabled; 5+3 new arches. To climax of early c17 pub, 1592 Canongate Tolbooth (museum), jutting out with turreted steeple, steps up to council chamber (carved dormers, one 1591). Opposite, 1570 Huntly House (museum), timber overhanging stone, between c17 harled on left, 2-storey toothed surround over arch on right; behind, delightful Bakehouse Close to 1634 Acheson House (initialled dormers, re-erected 1672 doorway).

Then 1688 church (3) – curved ends, Doric porch; recreated c17 garden; under 1968 infill to c17 Panmure House; early c18 mansion (4) – scroll roof ridge, wings. s side: 1886 school; reconstructed 1619 house; 1682 harled Queensberry House (remodelled as barracks 1808) – eared central doorway, quoined wings. N side: hidden 3+3+3 c18 Whitefoord House (5) – triglyph porch; 1960s arcade to picturesque White Horse Close; corner 1697 with 3 stepped gables. Abbey Strand: 4-storey c16 mansion (remodelled, rear round stairtower); c17 (external stairs); remains of gatehouse vaulting; c17 gable roundtower facing LH round towers of original 1500s Holyroodhouse (Palace), heavy 1670s pilastered entrance with crown; tiny late c16 pavilion/bathhouse (6); at back, superb c13 abbey nave ruins, c16 house (7) with conical turrets.

South Side (Map IV)

Into Edinburgh's other Georgian expansion. Under Robert Adam's 1789 facade (dome 1886) into fine 1818-34 university Old College courtyard (imposing Upper Library, Soanian domed Arts Centre). Along Chambers Street (since map) to 1861 Italianate Scottish Museum (1) with delightful 3-storey glass/iron interior. E past 5-storey 1790s (2) with chimney/gables, past Roxburgh Place chapel Venetian windows, to pantiled 1930s brewery conversion (3) plus 1781 chapel. Back w through 'New Town' Hill Place to (4) – 1815 chapel. N to 1832 'pure Greek revivalist temple to medicine, fronted by an Ionic portico flanked by footgates'. s to 1981 neo-c18 and Georgian frontage (5) – 1966 courtyards (6); little square (7); 1823 church (8), now Queens Hall. Loop: Lutton Place 1860s Early English church, N of (9), terrace; 1967 Commonwealth Pool (10); gabled 1734 house (11); 1836 church; 'New Town' (12). s of (8) to more 'New Town', facing (13), the Meadows, as are 1770 house (curved gable, round window with twirls), 1839 school (14).

Past 1776 Archers' Hall (15) to c18 harled, 1861 church (16). Up 1770s Buccleuch Place – bow backs, quoins, varied doorways, 8 Venetian windows in two bays (17), rusticated ground floor. Into remains of 1763 George Square (18), sacked by university in 1960s: E side varied doorways (two double 4-column); w complete – 2-storey with slated mansard roofs, screen (Venetian window), 3-storey quoined; N side 1890s Renaissance. To 'university square' (19): to sw 1887 Baronial, 1858 Renaissance; to NE 1976 glass domed centre, 1858 church facing Old College. w past grandiose 1890s domed hall to 'Venetian Renaissance' (20) with courtyard (vaulted entrance), turreted 1870s Baronial Royal Infirmary incorporating 1738 original (21) plus huge spiky central tower.

Across and round Meadows/Links: more classical terraces (22), (23) plus 1981 housing; s of (24) 1870 Baronial Bruntsfield Crescent; to w Baronial, Regency villas; amazing 1864 Gothic Barclay church (25) with spire, 'stone as most people use plasticine'; 3 1880s corner tenement turrets (26), 1905 Baroque King's Theatre (27).

s of map are extensive Victorian suburbs. sw of (24), 1880s Renaissance tenements lead to Morningside's Holy Corner (3 1870s churches, one 1927) and c17 Merchiston House embalmed within 1960s Napier College – classical, neo-c17 villas to NW, W, S. Conservation Areas: Grange s of (22); Blacket s of (9), (10) – beyond **Grecian 1830 60 Dalkeith Road, w into curving, classical 1825-60 Blacket Place**; further s, villas and trees of 1862-93 Waverley Park.

West End (Map V)

From incongruous half-timbering (1), 'townscape sequence' into Charlotte Square. Back past curved ends into 1820s Melville Street

– 'motif' of recessed centre, pedimented window; facing street, Ionic front, Venetian doorways; pilastered splays (2), 1855, since map. Advanced corners to 'motif' on half-crescents, 1825 (3) with Ionic pilastered centre/ends plus Ionic porches. (4), 1886 school (5) with pilastrade – as in 1826 crescent (6); opposite 1857 cottage/flats, 1856 brick quadrangle. Union canal basin filled in N of (7), but towpath accessible s of (8) at 1920s lifting bridge. (5); 1869 Baroque church (9) plus campanile, pedimented corners (1-bay, 3-bay), from (2) to 'sublime, Teutonic visual stop' – Gilbert Scott's 1870s Early English St Mary's cathedral (10), 263ft long (rich vaulted interior), 3 spires, (central 275ft) – next to 1615 house.

Classical (1850/60s, since map) now becomes more Italianate, straight 1st-floor windowtops, *channelled* ground floor – as s of (11); but N side expresses new 1860s demand (as in Glasgow) for bay windows, here 2-storey, tripartite Ionic doorways. s, pilastered bow end (12), (10), (13) – s side classical (1+3+1 ends), w later; through oval (cast ironwork over bay windows) to (14) – 1840s neo-Tudor (24 turrets); (15) – scroll doorways, down to 1890 octagonal spire (16); back, past gabled mews, to (13). Best 1860s: rounded tripartite (cast-iron balconies) facing bay *and bow* windows (17); 2-storey square bays (Corinthian columns), classical, 'New Town' towards (2); to (18).

Pediment (19), down to Dean Village: restored warehouses; 1675 granary facing bridge; 1805 West Mill (20); 'c17 Scots fantasy' redtiled 1884 Well Court, across river to 1895 timberframe row. Follow river under Telford's 1832 bridge; 1789 well; (21). Across to more late classical (channelled ground floor); past delightful 1814 houses behind gardens, pedimented centres over Doric porches, iron lamps – to (22); amazing Doric crescent colonnades, 2-storey centre; along river (23). Beyond neo-Romanesque churchtower (24): 'New Town' rows, villas (often mutilated) to (25); villa with wings (26), to incomplete pedimented terrace (27).

Past (22), classical (28) – varying windowtops; to 1870s bay windows, 1890s Corinthian bows (29). Loop: 1845 cemetery, 1890s spire, river (30), to new hotel (31); leafy suburb to 1833 Baroque (32) with Archer-like towers; chaste 1828 Greek (33), now art gallery; huge 1850s Renaissance plus 1874 'Second Empire' mansion (34). Then 1860s facing gardens (35); Buckingham Terrace with clever 'breaks' for slope; to 1850s classical again (36), and along river. Across to superb 1820s New Town sequence from (18): crescent, terrace, oval – straight windowtops between advanced pilastered centres/ends – to climax of Moray Place (37).

North of New Town to Leith and the coast

Map I: down Leith Walk from (40); 1790s frontage (42) – centre with little pediments, flanked by bowfronts (Venetian windows); through square (made from c18 park) – 'New Town', pediment, early villas, to 1763 'parent' (43) – pediment, urns, curved chimney/gables; to 1840s (44) fluted Ionic colonnade, incomplete as on map.

Map VI Back on Leith Walk: 1796 Middlefield (1), pedimented between Venetian windows, behind tenement; 1812 'New Town' (2) plus pedimented houses (end Venetian windows, doorway, urns); early c19 villas (3), to 3-storey bowfront (4).

The port of Leith is an interesting town in its own right (though rundown, gaps), with a good warehouse area, elegant early c19 public buildings, villas round Leith Links. 1870s Gothic tenements to 1830 Tudor school, pilastered chapel (5) opposite mid c19 warehouse (blank arches). Past (4), through pedestrian precinct, to twin-columned 1816 Trinity House (6), 1848 Gothic church (c15 remains inside). Back to (4), past bowfront, Grecian doorway, to Ionic church portico (7). Explore round (8) – Georgian houses facing churchyard (5-bay), links (7-bay, recessed centre); 6-storey 1862 warehouse (9). Follow grassy links round anti-clockwise, ½ mile beyond (10): double Ionic porches, 'New Town'; 1860s 2-storey bay windows; nicely varied villas (from 1827), to cemetery. N to 1813 corner (facades with recessed centres, little dome). Back W, N side: 'New Town'; 1879 Renaissance warehouse (good side); more villas. Onto map (11): double doorways S; pilastered houses, little terrace into town centre at 1828 Old Town Hall – Doric porch, columns 'in antis' (on corner with nice shopfront, pedimented and pilastered Grecian).

Constitution Street: Grecian Venetian windows opposite 1863 Gothic church, 1850s palazzo GPO, Grecian doorways; to grand 3+2+3+2+3 1809 Exchange, 1871 Italianate bank, 1860 Corn Exchange (12) with frieze (cast-iron roof behind). Bernard Street: 1804 domed bowfront plus symmetrical tenements (varied window-tops); double bowfront between more good c19 banks; to early c18 chimney/gabled corner (13).

S along The Shore, behind 6 tripartite windows, to early c17 Lamb's House (warehousing above and below merchant's quarters), round fine warehouses (14) with rusticated pilasters, to interesting dense warehouse area. N of (13), along shore to more warehouses right, 1685 Signal Tower (originally windmill). Then Albert Dock (15); c19 drydocks (16), yellowbrick range (tower); 1890s swing bridge; 1840 lock (17) – docks filled in; to emerge by superb 'magisterial Greek Doric' 1812 Custom House – opposite

tenement recessed centre (18). (Across to The Shore, s to 1891 corner (19), 1840s Baronial almshouses (20), facing 1850 hospital porch). c17 timber turret, gables, 1600s stonework embodied in waterside granary/mill (21). (Past burial ground to 1900s tea warehouses (22) – start of riverside walk into Warriston, (17) on **Map VII**). To arched gateway of Cromwell's 1650 Citadel, behind 1830s turreted Gothic chapel, opposite 4-storey warehouses (23).

Past one-storey corner (Grecian doorway) to (24) and up simple classical street (since map) to 1813 church with good steeple; s to 'New Town' (25); c19 Gothic spire; past (26), (27) with pilasters separating houses, to 5-storey end bow (28). Along coast (new housing on site of c19 fort), past (29) to 1800s terrace/row, between maps.

Newhaven, Trinity and Inverleith (Map VII)

Delightful redtiled roofs, white harling, gables to sea, of c18 restored and infilled 'fishertown' of Newhaven (1) – fish market on little harbour. Along coast: corner pediment/chimney (2); 'New Town' next to balconies; classical row, 7-bay 'New Town' pair; to pairs (3) with channelled ground floor.

Back to (2) to explore inland uphill delightful leafy mid c19 suburban villas (high stone walls) of Trinity. Gothic with deep eaves (4), now park, to pairs (5) – quoined, then arcaded with tall 1st-floor windows; bowfronts to 1820s bungalow (6). N down York Road: Grecian porches; gabled, Gothic, pilastered – not on map; Italianate, recessed between pedimented wings (trelliswork), pinnacled – on map; to 1854 orange Italianate (7), with two 1870s mansions (towers) beyond. Across railway to 1870s gabled (8); opposite 3 superb Gothick – best bungalow with Gothick ironwork. Varied 1850-70s villas – bargeboards, Italianate with square towers, bow, oriel to (6); back to (8). Huge neo-Renaissance octagon (9) with 'Scots top', to bow, square tower (10).

Then big villas (11); Gothic churches – orange 1920s (12), 1888 (13) – at start of amazing 1823-50s houses backing onto Arboretum: semis in pairs – Doric, Ionic, Italianate, scroll doorways and porches, to Egyptian columns next to gardens building (14); then single villas – Ionic doorways 'in antis' alternating with twin pilastered (pilastered centre); Doric porch. Pairs again to 1809 'New Town' (15), opposite colonnaded villa and entrance to Botanical Gardens: superb curved iron and glass 1834 and 1858 palmhouses (plus tensioned 1965); 1774 house (16) with bow/entrance. End at simpler 1818 (17) – string course instead of rustication. Return to city centre, over bridge, past (24) on **Map I**.

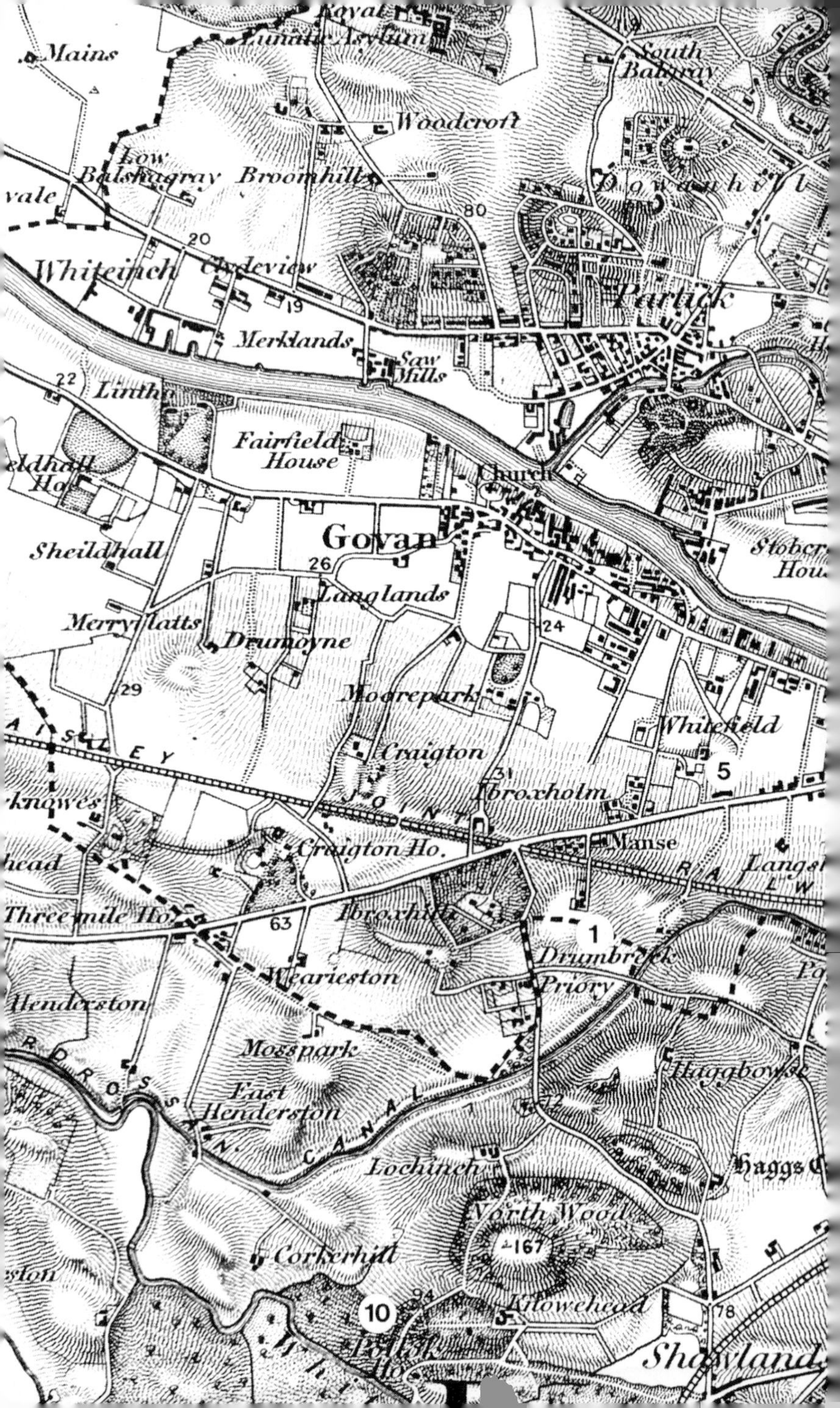

Royal
Lunatic Asylum
Mains
South
Balgray
Woodcroft
Low
Balshagray
Broomhill
Dowanhill
vale
80
20
Whiteinch
Clydeview
19
Partick
Merklands
Saw
Mills
22
Linthouse
Fairfield
House
eldhall
Ho.
Church
Sheildhall
Govan
26
Stobcross
House
Langlands
Merryflatts
Drumoyne
24
29
Moorepark
Whitefield
PAISLEY
Craigton
5
31
knowes
Ibroxholm
JOINT
Manse
Craigton Ho.
RAILWAY
head
Threemile Ho.
63
Ibroxhill
1
Drumbreck
Weirieston
Priory
Henderston
Mosspark
Haggbowse
ARDROSSAN CANAL
East
Henderston
72
Lochinch
Haggs
North Wood
167
Corkerhill
ston
10
94
Knowehead
78
Pollok
Ho.
Shawlands

Glasgow

Scotland's commercial capital and largest city, centre of a conurbation of two million, Glasgow is of great architectural interest – despite a bad 'image' of industrial decay and rundown tenement blocks; in an attempt to be 'progressive', the city has built many bad new office blocks, replaced slums by equally degrading tower blocks, and constructed an Inner Ring Road (M8) which cuts off the early Victorian Park Scheme from the centre and whose completion threatens the Glasgow Green area. However, despite all this (recently the city has become much more conservation minded), to me Glasgow is still a great late-Victorian world city (which reminds me of Barcelona) expressing its industrial, commercial and shipbuilding peak in 1880s (when a third of all world shipping registered was built on Clydeside) in the great steel Forth Railway bridge (NW of Edinburgh), with a Glasgow designer and a Glasgow contractor using shipbuilding and boiler-making techniques.

So Glasgow, along with Edinburgh, has more to seek out and explore than any other city in this book – from Scotland's finest medieval cathedral (with the Necropolis as an extraordinary 'backdrop'); fine Georgian buildings with Georgian Blythswood New Town; the Park Scheme, the finest mid-Victorian development in Britain, with, beyond, the University and the amazingly inventive, varied and extensive terraces up Great Western Road – some of them by a local, Alexander 'Greek' Thomson (1817-75), architect of the 'finest Romantic classical churches in the world' (Pevsner), two of which survive; to the work of the Art Nouveau designer and architect, Charles Rennie Mackintosh (1868-1928), and his masterpiece, the Glasgow School of Art. Excellent booklet 'Glasgow at a Glance', from which I occasionally quote, and leaflets on Mackintosh, etc. from City Information Office, George Square.

Map I

This map is a reduction of 6″ maps made at the time of Glasgow's greatest growth and the building of its finest terraces, with a surprising amount of interest outside the central area (covered in 6″ maps later).

West Pollockshields, with its trees and great Victorian villas – which extends W to the canal (later railway) with similar Drumbeck area (1) beyond – has three villas by Thomson: 'The Knowe' (2), 301 Albert Drive (N of 1875 Thomsonesque church), 1851 Romanesque before he went 'Greek'; and, 20 years later (3), in main Nithsdale Road, one-storey 200 with 'Egyptian' columns, and 202 (now a school). To S, facing railway in Strathbungo (4), is Thomson's finest terrace, 1859, 1-10 Moray Place, with his characteristic square pilasters between windows – the 'pilastrade' (with incised ornament) under end pediments and along 1st floor between (plus three terraces, not by Thomson, of decreasing quality to right); and, in poor area on Paisley Road (Cessnock underground station), his subtle 1857 Walmer Crescent (5) with pilastrade plus square bay windows. N of (6), shortly to become Queen's Park, was Thomson's most exotic church, destroyed in Second World War, but that at Caledonia Road (7), with its inventive tower, survives (just) as a facade amid the traffic.

Off **Map I** to s lie: sw of Queen's Park, Thomson's unusual 1856 double villa (25, 25a Mansionhouse Drive, Langside); ¼ mile s, Thomsonesque (Egyptian motifs) 1876 Millbrae Crescent, backing onto White Cart Water – as does Thomson's finest house, again 1856, 1½ miles SE, 'Holmwood' (now a convent), Netherlee Road, N of Cathcart cemetery. Back on **Map I**, in South Glasgow, (8) and (9) mark the better-class tenement/flat areas, now Conservation Areas, of East Pollockshields and Crosshill (facing Queen's Park); (10) marks William Adam's superb C18 Pollock House (art gallery with superb paintings plus new gallery for the Burrell collection); and (11) Mackintosh's 1904 Scotland Street School (Shields Road underground station), with its symmetrical bow staircases. On **Map III** it is just w of (16) – along with, in a depressing area, three warehouses: 1900s Venetian Gothic brick (15); 1897 French Renaissance with dome (13), 'a warehouse in scale and elaboration to eclipse all others and to boost the rising prestige of the co-operative movement', and the adjacent one, 1919-33 (14), 'almost equally grand' with 'more positive merits'.

Dennistoun (12) is a surprisingly attractive 1860s classical residential enclave, (**Map II**, just E of the Necropolis), with villas and trees behind 1840s terrace (Annfield Place) on Duke Street. Along Maryhill Road may be found: Mackintosh's 1897 Gothic/Art Nouveau Queen's Cross church (13) – at junction with Garscube Road; and ½ mile further out, right, up Ruchill Street, his 1898 Ruchill church hall. The nearby Forth-Clyde canal is worth exploring, along the towing path: 1 mile NW out over Maryhill Road, down 5 derelict locks to massive 400ft long 1790 stone aqueduct over river Kelvin; or 2 miles SE to Georgian and Victorian warehouses (14) of Port Dundas (above M8 and city centre), lifting bridge and strange basins (15) which once led to Monkland Canal (filled in for motorway).

Cathedral and High Street area (Map II)

The town, originally an ecclesiastical burgh round the cathedral, moved its centre s to Glasgow Cross, then w with subsequent Georgian developments to George Square; so the cathedral area is rundown, and 'blighted' by motorway proposals.

Start at medieval cathedral (1) with superb mid c13 Lower Church. N of 1900s Royal Infirmary (site of bishop's castle/palace) is Mackintosh's 1895 Martyr's School (2) with little cupola. Next to cathedral, over 'Bridge of Sighs', is the Necropolis, laid out in 1833 (1825 Doric column) with fine monuments, such as 1842 Romanesque Menteith Mausoleum; opposite, crowstepped Provand's Lordship (1471, 1670, museum); facing Cathedral Square (1735 William III statue) contrasting Barony churches – 1878 honey Baroque with tower, huge red 1890 pointed Gothic. E of (3) is Dennistoun Conservation Area mentioned earlier. Down High Street, past site of c17 Old College of Glasgow University, moved in 1870 to Kelvingrove; 1790s doorway facing (4) in street opposite. Left to fine late c19 warehouses – long stone 6-storey (5), redbrick giant arches, classical Thomsonesque with pilastrades, as also s, to Gallowgate and 1922 Ionic columns facing Glasgow Cross (6) – 1930 replica Mercat Cross, 1626 Tolbooth steeple.

s to mid c18 St Andrew's (fine interior) with slender steeple (7); decayed pediment houses out to (8) with frieze over doorway, to re-erected Ionic arch (9) from Adam Brothers' Assembly Rooms. This faces Glasgow Green – 1888 Doulton Fountain (10), 1806 Nelson monument, People's Palace (11) with palmhouse and Old Glasgow Museum, amazing redbrick and bluetile 'Doge's Palace' 1889 carpet factory (12). w of (9) along Green: 1896 giant arches, 1750s episcopal St Andrew's (rusticated pilasters, urns); N to 1876 gabled corner; nice 1887 row (13) on Saltmarket, back to (6).

s side of Trongate: stumpy 1593-1636 Tron church steeple (1793 church behind), to stucco palazzi dated 1857 and 1870s (14) with marble and ironwork. N between grand 1903 Baroque with octagonal corner tower capped by green dome (to be seen many times later) and 1855 Scots Baronial (15), to good mid c19 classical City Halls (16); past market in SE corner to neo-Egyptian splayed windows of back facade, then along Candleriggs (past front facade with giant arches) to 1824 Gothic St David's 'Ramshorn' – sited as focus of street, like many Georgian public buildings to be encountered later. End, by contrast, at shining glass facade (17), 1936 for 'the Daily Express' (as in Manchester and London), now a listed historic building Grade A!

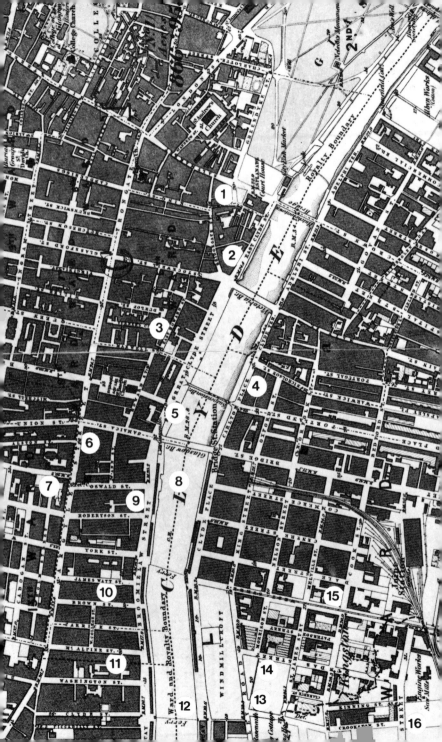

Clydeside (Map III)

Start, opposite Glasgow Green, at Jocelyn (once Jail) Square (1). Past impressive court houses with 1810 Doric portico, to 1871 Albert Bridge (3 cast-iron arches, previous bridge 1794) to follow N bank of the river to W. Under railway bridge to St Enoch Station (demolished), to 1873 classical facade of former Fish Market (2) with, embodied in it behind, strange 1665 Merchant's Steeple, a 'charming compound of Gothic and Renaissance features' – in Bridgegate, street to original medieval bridge (now 1850s Victoria Bridge with 5 stone arches). Beyond, attractive new quayside walkway and gardens, next three-masted 1864 wooden clipper; then 1816 St Andrew's RC cathedral (3), early Gothic revival (plaster vaulted interior); behind, 1900s Art Nouveau, facing (3). Across delightful 414ft 1851 suspension bridge (classical arch pylons) to two long 1800s stucco terraces – fine plastered interior in left-hand (4), pilastered and pedimented centre. Back to classical stone corner and 1840 Custom House (5) with Doric centre (by John Taylor who designed similar one in Dundee).

Now, from 7-arched 1899 stone Glasgow Bridge (previous ones 1836, 1772), one block inland, to savour fine c19 city centre commercial architecture (encountered much more later). Along W side of Jamaica Street: 1880s corner with pilasters and Grecian detail; 1860s cast-iron facades with slender columns and curving giant arches; superb corner 1855 ironframe Gardner's building with original lettering; 1864 palazzo; 1860s Thomsonesque; to main shopping Argyle Street. Left to 1863 ironframe (6) with more conservative facade; under 1900s extension (nice glass sides) of Central Station: 1900s palazzo pub (7); past pilastered warehouse, back to river at 3-arch stone 1927 George V bridge (8) – since map, as is 1880s railway bridge to E.

Continuing along Clyde at Broomielaw – late c19 Renaissance (9) with corner dome and side pediment. Superb mid c19 classical warehouses up James Watt Street: E side, best with balanced pilastered pediments, frieze, 2-storey window recesses; beyond, more conventional 9-bay with advanced centre, as also opposite; (10) similar 1854 greystone, heightened in red stone in 1911. Finally along quay, noting corner green dome and another classical warehouse (11), to under 470ft span 1970 Kingston Bridge (12) carrying M8 motorway. From here (and M8) can be seen two great Co-op warehouses mentioned earlier, (13) and (14) – the third warehouse (15); Scotland Street school being just W of (16).

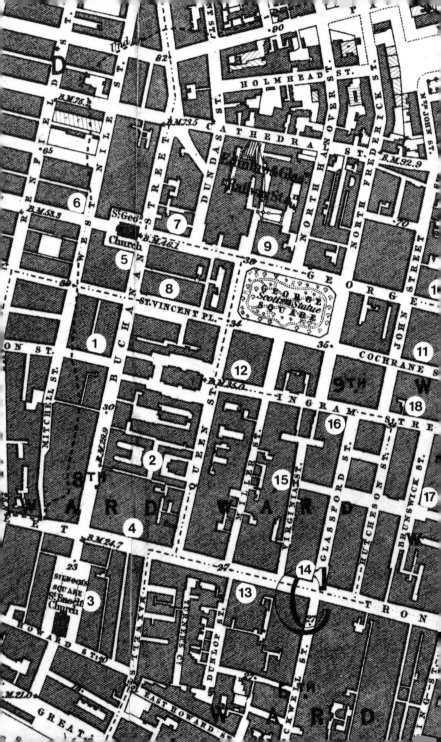

City centre (Map IV)

Start at canopy of Central Station, to me the city centre, where Glasgow feels most a large metropolis. E to monumental 3+5+3 palazzo bank (1) 'with the Farnese window theme at the first floor'. Then to explore fine pedestrian Buchanan Street. First downhill, both sides classical. Then on left huge 7-storey tall narrow 1898 development of burgage plot with recessed facade under elaborate gable (to be seen much later), in this case red sandstone with corner statues; opposite 1896 Renaissance gable with finials – bank, once famous tearoom (it had Mackintosh mural), 'exquisitely detailed François Ier to the requirements of Miss Kate Cranston's fastidious taste'. Into 1854 Princes Square with twin pilastered centre (2); then on W side, classical becoming Baroque with corner dome – to faceless c20 commercial architecture of main shopping Argyle Street. Cross to 'Jacobean toy-like' 1896 underground station, next site of St Enoch railway station (3). Back N (good view), via curving neo-Austrian 1899 bargeboarded gable (for Miss Cranston's Crown Lunch and Tea Rooms), along 1827 jewellers' arcade (4) with hammerbeam roof, to emerge opposite Frasers (4-storey 'arcade' inside).

Continuing Buchanan Street N of (1). 1887 Baroque corner tower/dome; 1884 palazzo; lavish 1900 with balconies over windows – on St Vincent Street. Then best group in Glasgow, from 1840s Italianate Western Club with square-columned tripartite windows and porch, eaves console brackets. Superb around 1807 St George's Tron Church with Baroque tower: Stock Exchange (5), 1875-7 *Gothic*, well-modelled corner and facing church; round windows, simple stucco – on corner with West Nile Street, where (on other corners) lavish red 1913 contrasts with severe white 1930 classical (6); richly detailed 1854 Royal Faculty of Procurators (twin fluted columns), its rear facing church; 'clean simplicity' of 1886 Athenaeum with statues on Ionic columns; big red 1909 Renaissance Liberal Club on corner; ending with two more tall 1890s narrow gables over recesses (both sides of Buchanan Street). Back down E side: 1877 shallow bay windows with tall Grecian corner — beyond, classical (7), exuberant Renaissance; good chunky new infill bank.

Left along St Vincent Place: huge 1906 with French roofs, opposite fine group – elaborate 1870s (8) with LH tower, not balanced because 'Citizen' newspaper got RH side and built 1890 'Netherlandish' gables; 1907 classical white tile; 1869 bank palazzo with curved pedimented windows. Into George Square – where this forms part of 7+5(higher)+7 frontage, RH end unbalanced by 1907 top to Merchants' House (dome with ship weathervane). Good view to Tron church, nice 1878 Queen Street station trainshed. In square: statues of James Watt (1832 Chantrey), John Moore (1819 Flaxman), Walter Scott 1832 (on column); original early c19 terrace (9); lavish 1883-8 City Chambers with 216ft tower and opulent interiors. To 1903 Royal College red facade (10) with interesting windows; s through arches linking 1924 City Chambers Extension to (11).

Back along George Square, past 1878 GPO (its 1892 rear replacing 1780s Assembly Rooms), 1860s palazzo (pilastered top floor) to superb 1830s classical area. Past fine 1834 7-bay with frieze over Corinthian pilastrade, to symmetrical frontage (round Ionic pilasters) either side of Stirling's Library, facing (square Ionic pilasters) its sides, with, at back, fluted Ionic columns of screen arches and 1827 bank portico (look at 1851 facade in Buchanan Street). To s, behind 3+6+3 stucco facade are two narrow courtyards, each with 'terraces' (windows picked out above doors, rusticated ground floor). The superb central block started as 1780 mansion (square pilasters) for one of Glasgow's 'Tobacco Lords', when Glasgow imported 40 million lb of tobacco a year, a reminder of the c18 Merchant City E of Queen Street we are about to explore (having seen part earlier); it was then added to in 1827 – at back (Corinthian columns, good interior) as Royal Exchange (Stirling's Library in 1954); at front fine fluted Corinthian portico plus columned clocktower; this faces 1844 Wellington statue and disruptive new bank (12).

W past (12), s down Miller Street: right, elaborate 6+3+6 1850 warehouse, with curved window pediments; stucco classical; left 7-bay 1860s former Stirling's Library with tall 1st-floor windows, pedimented Georgian house with 3-bay centre; to Greek Thomson's first (1849) pilastrade, with 1860s cast-iron corner (13). E to three good corner buildings (14): 1760s house with keystones, huge 1920s with green dome, 1903 Renaissance with 4 round towers. Back and N up Georgian Virginia Street: left under 7-bay with pediment/chimney into former 1819 Tobacco Exchange with Ionic 1st-floor columns; 1+8+1 Virginia Buildings with 3-bay centre (15) plus court. Right, nice 1860s palazzo; Georgian house with side and corner pediments; elaborate 1890s on corner with giant arches. Round 1870s classical Court Houses to Ingram Street and single-storey 1890s Baroque banking hall (16); back to (15).

E past 1790s Adamesque facade with coupled pilasters and pedimented ends, to fine 1844 Ionic portico of County Buildings. Go round it anti-clockwise – noting strange 1859 Baronial/Art Nouveau (17), 1854 gabled Baronial corner, Grecian 1805 Hutcheson's Hospital (18) – to original 1844 pilastered Merchant's House (part of County Buildings block.) This faces superb 1794 facade of Adam's Trades House, s of (16), reminiscent of his Edinburgh work – the massing and small central dome of the Old College facade (where bigger dome in fact built), the huge round-topped tripartite/Venetian windows of N side of Charlotte Square. Finally, via (18), to fine 1859 corner church with glazed colonnades (Baroque interior), facing (11).

Glasgow West central (Map V)

Back to Central Station. Opposite station canopy is Thomson's 1860s 'Greek' warehouse (1), with pilasters brought forward 2nd floor, eaves gallery with consoles (plus 1907 'Graeco-Baroque top hamper'). Then Union Street and his superb 1871 Egyptian Halls (2) – eaves gallery now colonnade, with two 1857 classical cast-iron facades beyond. Past 1872 cast-iron corner (mansard later), opposite good frontage, to two newspaper offices by Mackintosh: 1893-5 Glasgow Herald with strange corner water tower (3); 1900-1, hidden in Renfield Lane behind (1), white and redbrick, with Art Nouveau stone top; contrasting 1894 French Renaissance to W. S past 1880s Central Station tower and 7-storey side, 1899 with eaves gallery (4). Waterloo Street W: 1899 with recessed top, functional rear of (4), to 1900s parcels office (5) with huge round windows. N at 1927 corner. Rothwell Street E: huge 1927 block (6) – US classical (like King Street, Manchester, and Water Street, Liverpool); and 1898 with balanced gables and Renaissance corbels, opposite terraces (1890s red, classical 1849 stucco); then, past (1), along now familiar Gordon Street.

Now St Vincent Street, W from Buchanan Street, block by block. Left (corner already noted) pedimented windows, 1840s classical corner (7). Left, 1890s curved gabled corner, 1860s Thomsonesque, 1920s classical with sculpture (Renfield corner); right, 1913 classical corner, 1908 steel-frame (7-storey bay windows – 'functional' rear), corner 1853 columned classical. Left, corner 1870s pilastered 2nd/3rd floors, 1860s palazzo (balustrade), red Hope corner tower; right, corner 1927 US-style classical, 1904 pilastered Renaissance (varied top, 'functional' rear), 1870s pilastered corner. Left, 1929 middle (tall arched recesses), classical 1931 Wellington corner. Right (beyond corner) most famous tall narrow development – 1899-1902 'Hatrack' with ingenious windowed facade, 'ten storeys on a single house plot 29ft 6in wide but 109ft deep'; good new chunky glass infill beyond, (8). Left 1904 red corner, 8-storey 1931, early C19 corner – reconstructed 1860s with Thomsonesque details; right, chunky new, early C19 stucco, to last of great US-style blocks, 1926-9 on West Campbell Street corner.

We now enter smaller-scale Georgian residential area (now

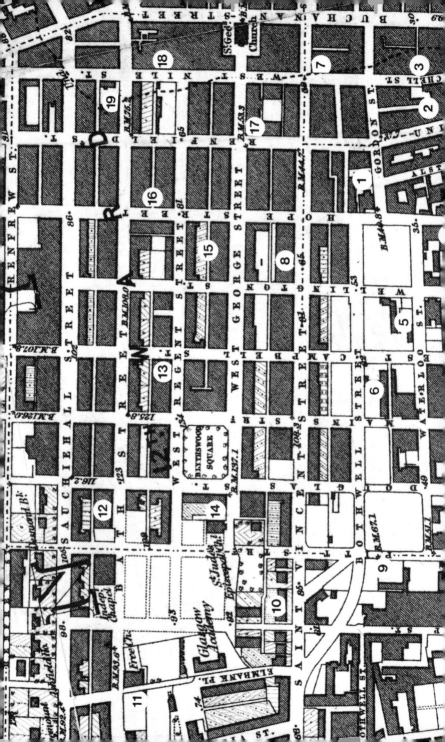

offices), with 3+6+4+6+3 terrace (eared windows) right. Next block, another terrace, 3+6+6+6+3 on left (part raised later), but, opposite, only fine 5-bay central house and RHS (cast-iron balcony). Then 3-bay Georgian houses with good porches (as uphill to square) to Thomson's superb 1859 church on podium (blank on map) with extraordinary 'free-Egyptian' tower. Down to 1854 Eagle Buildings (9), back N (best view of church), W to 1904 spire (10) plus good infill.

N past classical houses, fine Italianate original Academy, to 1903 King's Theatre (11). Back E down Bath Street to four corner churches: 1850s Gothic with spire, opposite classical (to S, classical with round windows, 1938 back Academy gatehouses); classical (on map) with fine portico, with round windows (opposite, since map), facing pilastered terrace (12); to terraces both sides – 5-bay centre with twin porch, 6-bay centre with fluted Ionic porches.

Finally zigzag across Georgian grid. S (1894 Baronial (13) to E), to terraces round Blythswood Square (3-storey, channelled ground floor with recesses, Ionic porches); 3+15+3 N side (no. 5, 1905 doorway by Mackintosh) and S; 5+12+5 E and W. From (14), with splayed 'Egyptian' windows, E: vista to church; Georgian houses with good porches. N and E round good corners of block (15) to West Regent/Hope (1900s Art Nouveau copper bay windows). Back to commercial scale with 90ft 1905 concrete (16), 4in thick walls and floors, S down Hope Street to 1902 West George Street corner 'mighty commercial alcazar'. E again: fine classical Northern frontage – 1879 tripartite windows and pilastrade, 1860 palazzo, 1867 corner, 1869 corner palazzo with varied shell-topped windows; opposite, 1890s French Renaissance corner (17). N to West Regent/Renfield's 3 good corners: tower, 1890 gabled Renaissance, 1860 Baronial. E past hideous Odeon. N past 1837 pilastered former Victoria Baths with pedimented ends (18); 1858 Thomsonesque corner with pilastrade. W to end at 1861 Mechanics Institute (19) with huge Ionic columns, 1910 top.

North central area (Map VI)
Of less general architectural interest because of commercialisation, but includes Mackintosh's Willow Tearooms and College of Art, and decayed but strangely attractive early C19 residential Garnethill. (R) marks Inner Ring Road (M8), which severs this area from the canal warehouses of Port Dundas (1) mentioned earlier, and 1840 Queens Crescent (2) covered later.

Start at pedestrian stretch of Sauchiehall Street (3), noting classical Crown Halls (lettering on top), corner. Left past 1904 Pavilion Theatre (4), to gabled Art Nouveau 1907 row opposite 1895 Theatre Royal (5), reconstructed for Scottish Opera, facing

1872 Italianate tower, exotic 1895 Orient House (6). Back to Sauchiehall Street: 1895 Baroque (7) with recesses; s round new shopping centre to 1912 Education Offices (8); note 1880s 'Venetian' (9) – bottom Gothic, colonnade top; to Mackintosh's 1904 Willow Tearooms (10), now jewellers, Art Nouveau interior reconstructed in 1981. Then 10+11+10 classical 1850s McLellan Galleries (11) to 1865 Thomson corner (12) with top Egyptian colonnade.

N into Garnethill up to clifflike side (library bay windows set back to end up flush with wall) of Mackintosh's School of Art (13), whose original fusion (1897-9, 1907-9) of curvaceous Art Nouveau, sturdy Scottish Baronial and modern Functionalism makes it one of the key buildings in world architecture. Past its front to zigzag around Garnethill grid, noting early c19 classical houses and terraces, many in bad condition: E past back of (11) to 1939 'Scandinavian' brick cinema, finely composed 1925 to right; round 1910 RC church (14) with tower, dome and lavish Baroque interior; w past its Italianate school facade; N past 1882 school with roundel (15); E; N to Gothick chapel (16), next to 1884 neo-c17 (another roundel). Across grass, Britain's first teacher training college, grand 1837 (17) with pilasters and square tower, like Leeds Town Hall; and 1906 Baroque corner (18).

Returning uphill: up steps (19); w to Italianate square buttresses/ columns (20) – plus symmetrical school facade with tower; s to 1845 terrace (21), opposite terrace/tenements – both with varied 1st-floor windowtops; along ridge (Hill Street) past richly moulded synagogue facade (22), to terrace (Doric porches) and view over Inner Ring Road to Park Scheme and University. Return E; s past (22); E past terrace and tiny Gothick church opposite 1931 hospital (cast-iron panels), to revisit Mackintosh (13) and Thomson (12). Finally w along Sauchiehall Street: 1900s Renaissance gabled (23), to 1903 narrow gable and 1890s group – asymmetrical 1897, Renaissance gable, spectacular 'Parisian' curve facing IRR.

The Park Scheme and Hillhead (Map VII)

Over IRR(R) on footbridge (1) to classical 1830-60 residential area – starting with two terraces in Sauchiehall Street, 1864 3+18+9+18+3 (continuous cast-iron balcony) facing 1837 6+30+9+30+6 (2). Good loop s to James Sellars' superb 1870s Ionic facade with caryatids (3); 1858 tenement terrace (4) with 5 pairs of 3-storey bay windows above channelled ground floor; 1911 Baroque front and green dome of Mitchell Library (facing IRR). w of (2), grass and trees; varying heights on left – columned porches, tripartite windows, eared Egyptian doorways; right 6+15+6+15+infill; crescent (5) with pilastered ends and centre. s

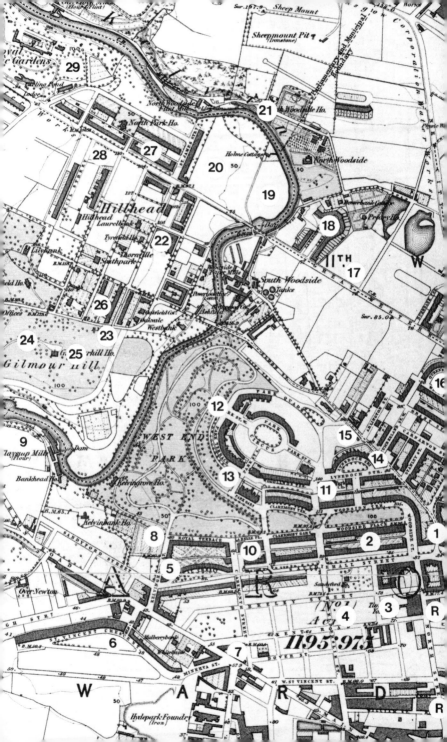

to 1850 development (6) – rusticated ground floor, square porches, straight 1st-floor windowtops, eared 2nd-floor, balustrade; concave curve to w, convex E, becoming 4-storey (pilasters) to corner (7).

Back past (5) to Sellars' 1878 church (8), again with fluted Ionic columns; (behind, huge 1901 Art Gallery and Museum (9), with 1920s Kelvin Hall opposite). Following gardens round: Corinthian bay window columns; Doric, then Ionic, porches; advanced end; strange round openings to go with 1857 Queens Rooms with frieze (10); across gardens to 1850s 3-storey bay windows over large tripartite, continuous balcony left, right 1847 crescent (despite name, centre 1842), with scroll windowtops, Ionic porches; 1857 with 1st-floor bay windows alternating with scroll tops; 6+30+12+30+6 with Doric doorways; nice curve up from (1); terraces with doubled fluted Doric porches at ends; up steps to amazing Lombardic towers of 1856-61 Trinity College (11).

Past Victorian church tower, through Park Circus, designed 1855 by Charles Wilson, 3-storey with frieze/band above rusticated ground floor and at top (roundels) – the hub of 'probably the greatest town planning enterprise in mid-Victorian Britain'; to statues (12), view of University. Turning back – both sides with elaborate roofs. Follow gardens to (13) – 2-storey bay windows, tripartite doorways, round and Venetian attic windows. N to circus; past Trinity College; down crescent (two centres with double porches) to emerge in busy tenement area at (14); to NW fine 1870 Burges-like Gothic church (15).

Past Ionic porches, through 1840 Queen's Crescent (16) – 2 storey with 3-storey ends, to first part of Great Western Road: Gilbert Scott's 1871-84 episcopal cathedral (17), well-proportioned interior, crescent (alternate bay windows) behind; into crescent (18); another good Victorian spire; 1891 iron bridge over Kelvin. N to 1890s Glasgow Academy (19), 1869 crescent with top frieze (20), 1900s crown steeple (21). S past three terraces – simple 1840s, superb Thomson 1865 (22) with pedimented ends and pilastrades, small 6+9+6 – to University: 1888 gatehouse (23) with parts of original c17 buildings (see **Map II**); 1690 staircase rebuilt right of 1923 Gothic chapel (24); Gilbert Scott's 500ft 1870s Gothic frontage overlooking Kelvin Park, with 300ft tower (like Albert Institute, Dundee) and fine vaulted undercroft of Bute Hall (25); 1883 'Madeleine' church (26).

Now to start the great terraces of Great Western Road, set back behind grass and trees, in which mid c19 Glasgow architects kept classical terrace alive by inventive designs incorporating the increasing demand for bay windows: 1856 Belgrave (key door ornament) facing 1855-8 Ruskin (27) – 3-storey with top balustrade,

4-storey round corner (explore N to river), houses with urns; along 1870s Alfred (28) over shops (noting 1884 school facade with caryatids up to left), with view across to Rochead's superb Italianate Buckingham Terrace (bay windows and balconies over advanced ground floor). Cross to it, then past huge villas (one BBC), to superb curving 1860s glasshouses (29).

The West End (Map VIII)

Back to the great terraces at Rochead's 1855 Grosvenor (1), with its identical 10+65+10 Venetian bays – followed by his more conventional 1849 Kew (3), with scroll doorways; behind, Sellars' 1875 'Sainte Chapelle' (2). Across to the earliest, Charles Wilson's superb 1845 Kirklee (4) – 'crisp Italianate' with eaves frieze, balustrades, delightful mews cottages behind.

Now into area with huge villas: 1900s (5) with Baronial/Art Nouveau ends; Sellars' 1877 Thomsonesque Kelvinside Academy (6); terrace (7) incomplete; (8) with fine 1880s villas all round. To sophisticated 1876 Cleveden Crescent (9): roundel frieze, using bay windows to build up to centre. Along edge of conservation area – 1930s Gothic church (10), back to two 1870s terraces – Corinthian bay window columns, 'Venetian gables' (11) and French pavilion roofs, tripartite bay windows; opposite, 1878 'great Victorian ironfounder's palazzo' (Centenary Club).

Now long loop S to Partick Hill: Greek Thomson's last terrace (12), 1874, groundfloor bay windows linked by Ionic porches to support those above, fine ironwork; 1900s St Bride's opposite nice rhythm of 4-storey pilastered bow windows (13). Into unexpectedly leafy 1840-70 villa area with front gardens (14); down; round curve past little terrace (15); up steps (16) – good villas to E top and bottom – back to (14). Cross to 1870s terraces (17) with elaborate bay and attic windows; to S, terrace near 1865 church (18) with spire. Round 1858 circus (on map) with colonnade, to 1870s terrace with advanced ground floor (19). From (20) explore E to terrace (LHS unfinished), and round villas shown on map, via Sellars' 1877 Early English church (21), (22) in attractive area. Back via crescent (23) with *bow* windows, N to (12).

Right into gardens (window balustrades), 1880 Renaissance church, out to terraces again: left 1870s Lancaster (caryatid doorways) – opposite 1900 Renaissance houses and, later, gable and gabled dormers; right; subtle massing of Thomson's superb 1869 Great Western Terrace (24) – intermediate 3-storey blocks, Ionic porches, fine ramps and 'Egyptian' ironwork – as in (12). To end with more elaborate contemporary Belhaven terraces, segmental windowtops, Corinthian bay window columns – fluted in later half, unfluted in earlier (25).

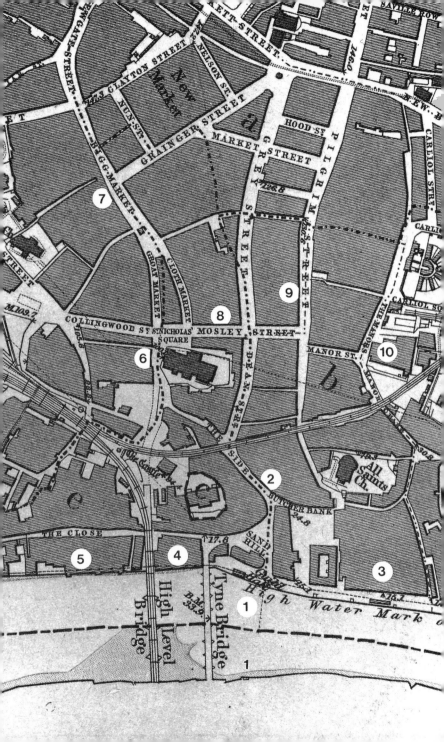

Newcastle-upon-Tyne

A Roman bridgehead, the town originated in a Norman 'new castle';
growing on its wool and famous coal-exporting trade to become a
county in 1400; the 'strength and magnificence' of its c13/14 town
walls (besieged by the Scots in 1342) 'far passeth' all the cities of
England and most in Europe (Leland, 1540). Newcastle became a
major c19 engineering and shipbuilding centre (and port) but,
remarkably, gained from this growth a superb classical planned
centre, with new streets inserted in gardens within the medieval
plan, by speculator Richard Grainger (1798-1861) and architect
John Dobson (1787-1865); by contrast denser medieval textures,
steps, bridges overhead, down steep slope to river. With new Metro,
Newcastle is 'capital' of the North East; Kings College in 1963
became a university – near striking new Civic Centre.

City centre (Map I)

Start at Guildhall (1): pediment, Dobson's Tuscan apse, arcade,
cupola; inside, 1650s hall, parlour, pendant ceiling (rebuilt), 1636
chimneypiece; bridge now 1876 swing. Superb Sandhill: Georgian,
1840s stucco; redbrick over timberframe; late c17 timber/glass
'curtain-wall' Surtees house (crude pilasters), similar 3-bay, Red
House; Victorian stone commercial up curve.

Under 1928 Tyne Bridge (531ft steel arch) to late Victorian/
Edwardian commercial quay area like Glasgow: inland between
elaborate tripartite windows, narrow plot; left to 1912 Baroque
curve (2); good frontage to (1) – one 1881, varied roofline
contrasting with crude bridge details. Along to 1840 classical
Custom House (3). Up alley to 1786 almshouses, under 1753 school,
into delightful Trinity House courtyard: segmental windows; 1800
porch to 1634 chapel; ranges redbrick (1787), stone (1721); out to
1841 Gothic between warehouses. Past Guildhall, under 1770s
bridge arch to redbrick, stone, iron 1880 Fish Market (4); under
Robert Stephenson's superb 1848 two-level bridge, to stone
warehouses (5) and courtyard; Georgian redbrick, steps, exposed
overhanging timberframe.

Loop into centre Up steps from (4); through castle postern gate; to
1810 Doric Moot Hall, 1170s keep, 1247 barbican Black Gate, huge
cruciform St Nicholas (now cathedral) with 194ft 'crown' (1736
library); w late c19 classical symmetrical about GPO (6). Explore
medieval marketplace (Georgian/1900s) past island (offices replace
Town Hall) to (7); back past White Hart (yard) to (8). Between mid
c19 classical stone, 1780s brick, across superb Grey Street, to early
c18 brick (9) with recessed centre. s to views from Tyne Bridge.
Through underpass, to Dobson's 1831 Royal Arcade, recreated

within island block; 1680s brick almshouses (10) – museum, loggia, shaped gables, c13 friary tower; superb oval 1790s All Saints (intricate spire); down to quay.

Along line of town walls (Map II)

For general picture of city centre, excellent surviving Western stretch, and surprising number of isolated remains (gate, two towers adapted as 'guildhalls'). c13 stone bridge (gatehouse N end) replaced by 1770s (1) on map; waterside houses incorporated in defences to (2); downstream, wall built behind quay to Sand Gate(16); nearly all 2-mile line shown on maps.

Start at site of Close Gate (3) – plaque, remains (wallwalk) above; up steps amid 7-storey 1840s redbrick warehouses to Hanover Street; up steps to stretch in new building, to stretch facing railway arches; here wall went N, W round (4). E to early c18 redbrick (5) with 2-storey bays, 1822 Tudor chapel; SW past pedimented doorway to stretch in brewery yard. Along 'intramural' lanes (6), across Grainger and Clayton Streets centred on Dobson's 1846-50 railway station. From pediment (site of West Gate) finest stretch: four towers (round external, square; c17/18 Morden top for Plumbers, Glaziers, Pewterers); past (7), through gap to see outside, to (8). E, into churchyard to see wall – plus stretch N of church, next to site of New Gate (9). Along (line just S) to remains of 1825-31 Eldon Square – 5+17+5 pilastered stone terrace, continuous cast-iron balcony (10), contrasting 1820s brick chapel, behind 1904 Art Nouveau Emerson Chambers; to 135ft 1838 Grey column (on line of walls), focus of Grey and Grainger Streets.

Past site of Pilgrim Gate (11) to 1904 Baroque/Art Nouveau Art Gallery (tower), facing Georgian pedimented doorways, Dobson's Grecian stucco house (frieze, scroll window), where wall turned S (12) – facing 'wall' of offices across road. SE past 1826 Tudor (BBC) to redbrick house, Plummer Tower (pilasters, Venetian window), rebuilt 1742 for Masons, rough townwall (13). Past 'wall' of offices, across motorway footbridge, tunnelling under railway to corner turret (14) – explore down garden to see stretch below road. 1900s tramways depot cupola, City Road to Pandon Bank (site of gate): 1900s gabled warehouses (Gibbs round windows); view onto Georgian brick warehouses W of (16). Up steps, to Sally Port gate (15) with 1714 top (for carpenters, ship over doorway), and 1701 Keelmen's hospital – strange stucco tower, curved gables, redtile roof, attractive purplebrick courtyard. (**Map IV** – along City (New on map) Road to fine 1768 classical St Anne's). Down past good Milk Market warehouse facade (hoists) to 1891 obelisk (16).

West central area (Map III)

Along quay under Tyne and High Level bridges to overhanging

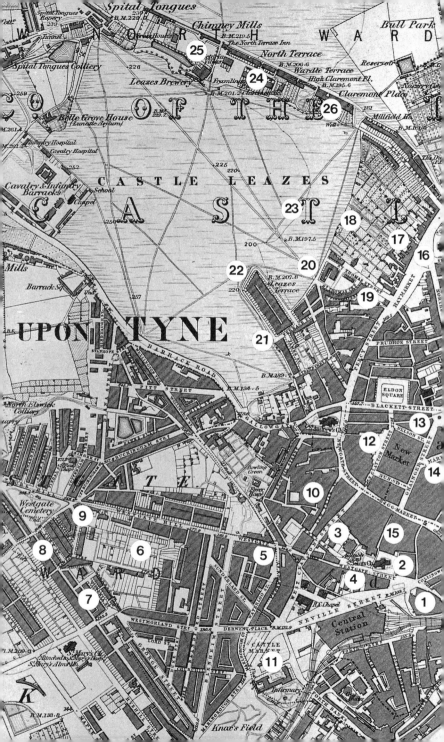

timberframe house; up steps, under railway; to right, views – of castle keep, down onto quay from High Level bridge.

Now pre-Grainger Westgate Street out from centre. Late Victorian/Edwardian commercial (back of GPO) opposite (1): 1890s Renaissance, 1910, lavish classical. Pedimented (Doric columns 'in antis') 1825, 1870s corner Gothic. Across, past Stephenson statue, to superb frontage: Loire-style 1877 (2); St John's (c14 arcade like St Nicholas); fine 1860s classical banks, County Court; 1770s Ionic Assembly Rooms (3) with pilastered ballroom. Opposite, (4): corner 1870s Italianate; Georgian redbrick (stone window strips); 2+3+2 1820s stone pilastered (also window strips); 1890s Baroque; Georgian redbrick. Past 1890s corners, pediment next to walls (seen earlier) to 1890s Stoll (refurbished interior), 1903 Pavilion theatres (5); then extramural Georgian (pre-Dobson, so redbrick) – tatty, shops in front.

Left into unexpected grassy 'square' with trees (6): N side Georgian, cast-iron balconies; later mid c19 brick other sides – E 2-storey with stone scroll doorways, S 3-storey in pairs plus stone 'ecclesiastical' convent, W (unfinished on map) like E only grander, iron balconies. Out to classical school, (7) with scroll doorways; nice streets – cobbles, stone surrounds (8), to 1904 churchtower (9). Back Westgate Street S side, twice under frontage to delightful cul-de-sacs facing 'square'. Past (5); left into Georgian Charlotte Square (good doorways); to medieval Blackfriars (Smiths' Hall) recently restored from squalor – courtyard (10), museum, crafts. Georgian Fenkle Street (look left), superb frontage again to (1).

Now early c19 classical Grainger developments. Past 1890 hotel iron canopy, Dobson's superb 1865 station portico (since map), to 1840s Italianate house (11). Along simple 1835 classical Clayton Street (channelled ground floor, stone front, purplebrick back), past Pugin's 1840s RC cathedral (Hansom's 1860s 222ft spire), recessed Fenkle Street corners; to 3½-storey double bowfronts facing streets either side of (12). Round grand pilastered market facades (inventively different), four clerestoried 'naves' inside (plus late c19 hall). Then (13) – Cordwainers' Hall, symmetrical about 1900s Art Nouveau, 1838 giant arches; 1+6+5+6+1 (tripartite) to sharp corner facing column; superb triangular block – Corinthian domed corners (acanthus finials), pilastered centres, 1906 tiled Central Arcade. Follow long fluted and columned Ionic facade up (14) and along Grainger Street. Its extension since map (15) has late c19 mixture found in other cities: left, Italianate, Renaissance dated 1874, Dutch gable plus pilasters, 1880s dormered Renaissance (oriel) – facing St John's; right, 1870s Gothic and Venetian, superb 1861 bank (pedimented centre, rusticated ground floor).

Newcastle-upon-Tyne III   OS 6″   1864   **81**

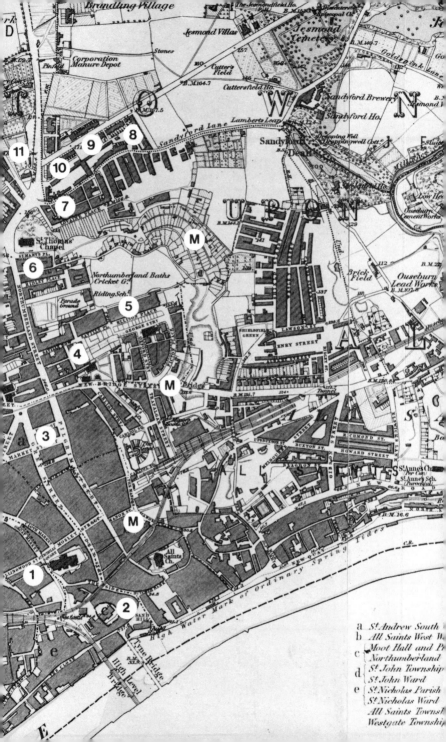

East central area (Map IV)

Between good 1900s corners (chunky groundfloor arches); past 1891 bank (1), with alternately pedimented Gibbs windows. Past St Nicholas; two parts of castle; *down* Castle Steps, to (2). Under impressive railway arch, up Dean Street: pre-Dobson Georgian redbrick right; left tall 1900s brick/timberframe 'Norman Shaw', fine 1870s classical corner bank.

Now up Dobson's masterpiece, superb stone sloping curving classical Grey Street, built after 1835, one of the finest streets in Britain: left side articulated by fluted Corinthian columned 'chunks' (central 10 bays with pedimented windows for Bank of England), Ionic hotel, 'triangle' seen earlier; right more varied, many with recessed centres (laurels), 1837 Theatre Royal portico (1899 interior), culminating in Corinthian bank block (3); up to column. Note inventively different facades (Doric porch opposite one) round (3), and to left and right in Pilgrim Street – where late 1920s/early 1930s blocks marked new through-route to Tyne Bridge, emphasised by recent urban motorway (M).

Up pedestrian shopping Northumberland Street; along Georgian brick Saville Row, across new road (4), to pedimented doorways (5) abutting glass offices. N into polytechnic area: 1887-95 former Medical School (gatehouse), 1880s 'Norman Shaw' school, 1884 cruciform church (octagonal tower). NW to mixed Georgian Ridley Place; late 1820s Dobson Gothic for a change – gabled Tudor (6), delightful spindly Early English St Thomas; striking 1968 Civic Centre with quadrangle (7). (Attractive early C19 brick terraces to N: with stone band facing motorway (8), (9); (10) facing underpass). Dobsonian classical 1878 pilastered stone museum (11).

Back onto Map III

Back to St Thomas' (16) and into university area: lively neo-Jacobean Students' Union (17); neo-Tudor redbrick Armstrong College – 1887 tower (4-storey oriel), 1910s quadrangle, 1904 front (18). Back to Haymarket; into good 1820s residential area: purplebrick with stone doorways (19); crescent, stone arch, to terraces (20) – first 1+6+3+6+1 brick, then stucco (pilastered end house, segmental recesses), as also (bow, advanced centre), facing 86-bay E facade of Leazes Terrace. Explore round this amazing 1830s stone 'superblock', channelled ground floor, fluted Corinthian pilastered ends, 21 bays S, 69 W – facing cantilevered concrete football stands (21), to 20 bays with pediment (22). Across Castle Leazes (reduced since map), noting 1900s Infirmary (23), past later hospital buildings and housing, to 1850s Italianate yellowbrick and stone terrace (24). To Town Moor and 1782 former windmill (25); back 'inland' past 1850s greybrick terrace (26), into university area.

YORKSHIRE

Bradford

A medieval cloth town, with fine parish church (now cathedral), some early c19 classical buildings; but, despite nasty 1960s shopping redevelopment, Bradford is primarily a fine Victorian city (when wool capital of the world), later than map, most important buildings designed by local Lockwood and Mawson; they designed Sir Titus Salt's 1850s New Town of Saltaire, 3 miles N of city centre, up the canal shown on map but abandoned in 1922.

Start with flourish of Victorian Gothic, at 1860s Venetian Wool Exchange (1), with spiky bank behind – s of site of 1773 Piece Hall in Kirkgate (on map but demolished shortly after); s to superb 1873 Town Hall (2) with 200ft campanile, more Gothic N to red terracotta Prudential Assurance – but Renaissance beyond to corner (3). Across traffic to Victorian classical Italianate: 1850s columned St George's Hall next to palazzo offices, facing elaborate Victoria Hotel (4); railway station on map replaced by 1977 bus/railway station with impressive glass roof (5).

Back to do good loop from Wool Exchange. Past its corner tower and bank corner dome to neo-Renaissance block (6), late c19 warehouses (7). Then four smaller classical buildings: left 1859 courtroom (set back), house with good porch; right registry, chapel; to corner (8). s to (9), near covered market, E to return to (1) down Piccadilly: nasty shop backs but fine 1830s warehouses with pediments and pilasters, to emerge in fine Victorian Italianate townscape of Kirkgate.

Then E to parish church cathedral (10), with elaborate GPO in front, pilastered warehouses to N; behind its 1950s Gothic extensions, Georgian house with Gibbs doorway to c17 Paper Hall (11), being restored. s to explore in detail splendidly dense 4 and 5-storey Little Germany warehouse area, built largely in 1860s and 70s (since map) by émigré German wool merchants – in triangle bounded by road past cathedral, East Road (since map) from (11) past huge 1870s RC church to (12) – plus Peckover Street to columned 1873 chapel (13), and by Leeds Road to s. Largest warehouses are at (14); the best streets Burnett to NE, and Chapel – beyond 1840s houses (15).

Mid c19 classical suburbs, developed just before and after map, can be explored to NNW and sw. sw: past 1880s Baroque technical college (16) – now extended to become university, and to s (17) to (21), with nice terraces and classical villas. To N these occur beyond Inner Ring Road along Manningham Road: 3-storey classical at

Eldon Place (22); two pedimented squares – 1851 Peel since map (23), Hanover on it (24). Beyond (25): to w Southfield Square; on left Apsley Crescent; becomes leafier with villas out to Lister Park (1900s Museum and Art Gallery); to w in Manningham, amazing 1873 Italianate mills, 350 × 150 yards in plan, 250ft campanile.

Sheffield

City of steel, Sheffield vies with Leeds as the largest city in Yorkshire. Geographically confusing with numerous valleys radiating from the centre, it is famous for its post-war redevelopment, in particular the extensive slabs of flats clustered together with bridges linking across – Park Hill, (1) on **Map II**, and Hyde Park, off map to E. Nonetheless there is a surprisingly good Georgian quarter in the centre, a number of good Victorian buildings and a mid c19 'West End'. My exploration starts with the West End, moves into the city centre – both with 6″ maps; 1″ **Map III** later shows how they fit together (see page 94).

The West End (Map I)

First red or purplebrick 1830s terraces – in inner city area, with decay, blight, new roads, roads blocked off. Nice purplebrick (1), new road, area of classical 2-storey brick terraces (2), stone terrace (centre missing) with porches on columns (3). N to redbrick villas (4), little terrace with pedimented doorways since map (5), to villas and terrace on Glossop Road (6). To NW 1900s redbrick neo-Tudor university buildings with library/chapterhouse (7), Ionic 1880s Mappin Art Gallery (8). Nice villas: 1830s stone classical (9); 1850s classical and Gothic with bargeboards (10); redbrick classical (11). Redbrick houses with laurels on porches (12) and terraces here and (13); 1860s villas with bargeboards (14); up to magnificent stone 1830s terrace (15) with Ionic columns at centre and ends, and fine classical villa (16). ½ mile W, S off Fulwood Road, stucco pairs in delightfully 'rural' Endcliffe Crescent, (1) on **Map III**.

s to grand 1837-40 school (17) – pedimented centre and ends, all with Corinthian columns. Classical villas (18), but down (19) to remarkable Broomhall estate, with trees and huge neo-Gothic stone villas, many with bargeboards. Best to (20); back round down to 1835 Gothic school (21) – now part of polytechnic; E to beyond Broom Hall (22), with 1500s timberframe gable and Georgian front.

City centre (Map II)

Start with Georgian quarter around and N of cruciform St Peter and St Paul with spire (2), now the cathedral (considerably enlarged); to W, good frontage with pedimented 1786 school. N into charming cobbled Paradise Square (3) – segmental porches E side, N side grander house with elaborate centre; out E side, down lane to redbrick corner house (tall pedimented windows, stone pilasters) next to classical house with splayed windows. Down (4) to classical 1854 courthouse (5) next to more redbrick Georgian. Back S up cobbled Fig Tree Lane: grand stone facade with Ionic pilasters, past its good porch; to 1728 Baroque corner house with pilasters, surrounds, twirls.

Along E side of churchyard: large stone school, good doorway and fanlight, delightful stone Gothick to late Victorian corner. Along S side, fine C19 classical: 1866 bank, Corinthian columned facade of 1832 Cutler's Hall, bank Doric columns; opposite, contrasting late Victorian classical redbrick and stone Gothic; 1795 stucco (6) with Grecian details.

Two loops from (2). First down pedestrian Fargate with more late Victorian to (7). Past 1840s Gothic RC cathedral with spire, more Georgian houses, to classical chapel with fine porch. More Georgian: (8) facing Town Hall; and isolated (9) facing new road (opposite Library and Museum). Back via two theatres – disused stucco Victorian Lyceum, 1970s Crucible (10); alongside 1908 redbrick Victoria Hall (tower), down lane (good banks on bend), back to (2). Second to public buildings (since map): past (7) to 1890s Town Hall (11) with superb tower and roofscape; W to 1920s City Hall (12) with Corinthian columns, 1867 classical, Georgian 'topshops' (13), to large 1804 chapel (14); back via Georgian factory (15), noting strange blank classical apse of City Hall and long varied late Victorian frontage (16) – part of it 1877 Firth College (from which the university developed).

E side of map, across new roads: new shopping centre/market on site of castle (17); 1819 canal terminal (18); medieval timberframe Queen's Head with carvings (19), isolated at edge of bus station; Midland Station (20), since map. In NW corner of map, S of river Don: some mid C19 factories with classical details.

Wakefield

A medieval town with an attractively irregular plan W of its fine parish church (All Saints), Wakefield then became a prosperous C18 clothing town before Leeds and Bradford – Defoe calling it 'clean,

large, handsome and very rich, with a larger population than York', as well as the county town of Yorkshire West Riding. So Wakefield has a number of impressive Georgian houses (with a 'typical' 2-storey round recessed centre), plus the remarkable St John's Square scheme, beyond the exceptionally fine late c19 public buildings (since map) that give it, together with the 247ft spire of All Saints (now the cathedral), such a distinctive skyline.

Start at All Saints; Georgian redbrick houses E to (1), and to N, facing new roundabout; beyond, 1598 Old Grammar School (2) with tall crosswindows. Sally first s to unexpected Georgian terrace (3) with fine doorways, plus good house and Italianate chapel across traffic (4). Back and w from All Saints past good corner to island, next to overhanging timberframe. N to explore the narrow burgage plots built on in c18: under Woolpacks Inn (crude Venetian window); to surprisingly grand pedimented house in Barstow Square; out to nice c19 Italianate (5); back past redbrick warehouses of Cheapside (to w).

Then explore largely Georgian Westgate w: good frontage (6) with 'typical' house (Venetian window), grand 1879 classical with Corinthian columns, neo-Renaissance White Horse, stucco with columned 1st-floor window (as also later near railway), redbrick with blank arches. N, next to 1894 Opera House (7), to grand Georgian house behind (Gibbs doorway); chapel with Gibbs and Venetian windows opposite 1780 Orangery (8); under railway, to impressive mid c19 jail entrance (9). Back to another good stretch of Westgate (10) with another Venetian window (on N side).

Back to island, and up Wood Street (11): little square with 1800 stucco Old Town Hall; fine Ionic pilastered 1820s Mechanics Institute; strongly modelled 1870s Town Hall with 190ft tower and tall oriel windows; 1810 Court House with portico; right, redbrick terrace with continuous balcony; elaborate 1890s County Hall with corner tower and green dome (12); follow its interesting long back frontage to three classical villas (13). N to three redbrick pairs (14), just after map, an introduction to superb Georgian St John's Square, started in 1790: fine church in centre with pilastered 'transepts'; pedimented w side (1st-floor balconies), N side (39 bays long), and (15) with balustrade details in centre; note fine doorways and fanlights. Return by two houses forming E end of the scheme (16); 1833 neo-Tudor school; Georgian group with columned bay windows (17); 5-bay house (18) with elaborate doorway.

s of town centre: c14 bridge (19) over river Calder, with lavish chapel; fine 1820s riverside warehouse (20), N of navigation cut.

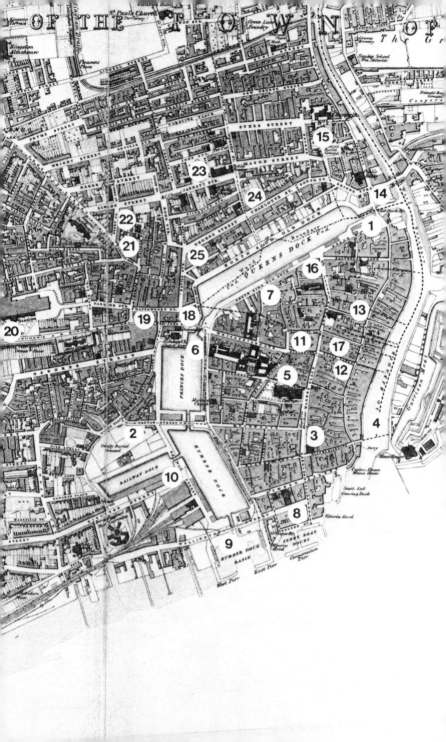

Kingston-upon-Hull

Previously Wyke, it was refounded in 1293 by Edward I as 'King's Town' upon the river Hull (still navigable, with movable bridges, up to Beverley). The medieval town was walled in stone, the extramural ditches being replaced – plus North Walls (1) – by three Georgian docks, starting with 1770s Queens Dock (in 1930s filled in as a garden, and Princes Dock is threatened). Since map, bridges have been added across the Hull, and the Old Town severed by a new road – (2) (3), over swing bridge at (4) – N of new tidal surge barrier. Nonetheless the Old Town still has much to explore, with historic houses, textures, warehouses and some welcome new infill housing and warehouse conversions; and, to NW, in the present city centre, are some fine c19/early c20 public buildings and unexpected Georgian houses.

Old Town

Start at Market Place, in front of Holy Trinity, one of the largest parish churches in England, much of it brick, with an impressive central tower. Round it clockwise: mid c19 yellowbrick Italianate; 1583 old Grammar School, redbrick with crosswindows; pediment with Venetian window over archway leading to curve of Georgian houses behind (doorways with console brackets); grand 1750s stucco facade with eared windows of Trinity House, whose buildings (not open to public) extend back (fine 1840s chapel) to Princes Dock; 1900s Art Nouveau Market Hall (5).

Three loops recommended, to and from (5).

First along Postern Gate, past pilastered side facade, converted warehouses, to fine Trinity House gateway with Ionic columns (6) and pedimented 1822 almshouses. Back along pedestrianised Whitefriargate with long Georgian frontage: three little terraces – stucco pilastered, redbrick with stucco pilasters, stucco with pedimented windows; superb 1790s facade of former Neptune Inn – round, tripartite, Venetian windows, cartouche over arch; redbrick with another elaborate design of pilasters, pediment, cartouche. N up Georgian street (tall pedimented doorways 'typical' of Hull, cast-iron balconies), along amazing 33-bay columned side of 1900s Guildhall (7); s back to (5) via charming Manor Street, Victorian commercial Land of Green Ginger, and lane with fine stone facade adjoining Trinity House.

Second, a loop s: to golden 1734 William III statue, near (3); across new road, past stucco pediment, into lively dock area, to corner 1820 Pilot Office (8) with tryglyph porch; along Humber frontage, across old lock (9) to gabled 7-storey warehouse (10); N to

look at Old Town across water, back past pilastered brick warehouse next to new road, E from (2).

Third, to N – up Trinity House Lane again, to Silver Street: N side, in alley, White Hart with elaborate late c17 side facade (11), s side 1894 arcade with dome on corner. Past good Victorian commercial buildings (many banks), timberframe cottage (12), to High Street, which runs N-S, its E side with warehouses backing onto the river. Fine stretch to (13): RHS hidden up alleys – Georgian redbrick house behind 1858 commercial, 1664 Crowle House with c17 pilastered and diamond-studded facade, either side of fine 4-storey warehouses; 1855 former Corn Exchange (transport museum) opposite 1744 Maisters House with fine doorway and staircase. High Street now loses any cohesion, but is worth exploring for individual houses: 1660s Wilberforce House (museum) with another pilastered diamond facade plus projecting porch; 1745 riverside warehouses near bridge; fine Georgian houses and building with pediment and cupola, old dock entrance, good doorway (14). Follow riverside warehouses to pedimented 1780 Charterhouse almshouses and house opposite (15) with curved gable. Back to (1); into gardens to see 1834 Wilberforce column, moved from E of (18); along old dockside to attractive warehouses (16). Then s past Georgian redbrick with good shopfronts; in front of Guildhall (square tower). Across 1900s Baroque street between Guildhall and GPO; back past St Mary's, into good Victorian commercial Lowgate, noting Georgian lane (17).

Hull city centre

Start from Queen Victoria statue and square: 1870 dock offices (18) now museum, with three domes; 1920s classical Art Gallery, 1898 terracotta Punch Hotel, 1900s City Hall with green dome and roof. w along City Hall (19), past Victorian Gothic arcade, to fine 1850s classical hotel and side facade of station, N of 1900s Art College with mosaic in pediment (20).

Then a loop NW from (18): up road (since map) past ornate frontage with green dome (21), to encounter first Georgian houses. Along (22), most redbrick with 'typical' tall pedimented doorways, to Albion Street – left 1840s stone house with fine porch (Institute), right terrace with keystones. Then RC church and, facing Kingston Square (23), pilastered and pedimented 1830s facade and stucco New Theatre (Ionic columns, former Assembly Rooms) – opposite more Georgian redbrick. s to two fine pedimented houses (24); down George Street to little 9-bay terrace (25) with panels (garlands); round former dock/gardens back to (18).

Leeds

The monks of Kirkstall Abbey started its wool trade, and Defoe in 1720s called Leeds 'wealthy and populous' and its cloth market 'a prodigy of its kind and not to be equalled in the world'. Leeds then became a major engineering and manufacturing as well as textile centre, growing to vie with Sheffield as the largest city in Yorkshire. It feels much larger than Sheffield and Bradford, a real metropolis – like Liverpool and Glasgow; and Leeds has developed recently as the commercial 'capital' of Yorkshire, with good dense new infill, especially in its West End (**Map III**).

The ruins of Kirkstall Abbey largely survive (superb c12 abbey church), 3 miles W of (1) on **Map III**. On **Map I**, they are 1½ miles W of (1), while 2 miles E of (2) is the largely c17 Temple Newsam House, owned by the city; late Victorian manufacturers' mansions tend to lie in the Northern suburbs of Headingley, Chapel Allerton and Roundhay – beyond (3), (4), (5), respectively. The maps show the early railways at the edge of the centre; they were then connected across it: from (2) on **Map III**; and on **Map II**, via (8) (3) (17) (18) to (19), cutting off in 1869 the parish church (4). Just after the maps, a civic area was developed N of the Headrow (widened and redeveloped in 1930s); while a new Inner Ring Road (R) curves round to N, in a cutting between the centre and the university. The outstanding local architect was Cuthbert Brodrick (1822-1905), who designed the Town Hall, Mechanics Institute and Corn Exchange.

East central area (Map II)

The original medieval/c17 town was round the parish church – Briggate its Western edge; the Eastern side became slummy, is largely now new housing – pioneer 1930s Quarry Hill flats demolished, site (20). Start at Briggate – between 1720s Holy Trinity (sophisticated 1839 180ft tower) and Brodrick's oval 1860s Corn Exchange (2), superb cast-iron/glass interior. Explore Boar Lane past Holy Trinity (1) – good Victorian curve and buildings S side; then E to (2), noting remains of 1775 Cloth Hall (severed by railway), to N stucco former assembly rooms (round, Venetian windows). Do two loops from (2).

First S of river Aire, starting and ending within the medieval street pattern with burgage plots still surviving (some Georgian fronts), to look at fine redbrick riverside warehouses. Down Kirkgate (3) to parish church (4), rebuilt 1838-41, attractive early Gothic revival, with apse and square tower off centre; redbrick mill buildings (5); across 1840 iron bridge, to good warehouses – corner (6), both sides (7), especially BWB right; across 1870s iron Leeds Bridge (once

Leeds I OS 1″×2 1858

medieval chapel like Wakefield) to best burgage plots NE of (8).

Secondly N into fine late Victorian townscape: city markets (9) – exuberant 1904 exterior and skyline, 1857 cast-iron/glass interior; then redbrick and terracotta King Edward and Queen Victoria Streets, with Empire, Cross and 1898 County arcades (10). Good isolated buildings across dreary neo-Georgian widened Headrow/ Eastgate: classical chapel (11); massive splayed 'Egyptian' (12) 1812 Hope Foundry; 1877 Grand Theatre (13) with tourelles, arcade to N, in New Briggate; 1630s Laudian Gothic St John's (14), good woodwork. (15) has two more arcades (1878 Thorntons figures, Gothic glass vault), 1900s City Palace of Varieties music hall. Finally two good early C19 streets (16): W along classical and Italianate Albion Place (1866 Gothic institute, late C18 pedimented house at end); E down Commercial Street with fine N frontage – stucco 1808 Library (Ionic pilasters, arched ground floor), then terracotta; to good stretch (C18 Turks Head hidden to S); back to (2).

West central area (Map III)

W to City Square (3) with many statues, 1847 Gothic chapel. S past City Station (2); over 1837 stone arch of Victoria Bridge; to 1827 terminus of Leeds-Liverpool canal – 4-storey stone warehouse with lunettes over hoists (4), locks, crane, bridge, tollhouse plus 3 C19 campanile/chimneys – octagonal topped, tall square, Florence duomo; inland to its factory entrance – stone coupled pilasters between redbrick round recesses, like round windows opposite (5); to amazing stone 1838 Egyptian lotus columns (6) – interior with cast-iron columns, little domes.

Back to (3). NW up LHS of 1896 stone Renaissance GPO (replacing Mixed Cloth Hall), redbrick and terracotta on left; in front of Loire-style 1897 Metropole Hotel, fine 1867 warehouse (giant arches) in York Place; to late Victorian corners (7). Now zigzag N through attractive redbrick 'West End' area: smart Georgian houses (on map facing gardens); fine 1850-70 warehouses – Italianate and Gothic, replacing gardens; good chunky new infill offices. W along Wellington Street to 1903 warehouse (oriel windows). N up Queen Street; to E Georgian house with fine porch (8). E along fine Park Place: stone pilastered centre (1st-floor balcony); lunette under pediment either side; varied Georgian doorways; pedimented centre; *greybrick* for a change. W along St Paul's Street – Italianate (9), 1930s neo-Georgian replacing church. To amazing 4-storey 1878 Moorish warehouse (10), facing Georgian square: N side – good pairs (3+4+2, laurel panels), two 5-bay pedimented houses, 6 tripartite windows; E side pedimented centre, curved pedimented doorways (laurels). Emerge in front of

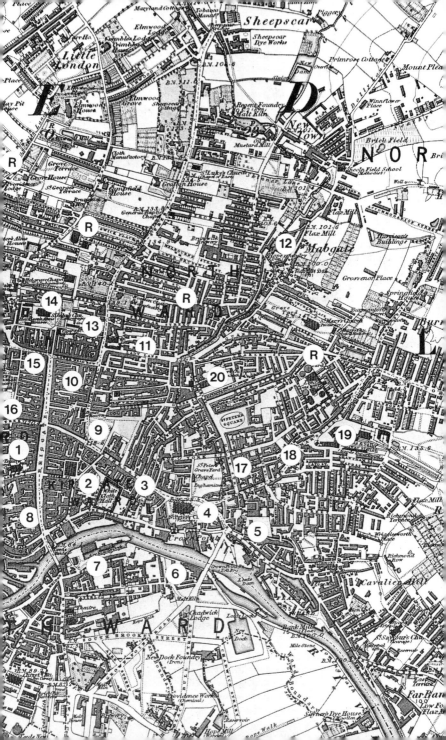

Brodrick's masterpiece, Leeds Town Hall (11), finest of all Victorian town halls, 1853-8, stone, giant columns all round, 225ft tower.

Back to (3) down East Parade: 1911 Gothic stone on corner, pedimented Georgian redbrick, 1898 terracotta next to stone round windows (12), 1894 bank with tower replacing infirmary. N up to Park Row: nasty 1960s Norwich Union; classical Victorian bank (13) next Georgian stucco; Victorian terracotta facing Georgian stucco (good doorway) in side street; fine classical 1860s bank (porch in South Parade), facing terracotta 1894 Prudential in good group (14).

Into area of fine public buildings – since map. Redbrick pilastered warehouse opposite 'Arts and Crafts' 1900s RC cathedral (15); Victorian classical – pilastered school (16), pedimented to N; Brodrick's 1865 Mechanics Institute (17) with large round windows (shell tops); good warehouse block (18) – huge round openings, rusticated ground floor; neo-Norman Colosseum (19); 1930s Civic Hall with two Wren-like towers (20). S to 1870s Italianate Library and Art Gallery (21), noting back and side of Town Hall.

Finally to early C19 residential areas N of IRR. W of (11) – 1890s Baroque chapel with tower, classical doorways, Victorian Gothic (22); huge symmetrical Gothic 1860s Infirmary (23); 1836-8 Gothic church; over IRR; to well-designed frontage (24) and pedimented corner of 1850-5 Woodhouse Square; Hanover Square – good houses (25) (26), stone pedimented and pilastered 1786 Dennison Hall (27) at top. Then redbrick Italianate villa (28) opposite 'Georgian' with back pediment; two pedimented houses; fine house (29), N of Dental Hospital. Now early C19 residential and university are inextricably mixed: left chapel with incised pilasters, early C20 Tudor priory (square tower) to 24-bay terrace (30) with pedimented ends, big scroll doorways; fine villa (31) with elaborate columned doorways. Past nice terrace to crossroads beyond (32): facing park, 1859 Gothic grammar school; NE cemetery with classical central chapel, Doric N portico.

Back past original late Victorian Gothic university buildings (33), earlier houses (stone with bow window, redbrick terrace pair) shown on map; emerging at two Victorian churches (34). Downhill: redbrick row (35) with pedimented porches; pedimented chapel (BBC); across IRR; to unexpected Georgian Queen Square (36) – pediment intended as centre of NW side.

York

A fine historic city – a Roman fortress and 'colonia', a centre of Danelaw (so streets are called ' – gate', gates 'bars') in which William the Conqueror established *two* castles, York reached its peak in 1377 when it was second only to London, expressed in the largest medieval cathedral in Britain (the Minster), famous for its stained glass (as are many of the churches). It had a Georgian prosperity with 'town houses' of the great country families, and then an unexpected c19 importance due to George Hudson, as headquarters of the North-Eastern Railway, accompanied by the severe overcrowding and poverty documented by Seebohm Rowntree. It acquired a university in 1960, mostly outside in Heslington but now partly 'downtown' in King's Manor.

The famous city walls, 2½ miles in extent, in parts on Roman foundations, are mainly c14, much renewed since. Within are superb streets and, surprisingly, industrial areas, bad new shops, dreary municipal housing plus disruptive late Victorian and c20 streets since the maps; but, outside the walls, are some fine Georgian/early c19 streets, with 'characteristic' purple/greybrick houses and tall classical doorways. Lord Esher's excellent 1968 report identifies the planning problems and is slowly being implemented.

My exploration starts from the 6″ double-page **Map I** with the circuit of the walls (an unusual, traffic-free way of getting the 'feel' of the city), plus Museum Gardens and streets w of the Minster and a sally within and outside Walmgate Bar; moves within the walls to **Maps II** and **III** at 12″ to the mile, to end on **Map IV** (at 24″) with the three most famous streets.

City walls (Map I)

Ascend at Micklegate Bar to start walls walk clockwise: over old railway approach, past present 1877 station (1) – 800ft long curving trainshed – and lavish hotel; 'grand Edwardian William-and-Mary' (Pevsner) to right in larger scale office area; down to riverside towers (a chain was stretched across in emergencies).

Then 1860s 'processional way' to the Minster. Iron arch bridge with Gothic details; neo-Jacobean opposite walls. On left, c13 ruins, 1927 library; Italianate contrasting with 1840s stucco crescent (cast-iron balcony); medieval side masonry to 1714 house (recessed vertical strips between windows); 1860s RC church and houses (Gothic of course); nice curve replacing precinct gate (demolished in 1827). On right, good 1860s corner; 1899 Gothic fiery redbrick and 1885 stone (2); to 1830s Gothic Minster Chambers and Song

School, on 1903 through-route (3) which completed the destruction of the precinct.

As a welcome contrast, explore NW of (2): Precentor's Court past Georgian row to 1680s (advanced centre, hipped roof plus staircase tower). Medieval Petergate – with mixed overhanging timberframe houses (as elsewhere in York), plastered and exposed 'black-and-white', past bow shopfronts, Georgian 7-bay with fine doorway, to Bootham Bar, the only bar without post-medieval widenings. Through to 1879 neo-Renaissance Art Gallery (4); into superb medieval-c19 abbot's house/King's Manor with two courtyards; note 1840s stucco rooms with pedimented windows and 1879 Gothic theatre (festive 1960s concrete canopies), opposite crescent seen earlier. Along walls to Roman/medieval corner in gardens – with 1830 museum portico, little 1833 observatory, and fine late c13 ruins of St Mary's abbey church with its guesthouse near river; through gatehouse to (5); follow impressive *abbey* walls, first down to river and water tower, then back past Georgian houses round to (4).

Back up along city walls at Bootham Bar (portcullis): left, older backs of Georgian Gillygate, 1840 neo-Tudor college (6); right, famous views of Minster; Monk Bar. Then right, decayed Aldwark area; foundations of Roman corner walltower; Merchant Taylors' Hall – level with 2-storey bow windows (7) in front of classical former hospital; much needed good new infill housing, back (brick pedimented windows) of St Anthony's.

Descend to cross river Foss and follow it (no walls because river and swamp), back onto walls at Red Tower (8), round to (9). Through bar and external barbican (the last left) to Georgian house with wings (10); opposite old church tower, 4-storey 1817 flax mill (11). Back through bar (1580s timber, Tuscan and Ionic columns) down Walmgate, once notorious for its slums. c14 timberframe opposite good infill, with St Margaret's (moved Norman porch) behind. It becomes a coherent street with another exposed timberframe (12); left, 1840s purplebrick rows of George Street; right, 5-bay Georgian (1783 rainwaterhead, panelled 1st-floor room); to bow windows (13) opposite St Denys, with Norman doorway (again moved).

Back onto walls at (9); past new pyramid swimming pool (14); down, near good infill, at Fishergate Tower (15), to cross the Foss again. Round castle wall (which covered this sector) to Eastern Norman castle mound (under Clifford's Tower); stretch of wall (16) with delightful Regency terrace (bow windows) behind; over 1878 bridge (17), another iron arch with Gothic details. Finally onto last stretch of walls: past Western Norman castle mound; between nice mid c19 purplebrick terrace housing; back to Micklegate Bar.

Micklegate, the river, the castle area (Map II)

Explore in detail superb Micklegate: plastered timberframe near Trinity priory church; grand 1750s town houses, two pedimented and quoined on the outside of the curve, opposite 5-bay with 3-column doorway (all with fine interiors); tattier mixed towards St John's. Return.

Then timberframe (1) with strange door canopy (moved), nice curve into c19 warehouse area; St Mary's (Saxon tower); Georgian 5-bay (2) with good doorway. Down Carr's Lane (3) to Skeldersgate: pedimented 1829 almshouses plus Arts and Crafts wing in front; pedimented 5-bay with elaborate central windows; Georgian group with 1+3+1 warehouse (groundfloor arches); views across river. Round fine 1875 bonded warehouse (4), across bridge; back past corner walltower and gazebo, to mid c19 purplebrick (5).

Inland beneath c13 Clifford's Tower to monumental Baroque Castle Square (6), best when floodlit: sombre 1705 Debtor's Prison with cupola behind curved pedimented wings (pilastered throughout) between festive 1770s (Ionic columns recessed at ends, in central pediments) female prison (now museum) and Assize Courts (urns, fine domed courtrooms). Then Castlegate and two 1750s mansions: pedimented (7), 1st-floor windows straight-topped over panels; opposite, in arched recesses with 'balustrades', railings in front, back Venetian between 3-storey bay windows; St Mary's (Heritage Centre); more Georgian – left with pedimented window, right (dated 1789) with huge stone doorway – to (8). Return to (5) down late Victorian Street (9) with Technical College (gabled centre) and Courts of Justice (turrets).

Then textures of King's Staithe; streets either side of 1700s Cumberland House; onto handsome Ouse Bridge (replacing c16 one in 1820) with views, upstream and downstream, of Victorian riverside warehouses. Inland to (8); along commercial Coney Street – church clock over street, mixed timberframe group, some Georgian and Italianate – to (10); beind grand 1725 Mansion House to c15 Guildhall (rebuilt after war) fronting river. Then Lendal – 8-bay with segmental windows and fine porch, 1816 former chapel facing strange narrow 1720s house with pilasters between gables and window linked to Venetian doorway; across bridge.

Finally – near hideous 1960s slabs (offices, hotel) – to riverside garden (11) with view of Guildhall. Turning inland: All Saints and good mixed group; past carved cornerpost and exposed timberframe side, to attractive space behind railings, between exuberant 1906 redbrick and stone North Eastern Railway Headquarters (12) and yellowbrick facade of original 1853 railway hotel; uphill along 1842 station (Tuscan colonnades), back to (1).

Map III

Across river to High Ousegate: corner 1850s palazzo; 1760s houses (1) with pilasters (Ionic, then Corinthian) at ends and flanking central pedimented windows; beyond All Saints (octagon), plaster timberframe houses, near 1912 Piccadilly (2). On The Pavement lavishly carved c16 gabled timberframe (plus 1670s brick, in yard, with ovals and 'Ipswich' windows), to appalling concrete (3) of 1960s Stonebow blitzed through (4). Turn thankfully down Fossgate: purplebrick opposite timberframe – exposed, then plastered (bow windows, shell doorway); good shopfronts and c17 entrance to Merchant Venturers' Hall – c15 timberframe interior, view from (2); 1812 bridge and almshouses with blank arches; to c18 row facing timberframe inn (5); back to (3). (Down Stonebow, by telephone exchange, to riverside view (6) of 1896 mill with tower.)

From (3) down Colliergate (1748 rainwaterhead, two gables, timberframe, bow window) to King's Square (7), church demolished in 1937. Noting early c19 Church Street, down curving Goodramgate: on left 1320 timberframe row backing onto churchyard, right mixed timberframe group (8), behind right, in Bedern, restored chapel; to Monk Bar. Good loop: rebuilt c17 brick, 1700s (9) with vertical recesses between windows; corner timberframe; into courtyard with shaped gables; cobbled lane up to vast bulk of Minster; right to c17 facade of Treasurer's House (curious windowtops), Georgian houses, late 1930s Deanery (10), c13 archbishop's chapel (now library) and Norman palace arcade.

Then good houses facing Minster East End: good doorway, timberframe with shaped gable behind, grand early c18 (11) with pedimented window linked to console doorway, bay windows – before disruptive Deansgate. To N c15-18 amalgam St William's College facade – stone with bow windows below timberframe (good courtyard), to overhanging timberframe. Back to (7).

Finally into area with good new infill housing: 5-bay pediment (garland, oval), window over door in recess (12); former church and side Venetian windows; pilastered ground floor; to Merchant Taylors' Hall (13) – 1400s timberframe hall within c17 brick exterior, low 1730 row. Then Aldwark to SE: Georgian with stone doorways (huge Gibbs, surround with keystone); stone gatepiers and round Gibbs doorway; to St Anthony's Hall (14) – c15, c17 exterior; across busy road, timberframe Black Swan; restored 1752 Peaseholme House (15). Bad office blocks in St Saviourgate – replacing Salem Chapel at end, (16), next to 1840 chapel with Ionic portico. Between, good Georgian street with dated rainwaterheads: 1740 centre picked out, 1763 with bands, terrace, 1840 almshouses facing church; 1693 chapel (unusual cruciform plan). Back to (7).

Map IV

The three best streets, mixed Georgian with many overhanging timberframe houses. First the picturesque *Shambles*, between (1) and (2), the houses almost touching. Then into market stall area, newly created around an exposed timberframe; out to windswept 1830s link between market place near All Saints' Pavement and Thursday Market (3); Victorian 3-storey iron and glass shopfront (4); past Georgian house to 1740s terrace (5); back to (1).

Then *Low Petergate*, its timberframe plastered: right bulky new shops; former Talbot Inn (dated 1743) over pavement on columns (timberframe from churchyard); mansion with triglyph centre, later wings and porch; bow shopfront with garland opposite 1772 pair. Across Stonegate (Minerva statue) becomes Georgian High Petergate: right central window picked out, St Michael-le-Belfrey; left pair, advanced centre (6). Finally superb *Stonegate* with many fine shopfronts. Purplebrick to Minster transept facade. To sw with interesting alleys off: long row with oriels, to remains of Norman house, Victorianised black-and-white like Chester, Coffee Yard, 1437 with carved bressumers and bargeboards, pedimented central window; to 1851 chapel (7); overhangs with Victorian tiles, Gothick details. Out to fine classical stone frontage (8); round 1830 corner, past good doorway, to Lord Burlington's 1730s Assembly Rooms (9) with its famous columned interior.

Back to **Map I** for the best extramural streets. To sw Blossom Street: row with identical doorways, varied bow windows, South Parade – (18) fine 1896 school, becoming Italianate 1840s with debased pilasters, out to (19); attractive curving mid c19 (20); returning to fine group of Georgian convent plus pilastered extension with Micklegate Bar.

Then Bootham, the best: varied Georgian windows (21) – lunettes above round Venetian above bows with columns; 1739 almshouses with giant arches; good frontage (tripartite window over columned porch) to Venetian doorway – opposite pilastered greybrick, pilastered groundfloor windows (22); 1777 portico (23); 1840s stone with bow window (24), terrace; to stucco pedimented and pilastered house (25), like chapel. Victorian cottages and villas to new bridge (26). Returning, impressive stone collegiate 1838 school (27); 1630s almshouses (28) with Norman doorway (moved).

NE *Monkgate*: pilastered house, little terrace, to bow windows (29); returning, SE side, 1840s terrace with round Gibbs doorways, tripartite and rusticated pilastered doorways; to house (keystones, quoins) in group with bar. Finally nice *loop* S: along embankment (30), to 1750 stone well (off map); inland past Regency terrace (31); twin pilastered villa (32); pedimented Georgian house (33).

Magazines
Life boat house

V

Zigzaghall

Bootle
view
Sea bank

North Egremont

Egremont
Ferry

Egre
mont
Codling gap

Liscard

Oak
Cottage
Seacombe
Seacombe
Ferry

Quay

3

2

BIRKENHEAD
Station

Monks Ferry
Priory

Birkenhead
Ferry
Pool

Tranmere
Ferry

Hotel
Hamilton

Holt
hill
Mill
Tanyard
Sloyne

Birkland

Ganal road

T.G.

Tranmere

Bank Hall

Graving
Dock
Sandon
Basin
Wellington
Half tide Dock
Bramley Moore
Dock
Nelson Dock
Salisbury
Dock
Graving
Dock
Clarence Half tide
Basin
Trafalgar Dock
Victoria Dock
Waterloo
Dock
Princes
Basin

Sandon
Br

Leigh
Bridge

St Mary

Princes
Dock

St Georges
Basin
Georges Dock
Ba. 1

Canning Dock

Albert Dock
Dukes Dock

Woodside
Ferry
Tobacco
Warehouse
Kings Dock

King & Queens Basin

Brunswick
Basin

Brun
Do

Graving Docks

Harring
Do

Hercu

V
F
E
R
R
I
L
M
E
R
S
E

Liverpool and Birkenhead

A seaport and the regional capital of Merseyside, Liverpool, has (like Glasgow) a bad 'image' and massive problems of dereliction and declining industries, but it has also, like Glasgow, considerable vitality and a real metropolitan scale, with particular fine public buildings and much to explore.

Founded by King John as a point of embarkation to Ireland not controlled by the earls of Chester, Liverpool's growth really started in late c17. The first dock was opened in 1715, its c18 trade being sugar, tobacco, increasingly cotton – and slaves. The docks expanded to a 7½-mile frontage served by an overhead railway (now dismantled), Liverpool reaching a late c19/early c20 peak as Britain's main Atlantic port. Birkenhead similarly grew rapidly in early c19 as a rival on the other side of the Mersey (its main docks, running inland, along Wallasey Creek, re-named the Great Float), until the joint Mersey Docks and Harbour Board was established in 1857.

Map I

First explore Liverpool's Docks (their extent in 1855 shown in Map I opposite), in particular those constructed between 1824 and 1860 by Jesse Hartley, with an unequalled new solidity, strength and scale – in granite and cast iron; though the older docks are semi-derelict and under-used, access is often difficult. N of modern Pierhead (1), on the site of St George's Dock, nothing much for first half mile; then fine warehouses E of docks road, and 1867 grain warehouse with groundfloor arcade and hoist turrets along Waterloo Dock. Finally, connecting with Salisbury Dock but E of the road because linked to 1840s locks of Leeds-Liverpool canal, Stanley Dock and associated warehouses: 1880s Bonded Tea; Hartley's 1848 S warehouse, cut off from dock by later 11-storey red and bluebrick tobacco warehouse; Hartley's N warehouse facing dock; in 'random' stone, Hartley's dock entrances and watchmen's hut, hydraulic tower and basin entrances next to sea.

Then S of Pierhead to explore in detail the finest historic dock complex in Britain, Hartley's superb 1840s Albert Dock, a new attempt to integrate warehouses and docks, now being restored; office portico is of cast iron, and at the groundfloor level of warehouses, massive cast-iron columns with entasis contrast with huge segmental brick arches. Further S, along docks road, the similar 1858 Wapping Dock warehouses face King's Dock on map.

Then take 'metro' from James Street, just inland from Pierhead, under the Mersey to Hamilton Square, Birkenhead, emerging under station tower (2), built to house hydraulic lifts; Birkenhead's

ambitious early C19 grid-plan initiated in 1824 extends another mile off map. By contrast with Liverpool, main docks are excitingly inland – worth exploring from another hydraulic tower, of 1863 (3), s of two swing bridges.

Birkenhead (Map II)

Now explore using 6″ maps opposite. From 1886 station (1), classical buildings lead into 1825-44 Hamilton Square (3), designed by an architect of Edinburgh New Town, James Gillespie Graham – so stone, with a 'dour dignity' (Pevsner), terraces pilastered at ends (round) and centre (square), and a rusticated ground floor (cast-iron balconies above). Three long terraces; two short ones and small terrace facing Town Hall (2) – 1887 classical with fine tower plus pilastered sessions house behind. To s, Italianate triangular block E of Market Square; 1820s church (4) next to priory ruins.

Then on 'metro' to station (5) for Birkenhead Park, laid out 1843-7, 'Paxton's most successful design and the first park ever provided at public expense' (Pevsner). It has a lake plus boathouse and Swiss bridge, artificial hillocks and marvellously varied entrance lodges and Italianate or Gothic villas incorporated into the attractively irregular layout. Recommended tour: to villas (6); E via lake to monumental main entrance (7). Lodges – Gothic plus good houses (8); Italianate plus terrace with pedimented ends (9); castellated (11), to classical pair (12) – despite name 'Norman', via varied villas both sides (10).

Return by emerging again at Hamilton Square (1), past more Italianate and (13), to catch ferry back across Mersey with famous view of Liverpool's waterfront and the two cathedrals behind – before exploring the central business district inland.

Liverpool city centre (Map III)

At Pierhead are three spectacular buildings of 1900s, height of the city's prosperity, which 'represent the great Edwardian Imperial optimism and might indeed stand at Durban or Hong Kong just as naturally as at Liverpool' (Pevsner): Royal Liver building (1), reinforced concrete faced in stone, in a free neo-Byzantine style with two 295ft towers capped by the legendary Liver birds; Dock Offices, whose Renaissance dome (good central space under) comes from a rejected design for the Anglican cathedral; and, in the middle, the palazzo Cunard building, whose US style (reminiscent of upper King Street in Manchester) is continued in two later interwar buildings – India (4) with shopping arcade inside, and Barclays (5).

Across the wide new road (incorporating site of overhead railway) is parish church (postwar Gothic, 1815 open spire); 1860s offices face churchyard and Chapel Street behind – round-arched Venetian Gothic (3) by Liverpool's leading commercial architect, J. A.

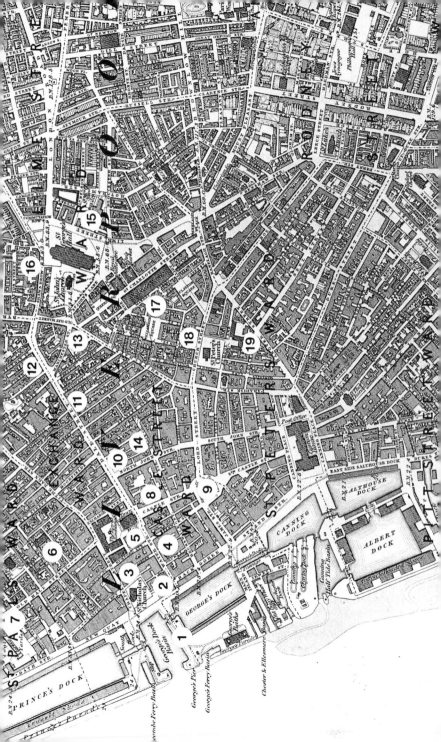

Picton. The 1900s White Tower building (2) occupies site of a fortified tower built by the Stanleys in 1406; and (9) was the site of the castle, from which Liverpool's main medieval street ran to (7), with Chapel/Tithebarn and Water/Dale as cross streets. The original anchorage was a creek on the site of Canning Place and the 1830s Custom House (destroyed in Second World War), with an inlet along Paradise Street/Whitechapel.

Up Water Street to another 1860s building just before (5), but totally unexpected – Peter Ellis's extraordinary pioneering glass and cast-iron Oriel Chambers of 1864; then, beyond (4), two fine banks – typical of the well-mannered mid-Victorian classicism of the Liverpool 'gentlemen', as opposed to the Flemish Gothic cloth-hall style preferred in Manchester; to the superb Georgian Town Hall, main body 1750s by John Wood the Elder of Bath, dome and portico added by James Wyatt (to face Castle Street, widened in 1786). Behind, towards (7): Exchange flags; redbrick 1856 Albany Chambers (cast-iron courtyard bridges, tall top-lit corridors) opposite stone classical and 1906 corner cast-iron and glass remodelling; ironframed back and sides of 1900s Cotton Exchange (6), its lavish front gone.

Back to Town Hall to explore in detail fine varied Victorian Castle Street. E side: corner redbrick with frieze because built as art gallery; redbrick and terracotta gabled insurance building, facade to arcade; stone; then two fine 3-bay mid-Victorian classical – correct columned portico, contrasting with Cockerell's inventive 1840s Bank of England (8), similar to that in King Street, Manchester. This faces Brunswick Street, which follow to two classical banks – one 1800, one dated 1835; S to another on corner facing (9) and Victoria Monument. From elaborate corner also facing (9), Castle Street has good Western frontage: 1864 building by Picton inserted between earlier Georgian; to end with later lively Loire-style 1890s, with turrets either side of Brunswick Street, continuing to corner, broken by Norman Shaw's massive rusticated entrance and pedimented classical villa at 3rd/4th floors. (See drawing on next page.)

Similarly fine Dale Street starts with 1857 palazzo by Cockerell (next Town Hall) contrasting with, on next two corners (nice lanes behind burgage plot between) round-arched by Picton and 1850s stucco. S side has more 1860s by Picton, then grand 1839 Royal Bank classical facade (another at end of alley), next half of 1900s Gothic/Art Nouveau front. Continuous good Southern frontage starts with a reminder of Pierhead – the huge Edwardian Baroque steel-framed, stone-fronted Royal Insurance (10) with tower and long side facade; then 1860s Italianate by Picton; 1880s Prudential

Castle Street, N end of w side, Nos 2–18

Assurance (spiky Gothic by Waterhouse in redbrick and terracotta of course), brick on corner (nice stucco classical opposite); then two more Gothic (plus a third beyond Municipal Buildings) and Loire-style 1883 Conservative Club. Next stretch is dominated by late c19 public buildings: lavish Renaissance Municipal Buildings (11) with pyramid spire, like Halifax Town Hall; classical Magistrates Courts opposite (prison behind), plus, round corner, freer Edwardian Fire Station and Transport Offices. Finally, Georgian houses (12), with Venetian window round corner.

Parallel is Victoria Street, formed in 1867 w from (13). Exploring w: 1850s Midland Railway warehouse with giant arches down side street; 1890s GPO (1st floor demolished); 1860s round-arched by Picton (14); finally good offices (plus shops to s) all round, entering Cook Street, where No 16 is another iron and glass facade (of 1866) by Peter Ellis.

Then explore round superb St George's Hall, 1841-1856, Harvey Elmes completed by Cockerell, 'the climax of the Grecian phase in c19 classical architecture' (Pevsner), a complex of courtrooms and concert halls (fine interiors) surrounded by giant columns. Best view from (15) – from terrace of Lime Street Station (1867, 1879 trainsheds, 1870s Gothic railway hotel); towards (13), plateau with numerous statues, replacing (in 1887) St John's church; sense of enclosure spoilt by road approaches to 1930s Mersey road tunnel. NE side also disappointing, but from the Wellington column, along (16) series of magnificent classical public buildings was built as a foil: 1884 Sessions House (portico with paired Corinthian columns); 1877 Art Gallery reminiscent of Barry's 1830 one in Manchester; 1879 Picton Reading Room whose curved colonnade ingeniously turns building line; long 1860 Library and Museum with pediment modelled on s side of St George's Hall; ending with confident Edwardian 1902 College of Technology.

To s is main shopping area, with new precinct (450ft concrete tower) – w corner of which is 1865 theatre (17) with new extension; to s, Victorian shop buildings (18); and unexpected courtyard of 1716 Bluecoat School (19), with cupola, pedimented centre, round windows in pilastered surrounds; to sw – at junctions of Paradise/ Hanover/Duke/Argyll Streets – good c19 buildings (two next to warehouses) ranging from Regency pilastered stucco to terracotta.

Liverpool east central (Map IV)
The eastern 6″ map shows Liverpool's 'West End', developed from 1780s, with Georgian houses in very varying condition to be found almost everywhere on map; the typical material is brick, with a columned doorway with rounded fanlight in a round recess, as in Dublin. Since the map, alien intrusions have interrupted the Georgian domestic scale – the huge neo-Gothic Anglican cathedral (1) with its 331ft central tower, built slowly from 1904 to 1978; the 1960s RC cathedral (2), 'the Mersey Funnel'; but, most damagingly, the University, which pulled down St Catherine's church in Abercromby Square (for a Senate House which could have incorporated at least its portico). The University originated in Victoria College (3), 1880s redbrick and terracotta Gothic by Waterhouse, with his similar Royal Infirmary behind (4).

Tour recommended from (5), back to the huge 1912 Adelphi Hotel (6), with top pilasters like New York. First attractive Bold Street, now pedestrianised, leading up to bombed-out c19 Gothic St Luke's: fine classical 1800s club/library (the Lyceum) opposite cast-iron shopfront; handsome 1850s Italianate Concert Hall on corner; 1864 bank palazzo; little pedimented and pilastered stucco terrace. From St Luke's, s to fine church columned drum and dome (8) – direct. Or by loop through decayed area: down Seel Street (1800s house with wings and later porch; pedimented house plus stucco RC church); Slater Street to stone 1801 newsroom (7); back

down Duke Street with grand Georgian houses as reminders of its former glory; further Georgian houses (9), in Liverpool's Chinatown. Up to 1829 mortuary chapel (fine interior) and St James' cemetery, romantically situated in old quarry, beneath Anglican cathedral (1).

From here down fine Rodney Street: rows, grander pedimented houses (Gladstone was born in No. 62 in 1808), out to three houses with balconies (10), beyond fine church facade; returning, left up Mount Street to see 1830s classical Mechanics Institute, and 1910 School of Art bow windows (11) in Hope Street. Continuing s past St James' cemetery: monumental but incomplete 1830s stone Gambier Terrace with pilasters and groundfloor arcade; Regency villas; to Georgian terraces of brick again (12), in Upper Parliament Street.

At (13), Princes Road, laid out in 1846 as a monumental avenue to Princes Park (see later), starts with three 1870s ecclesiastical buildings – St Margaret's plus vicarage, synagogue, Greek orthodox church. Back to (12). N up Percy Street: at first brick terraces, but then, beyond stuccoed terraces of Huskisson Street, the best terraces of all, in stone, with neo-Greek and Egyptian details and incised ornament, two facing the church portico (with neo-Gothic villas at end), one alongside with colonnade.

Right along Canning Street – stone terraces at first, then brick again (with some pediments over pairs of houses); to delightful 1835 Falkner Square (14), with trees and stucco houses now with bay windows; to s, pilastered stuccoed terrace (15). From (14) N to glance down brick rows of Chatham Street; then w. N up Bedford Street South: past two contrasting pairs (16) – brick and stucco (set back with ironwork); across street into university area with three fine Regency stucco houses; into Abercromby Square (17) – brick terraces, 1st-floor ironwork.

Finally w back to city centre and (6): brutalistic infill, better later; elegant stone classical Medical Institution (on corner of Hope Street) and, beyond RC cathedral, Wellington Rooms; opposite Georgian house incorporated in Victorian Gothic convent. Down Mount Pleasant, past (10) – Georgian houses both sides (grand one on corner with recessed arch), to Victorian Gothic YMCA with tower (18); left, in Benson Street, is an unusual pedimented stone pair, with Grecian details, like Percy Street. E of St Georges Hall, in rundown area, Georgian brick houses survive (just) at (19), (20), (21) and at (22) next to 1840s Gothic school.

Princes Park (Map V)

s of the Anglican cathedral – in and around the notorious inner city area of Toxteth – is a concentration of interesting c19 residential areas. Princes Road leads 1 km past late c19 houses to the ornamental gates (1) of 90 acre Princes Park, laid out in 1843 by Paxton, just before Birkenhead Park. Around it are fine mid c19 stucco and Italianate houses: along (2); jutting into park (3), one with pedimented back; (4), plus redbrick and stucco terrace (5); 29-bay terrace (6) with cast-iron balconies and canopies; around (7). To E main entrance (8) of larger Sefton Park, laid out in 1860s (since map): 1896 palm house at centre; to E (N of iron bridge), grand late Victorian villas – as also E in the exclusive c19 residential suburb of Mossley Hill. All these are now Conservation Areas, as are also 1850s villas of Grove Park (9); Lark Lane – late Victorian (10) but with 1840s private street (11).

Awkward turns s off Aigburth Road lead to three more CAs: beyond (12) to 1840s villas of Fulwood Park; 1½ miles further on, beyond 1930s Otterspool park along Mersey, are the Victorian Grassendale (mid) and Cressington (later) Parks, with 'promenades' along river. The most remarkable is delightful Regency St Michael's Hamlet, with church and houses built by ironfounder John Cragg to display architectural uses of cast iron – so window and door frames, church parapets and finials, etc. are made of cast iron, as well as the usual verandahs and canopies. Cragg's original five houses survive and are on map; they originally had romantic names – the Nunnery on corner to W of church (with the Cloisters further s); to s, the Friary opposite the Hermitage; to N, Cragg's own house, Hollybank. Explore also good later villas to (13) and s to cottages opposite railway station (14), since map. Along the Mersey is the site of Liverpool's famous 1984 Garden Festival, held on reclaimed dock land.

Manchester and Salford

Manchester, in certain ways England's second city (with the second largest airport in Britain), is the regional capital of a conurbation of 3½ million people (the former county of Greater Manchester). It developed as 'cottonopolis', the financial and trading centre of the SE Lancashire and Cheshire cotton industry, with the numerous huge mill buildings that so impressed Engels in the 1840s and which continued to be built into the 1920s. Flemish weavers settled in Manchester in 1373, in 1422 the parish church was made collegiate, in 1847 a cathedral. But, like Liverpool, its growth really started in c18, fed by inland waterways; in 1721 the narrow river Irwell, still the boundary between the cities of Manchester and Salford, was made navigable. Then between 1759 and 1808 four canals were constructed: the Bridgewater canal into Castlefields (site of a Roman fort); the Rochdale; the Ashton; and the Manchester, Bolton and Bury into Salford – plus a crosstown link, from the Irwell through a tunnel to the Rochdale; all these are shown on **Maps II** and **IV**.

By 1819, date of the Peterloo 'massacre' in St. Peter's Fields, Manchester was, with 150,000 people, 'the largest village in Europe', without parliamentary representation or municipal government. Getting both in 1830s, Manchester continued to grow rapidly, proud of its laissez-faire economics, largely unplanned by contrast with Liverpool ('Manchester men' rather than 'Liverpool gentlemen'), finally expressing its rivalry with Liverpool in the construction of the huge Manchester Ship Canal (its docks in Salford!), which made Manchester England's third port in tonnage. The ship canal was finished in 1894, the peak of Manchester's prosperity, expressed in the Royal Exchange and the great cotton warehouses in Oxford and Whitworth streets.

Map I

s of the new, largely elevated, dual carriageway Mancunian Way, out on Oxford Road, is the university area: in Grosvenor Square (1) a Georgian house, 1830s Chorlton-on-Medlock Town Hall with portico, next to good 1880s College of Art; Georgian Waterloo Place with recessed columned doorways; 1870/80s Gothic original university quadrangle (2) by Waterhouse, opposite Hansom's 1869 RC church with amazing spacious interior. Further s is Victoria Park, laid out in 1836, but E side never completed as shown on map. Trees and mid-Victorian villas – some stucco classical, later brick Italianate and Gothic, plus delightful stucco gabled Gothic Addison Terrace (3).

Now central Manchester – with many fine buildings and much to

explore, but with much bad modern 'development', particularly the gimmicky blocks facing Piccadilly Gardens.

Architecturally, compared with Liverpool, Manchester's red-brick Georgian has broken pedimented doorways; and its Victorian banks and warehouses are more likely to be Gothic in style, like its superb 1876 Town Hall. Instead of historic docks, there are historic canals to be explored.

Manchester and Salford (Map II)

Start with the fine warehouses (1) of Castlefields terminus of Brindley's Bridgewater Canal – pedimented canal HQ at (2) – in the historic transport area, s end of Deansgate. These are difficult to find from Liverpool Road, so most appropriate access, as well as most dramatic introduction to central Manchester, is to walk w to them along the towing path of the Rochdale canal, from (16) on **Map IV**, from bridge over Princess (then David) Street; through an exciting chasm of modern functional backs to warehouses whose ornate neo-Baroque fronts will be seen later, under Oxford Street; dramatic redbrick warehouses up to junction (3) of former crosstown link (now filled in), with 1874 warehouse next to canal turn (4); down locks under fine cast-iron railway and Deansgate bridges to Castlefields.

'Break out' to Liverpool Road, and world's oldest passenger railway terminus (5), 1830 Liverpool-Manchester, restored as museum. (Across river Irwell to see, from Salford, redbrick early Victorian navigation warehouses (6) and (7), either side of former crosstown canal link, opposite filled-up entrance to MBB canal.) Back to (5), past 1877 cast-iron exhibition hall being restored as museum, opposite delightful little 1827 redbrick Sunday School, to c19 market hall (8). Up Deansgate and left down unexpected Georgian redbrick St John's Street to site of church – Gothick doorways to left (good new infill housing beyond), pedimented to right, to 5-bay house (9). To NW Georgian row (10), new law courts complex (11).

Past 1912 stucco theatre and good corner (12) to Peter Street: 1910 Albert Hall with tower, palazzo 1868 offices; opposite, 1844 Theatre Royal; superb 1850s Italianate Free Trade Hall (on site of 'Peterloo Massacre') by Edward Walters, architect of Manchester's finest mid c19 banks and warehouses. Then 1909 YMCA (concrete faced in terracotta) and vast 1898 Loire-style Midland Hotel (13). Follow side, appropriately, to 210ft span Central Station trainshed (14) (being restored) and 1894 Great Northern Railway warehouses (15), once connected by hydraulic lifts to crosstown canal below.

Finally Deansgate N of (12). Nice late Victorian both sides – 1878 Queen Anne contrasting with 1898 classical stone; 1890s redstone

Agecroft Hall
Agecroft Farm
Kersal Hill
Kersal Cell
CASTLE HILL
Pendlebury Ho.
Canal
Zoological Gardens
Springfield
Park Lane Farm
Print Works
Broughton
Stony Priors
Park Ho.
Castle Irwell
Chapel
Pendlebury
Chapel
Whitlane
HYLEWOOD
River Irwell
Transfield Height
Lower Broughton
Summerville
Colliery
Height Lane
Ford
Acresfield
Charlestown
Newhall Fold
Chusely
Claremont
Pendleton
Chapel
Hart Hill
Wakiness
Dale Hill
Weaste
SALFORD Chapelry
Highfield
Hodge Lane
Little Bolton
Station
Campfield
New Barns
New Barns
Maud Wheel Mill
Infantry Barracks
RIVER IRWELL
Ordsall Wood
Hall
Osiers
Ordsall Hall
Hornbrook
Park House
Throstle Nest Mill
Canal
Bridgewaters
Blind Asylum
Gnat Hall
Botanical Gardens
Old Trafford
Hulland Hall
Clappers
ROAD

Gothic John Rylands Library with superb vaulted interiors (16). More good Victorian on corners to N; up John Dalton Street (since map) to Victorian furniture warehouse (17), its back next to 1848 RC church. Deansgate ends with Victorian stone both sides (18) – Venetian round windows opposite exuberant pilastered facade to delightful 3-storey cast-iron shopping arcade with two domes.

To N, fine Perpendicular collegiate church/cathedral. s in Old Shambles shopping precinct, two historic half-timbered pubs; to N medieval collegiate buildings incorporated into Chetham's Hospital, with c15 refectory, cloister, dormitory adapted as famous library.

From here to explore Salford, down its main Chapel Street: 1750s Sacred Trinity church with fine Venetian and Loire-style Victorian warehouses (19). Then ½ mile W opposite a Venetian-style bank, sequence of fine public buildings: 1820s classical stone Town Hall with Doric portico (20) plus later redbrick and stone market building; 1895 education offices; 1855 RC cathedral with tall crossing steeple; 1825 St Philip's with round tower, plus, behind, 1860s Italianate Court House (21), opposite unexpected Georgian redbrick row with stone doorways. Just off **Map II** start the Georgian redbrick houses of The Crescent, facing the river (plus Acton Place off to left) followed by Victorian Library and Art Gallery, and 1896 Technical College, now part of University of Salford.

Salford (Map III)

On **Map III** opposite, (1) marks 1840s classical and neo-Gothic villas of Lower Broughton Road and Great Clowes Street; (2) fine c15-17 mansion; (3) site of main terminus docks of the Manchester Ship Canal.

Manchester east central (Map IV)

Back to Manchester parish church cathedral, to skirt the Manchester central area using **Map IV**, before exploring the fine King Street and Town Hall area with **Map V**.

Cut E between new Arndale shopping centre (1) and new 400ft C.I.S. tower (2) – 'best of new high blocks' (Pevsner) – to shell of old Fish Market (3), Georgian houses, craft centre – all in Thomas Street. To N classical 1857 Market Hall (4); Victorian bank and Gothick pub either side of Oldham Road, with fine 1870s saddleback steeple (5); 1939 rounded glass Daily Express (6). Past Georgian houses (7), across interesting Victorian redbrick warehouse area, to two canal warehouses – brick (8), Rochdale headquarters (9) of stone; across canal to 7-storey pilastered railway warehouse (10), behind approach to new Piccadilly station.

Past Edwardian Baroque corner (11); then left past front and side of dramatic Victorian Gothic Magistrates Courts (12), over canal.

Into 1890-1914 area of streets (most since map) and towering warehouses (with steel or reinforced concrete structures behind their elaborate facades) giving this part of Manchester (like Liverpool's Water Street) an exciting late Victorian/Edwardian metropolitan scale, when these packing warehouses exported goods all over the world. Past 1900s police/fire station with Baroque towers (13); w along new Whitworth Street, past grand Loire-style Institute of Science and Technology facing gardens on site of canal arm (14); to corner 1906 Lancaster House with tower (15).

Princess Street NW into city centre: 1880s Scots Baronial (16), facing access to canal towpath walk recommended earlier; fine Victorian warehouses both sides, particularly E side 1863 with segmental windows on shafts, 1854 Italianate Mechanics Institute, to Georgian row (17). Return to (15) and on to 1914 Orient House (18) in Granby Row; 'on the street elevation the windows are arranged as vertical strips fitted into a fulsome Greek Revival frame of white glazed terracotta, but this is just one face of a functional glass and concrete box that would have made Le Corbusier gasp' (Victorian Society booklet).

Back to (15), between 1910 warehouses of Whitworth Street again, to huge Refuge Assurance (19) with Baroque tower. Into town again along Oxford Street. Palace Theatre and two huge warehouses opposite each other: left 1898 red terracotta, and beyond it, next to canal, the last textile warehouse, late 1920s Lee House (20), intended as skyscraper; right 1912 Baroque stone, next 1860s neo-Romanesque. Finally nice curvy facade to left (21), to St Peter's Square and huge circular 1930s classical domed library (22).

Manchester city centre (Map V)

Past 1830 classical stone Friends Meeting house, on map, to Albert Square (1) and Waterhouse's superb 1870s Gothic Town Hall with 281ft spire (2), both since map: s side good mixed Victorian Gothic and Italianate, centre 1862 Albert Memorial (similar to London but by a local architect, Thomas Worthington); w side new redbrick infill; N side corner stone pilastered, Victorian Gothic, 1902 Art Nouveau with cupola. Follow Princess Street alongside Town Hall (noting skilful use of triangular site and 1920s extension with bridges and steep roof), past Georgian houses, Victorian giant arches; to Barry's superb 1824-35 classical Art Gallery (3), varied columned facade and square staircase block like Liverpool's later St George's Hall.

The Gallery uses Barry's fine 1837 palazzo Athenaeum Club behind – where turn left up George Street, right, left up Falkner Street, into interesting 1840/50s warehouse area, now Manchester's Chinatown. Past coarsely pedimented and columned warehouse

(4), to Edward Walter's three fine 1850s Italianate warehouses s side of Charlotte Street, elegant corner 1802 Portico Library (5). Back down Charlotte Street to Portland Street, huge 1851 Watts warehouse (6) surmounted by rose windows, 1845 Italianate hotel by Walters facing (7).

Across gardens (site of first Royal Infirmary) to 1836 pedimented and pilastered house (8), warehouse giant arches and Walters' superb 1860 palazzo bank (9) plus 1880s extension on left, introduction to attractively dense and intimate upper King Street banking area. Zigzag across it: w along York Street; left down Fountain Street – Victorian and modern to classical 1860 Freemason's Hall (10); up delightfully varied small-scale Kennedy Street opposite (carved heads and beast, 1885 filigree Gothic Law Library); into Albert Square; then back into commercial alleys at Booth Street; N of new block (11); along its side to front of Lutyens' fastidiously detailed 1929 Midland Bank – 'the king of King Street' (Pevsner), which introduces, with its 1920s neighbours, a new transatlantic scale. To E three 1890s neo-Jacobean, and 1902 with corner dome (12); opposite, 1870s Venetian Gothic Reform Club; up Brown Street at side to giant Romanesque arcade (13), stone neo-Baroque.

Back to upper King Street: good new infill and Cockerell's superb 1845 (former) Bank of England (14), an unusual design (as in Liverpool) with giant columns and round window under pediment. Beyond, red 1881 Prudential; opposite, 1915 stone (on site of old 1830s Town Hall shown on map, part re-erected in Heaton Park). Beyond Cross Street (w side 1911 Baroque corner, terracotta pub, 1875 stone palazzo), King Street becomes pedestrian and domestic in scale: 5-bay 1736 brick house with wings, and some first-floor cast-iron shop facades; explore to pseudo half-timbering (15) on Deansgate. Back under clock to delightful 1709 church and St Ann's Square, with fine 1848 bank (16) on corner (plus bank house on right). N to where 1871 Barton Arcade (seen earlier) emerges from Deansgate, to finish at the 1910 columned Royal Exchange, the third on the site: go inside the lavish domed room (claimed in 1920s as biggest in the world) for the amazing space-age steel structure of the new Exchange Theatre.

Norwich

Saxon Northwic was one of the largest English boroughs by the Conquest – when the Normans inserted a cathedral and castle, moving market place from Tombland. Norwich reached its peak (second English city) in 1520s, expressed in the Perpendicular flint architecture of 56 medieval churches (York 39). Its weaving trade kept it second city until 1662, but it then settled into a comfortable Georgian prosperity, its c19 cattle-market supplied half of London's meat, was bombed in 1942, and acquired a new university (on outskirts) in 1961, sealing its status as the 'capital' of East Anglia.

Like York, a fine extensive cathedral city, with many factories and even more shops and offices within the walls (and new roads since the maps) plus welcome new good infill housing; but Norwich has a proper cathedral precinct, a more extensive walled area (1½ miles from NW to boom towers at SE) and an Inner Ring Road which goes within this, ironically along line of earlier Saxon defences – on **Map I** from (12) over (6) to (4); so rather than *Georgian* extramural *streets*, there are *early* c19 extramural *suburbs*. Architecturally Norwich has timberframe houses plastered rather than exposed black-and-white, usually with 2 or 3 'Norwich' attic gables – found also with early c18 redbrick and red tiled roofs, with a 'typical' heavy pedimented doorway (often scrolls) with big keystones; early c19 houses are grey or yellowbrick, roofed in slate, only occasionally stuccoed.

A walk round the medieval city is a good introduction: the 2¼ mile line of walls is clear, but one cannot walk on the remaining stretches, though there are attractive walks along the 1½ miles covered by the river.

Map II

From (1) past round tower to (2); to N two Georgian mansions (blank arches, rusticated pilastered doorway, curved Adamish porch); late c19 chapel (3); remains next to site of gate (4). Best stretch down Carrow Hill: behind wall, past stucco house (5) and Black Tower; across 1922 swing bridge (6) – ships still come this far; down to river and boom towers. Along river – opposite King Street burgage plots/quays, to 1886 railway station (7).

Map I

1880s iron bridge, view (1) of ferry house and c15 Water Gate (to canal for Caen stone for cathedral); timberframe pub (2), 1340s Bishop Bridge; along water, view of c14 Cow Tower. Famous view of Norwich from Mousehold Heath (3), in front of 1880s barracks. Along IRR to pick up walls again (4): stretch from river visible through glass corridor; past octagonal tower, new housing (line of wall marked in flint), c19 rows, to site of gate (5).

Loop into tatty area N of IRR. s down Magdalen Street: early C18 brick and flint, redbrick, stucco; opposite, White Lion (timberframe rear), Georgian redbrick. Under IRR (6) to first 'Norwich' timberframe gables opposite C18 pilastered with head doorway under Venetian window. N across new Anglia Square (7) to C16/17 timberframe row overhanging flint (8). Then 5 gables, left good shopfront, into Georgian redbrick Sussex Street (s side 1824) to good porch (9); back to site of gate (traces of wall in lane to right) opposite swimming pool (10).

Along new gardens in front of long stretch, to corner (11) behind gable (Gothick window); s past C15 hall house (look into yard) to timberframe row (12). Follow IRR across C19 bridge, along river, to wall stretches near (13); good infill housing, another stretch. Across footbridge to late C19 RC cathedral (14) since map (cruciform central tower, vaulted interior).

Loop into early C19 greybrick suburb with trees: pilastered houses; up to terrace – round doorways in recesses (15); out to pairs/terrace (16) – quoins outside, pilasters in centre; across to pilastered houses (17) with parapet shells (laurels); more early C19, back to (14).

Around park: group with cast-iron verandah and columned porch 'in antis' (18); exuberant 1880s brick (gatepiers); 1712 almshouse wings; Georgian (19) with good doorway. Then stretch of city wall (20); Georgian redbrick houses (21) with straight columned doorways; 1858 Norman chapel (opposite round tower), back to (22).

Explore superb cathedral close from Tombland (23) through 1316 gate (rose window pattern): Georgian mansion (segmental doorway), C17 brick (crosswindows) and 9 gables. Back of Tombland (pelican doorway, 2-storey greybrick bay, 3 gables); 1420 gateway (sculpture); Georgian, C14 chapel (vaulted under-croft), timberframe (shaped gable) facing cathedral west front. Past 4 C17 shaped gables (24), to (25): s side Georgian redbrick – grand 5-bay, pair, terrace (balustrade doorways); N side mixed with flintwork; E 1682 8-bay. Past nice mixture (Gothick window), Georgian stables (26), to Water Gate (1). Riverside walks: to (27), past Cow Tower round to Adam and Eve (28). s past villa (doorway in bow), back into close (29); infill, 1862 Gothic, to (25). Good (gabled on Doric columns) to (30); N to Bishopgate (3 shaped gables) and C14-C19 Great Hospital: courtyard – 1752 pedimented, flint with 4 gables; 200ft long range with tower (behind, C15 cloister); early C19 ranges. E to flint, stepped gable, mixed timberframe (31).

South central (Map II)

From (1) into leafy early C19 suburb. NE side: redbrick rows (8); pedimented hospital wing, 1879 centre (9); redbrick, then greybrick to pilastered villa (10) with laurel frieze, terrace (strange doorways). Fine varied villas off map (school has domed centre, verandah), and across road to (11). SE side: pedimented and pilastered pairs (12), terrace with round recesses (13), as also among redbrick houses to (14).

N past new shops, into Surrey Street: inventive 1900s Baroque Norwich Union (15). Opposite, Georgian redbrick: grand 1764 (rusticated doorway); pedimented porch; terrace (16) with later porches. Then stucco and redbrick (good doorways, two pairs) to tripartite window and timberframe (17). E of All Saints, down Timberhill: timberframe, 1833 chapel, greybrick gunmakers, to castellated Bell Hotel (18); E to La Rouen (19).

Along wide Ber Street on ridge past isolated Georgian redbrick and stucco to (20) – fine redbrick (pedimented stone doorways) between timberframe (moulded bressumers). To S, 1840s church, 1860s facade (21) with advanced centre, redbrick 'close' (22).

Beyond walls to early C19 Bracondale: NE side greybrick villa, redbrick pair, cast-iron verandah, 4 triglyph porches (23). Cross to little terraces – greybrick above stucco, triglyph porches; 1578 Manor House (crosswindows, shaped gables, pedimented windows) plus tower (behind Georgian redbrick); fine frontage – Georgian 5-bay, 1700s brick ('Norwich' gables, eared doorways), greybrick, to stucco villa (24) with little dome.

Cross to early C16 mansion (25); Italianate villa with conservatory (26). Into interesting King Street: 4-storey 1830s mill (27) with blank arches; Ferry Boat pub; complex Music House (C17 pedimented windows, C12 undercroft, warehouse courtyard) opposite 7 gables, and Princes Inn bressumer (28); brick window surrounds, steep medieval roof and stone doorway (29); new brewery buildings; 1690s Howard House. (Grand Georgian house (30) behind warehouse). Becomes good street with exposed timberframe (31) overhanging brick and flint; redbrick pairs (3 gables between); Venetian, lunette windows; redbrick, warehouse (little hoist), C17 crosswindows, 4+1+4 shaped gables; opposite, timberframe and Ionic shopfront (32). Last stretch (**Map III**) has more Georgian (ogive porch, pilastered pubfront), 1866 pedimented windows – orange compared with red 1882 Agricultural Hall, turreted 1896 Royal Hotel (1).

City centre (Map III)

From (1), past US-style 1930 Barclays into pedestrian London Street: pleasant curve to 1924 cupola (2); Corinthian shopfront,

overhanging brickfaced row, stucco pilastered corner (to greybrick terrace); timberframe, becoming late Victorian terracotta, Baroque (shop), Gothic (3). Market Place: 1930s City Hall (4); N side C15/16 Guildhall, 9-bay (pedimented window); S side timberframe above Doric shopfront, bows, 1700s windows in strips; E side Italianate (balconies), Corinthian windows (arcade), 1700s 9-bay (strips between windows).

Through Davey Place (between City Hall and castle), clockwise round Norman keep (5); 3¼ acre outer bailey, later 4½ acre cattle market. Cast-iron balcony, recessed centre; 1820s Tudor Shire Hall; 1868 cast-iron and glass front (6); 11-bay Georgian (7). Through Royal Arcade (Art Nouveau entrance) to Market Place. S of huge St Peter's, past George and Dragon to 1750s Assembly Rooms (8) – fine interiors. Beyond new library, Georgian Bethel Street (good doorways): redbrick, 1899 hospital facade; grand 5-bay, pair (9) – greybrick terrace behind; C17 hood moulds; 1750 mansion (elaborate centre, Rococo interiors) on new road (10).

Mixed gabled and Georgian to balustraded window (11), by IRR. Round St Giles: 6 gables, infill; stepped gable, Gothic oriel window; down to strange recessed centre (12) with split pediment. Up delightful lane (pairs, 1827 chapel), to superb C18 street (fine doorways, triglyph porches, shopfronts). S side: stucco pairs (window surrounds, scroll doorway); mansion (blank arches); rusticated pilasters (twirly surrounds, C19 palazzo); rear Venetian window, doorway (13). N side from (10): cast-iron balconies, 1900s Baroque (redbrick between); double doorway 'in antis'; timberframe; nice lanes; timberframe overhanging Doric shopfront, set back 1835 library (Doric porch). N past (14) to timberframe, Maddermarket theatre.

Pottergate W from (14): Venetian window to yard; C17 gables (medieval doorway), stucco, C18 redbrick (rusticated pilasters), 'typical' doorway; infill offices. Gaps with groups: redbrick pair; mansion set back (15) – 3 rusticated pilasters (once 4), pilastered window above rusticated doorway; gable, stucco – opposite 5-bay (head doorway); 7-bay pair; 3 'typical' doorways – on corner(16), behind (12) under 6 gables.

N past church tower in new housing. Back E; thatched stone house (17) behind church; gaps; nice curve. Beyond (18), frontages with medieval interiors: Strangers Hall Museum; fragment by telephone exchange; Suckling Hall (19) and 1700s 4-bay, once 5 (rusticated pilasters). S down alley: Bridewell Museum (C14 flint wall); Victorian mustard shop; to delightful Bedford Street, from (2) to (14) across Exchange Street – redbrick (eared window), narrow columned facade. From (19), past timberframe corner (3 gables) to

spacious St Andrew's Hall (c15 Blackfriars' church), cloister part of 1899 Art School (20).

North central (Map IV)

From overhanging (angle brackets), down Princes Street: Georgian redbrick, porch 'in antis' (1). Follow 1869 pilasters s; Queen Street E (court with pedimented doorways, stucco pilasters, overhang). s to mansion (segmental windows, heavy Doric doorway); N along greybrick Georgian, turning redbrick (quoins) facing textures, trees of Tombland (2). Victorian greybrick (tripartite windows) between gates. Opposite: stucco (Doric porch, rusticated ground floor); purple and redbrick (7-bay with frieze porch); overhangs – brackets (explore behind), 4 gables with c17 Sampson and Hercules porch, 'the two most debonair and sleepy of English strong men' (Pevsner); Georgian (3). Marvellous curve of Princes Street; mixed timber-frame; pairs of Gibbs and Ionic doorways; tripartite windows; to (1). N down famous Elm Hill: overhangs (tracery), gables, crosswindows, carved lintel, 'typical' doorways, flintwork.

NE from (3): overhanging row (classical shopfront), gaps, Georgian, 5 gables; to White Lion (4), redbrick, c15 window; opposite, c15 Bishop's Palace gate (c14 porch). Across bridge to 1830s mill (5) with dome, blank arches, behind c13 arch.

From (3) N: Corinthian shopfront beneath overhang; over river; to crosswindows facing churchyard; (6) coupled pilasters, to right c19 warehouse (recessed windows – beyond, gabled house). Magdalen Street: left, Georgian redbrick; right, 3 gables (1612 spandrel), 3 gables (pilastered shopfront) to delightful Gurney Court (7) – gabled dormers, scroll doorways. Opposite (3 tall gables) to 1690 Doughty's Hospital (8), remodelled 1870. s down Georgian redbrick (plus infill) Calvert Street to Bacon's house (medieval windows, good back); 4 gables (9), 1784 bridge (good riverside infill). Then fine Colegate – (9) to (6). N side: gables, superb set back 1756 Octagonal Chapel and 1693 pilastered Old Meeting (galleried interiors); pairs, grand purplebrick ('typical' doorway). s side: c16 flintwork; early c18 mansions – gable and elaborate doorway (rear pilastered segmental window) facing L-shaped (infill behind) with Ionic pilasters.

w of (9), fine Georgian doorways. Past 5 gables, up curve to mixed timberframe (10) – courtyard. Then isolated houses: w past Anglo-Saxon church tower to medieval thatched (11); brick, flint, stepped gables (12); past (11) to timberframe facing St Michael's flint tracery (1660 oriel to E). Explore 1980s infill housing (13) – courtyards, giant arches, riverside walk. Cross river (1804 iron bridge) to classical shopfront, shell (being redeveloped) of 1860s brewery (14), round pilastered corner to 1578 Renaissance fountain.

EAST MIDLANDS

Nottingham

A thriving regional capital, which still has, despite a destructive Inner Ring Road, an attractive and surprisingly extensive historic core, plus remarkable C19 residential areas to W. See comments and Nottingham 6″ map in Introduction, pages 8 and 9, 14 and 15.

Medieval town (Map I)

Start exploring 'clockwise' round Market Place. Several Georgian houses either side of funnelling up to (1) – one with pedimented 1st-floor windows, good fanlight, next to pedimented stucco Bell; good views up streets to Theatre Royal (2) and either side of 1890s redbrick Prudential Buildings – on site of slums (3); round 1929 Council House (on island to E) with Wren-like dome and arcades beneath – note medieval Flying Horse. Nice loop to S: C19 banks framing Council House dome, Georgian house facing churchyard (4); Georgian row with keystones (5); pedestrianised stretch past lunette (6).

Out to SW by largely Georgian St James' Street (pedestrian), severed by IRR (right, towards (1), for underpass), to fine stretch and corner (7) – pedimented redbrick (elaborate centre), tripartite window (triglyph eaves frieze), groundfloor recessed shell windows. To S more Georgian: facing hospital (8), pair facing castle; 3-storey bow windows both sides (9); in lane to S. Up to castle (museum) with good views E and W. To moved 1450 timberframe cottage (10); medieval Trip to Jerusalem; C17 gables (11) against castle rock.

Follow best street E from (10). Castle Gate S side: C17 redbrick gables, Georgian stucco (fine doorway), little terrace with identical doorways (urns). N side warehouse (hidden) with pedimented centre (oval); splendid late C17 house with alternate straight and curved pedimented tops to all windows (including dormers) plus fine railings – overawed by new offices facing IRR. Across IRR, good Georgian with elaborate tripartite centre (12); up street opposite, Georgian house, C16 Salutation Inn; 3 Venetian windows opposite C19 redbrick warehouses; two fine C18 houses – tripartite doorway ('Adam' window, triglyph frieze), Venetian doorway (even quoins).

Then fine Low Pavement (13). Late C19/early C20 – stucco warehouse corner (Moorish 'attic' windows), redbrick and Ionic pilastered (heads), 1903 stepped gable, sculptural 1876 stone Gothic, lavish Italianate stucco, 1910 stone and brick (unusual curved bay windows). Then Georgian – 6 Venetian windows (ground floor pedimented), segmental doorway and fluted sur-

rounds set back behind good railings, pair. Opposite, 1836 stucco – Ladies' Assembly Rooms Corinthian columns, pilastered bank (laurels); 1858 Italianate – explore pedestrian Bridlesmith Gate to (4). Middle Pavement: Georgian Venetian/bay; chunky 1908 (2-storey bays, corbels) facing widened road (site of Weekday Cross).

Into Anglian burgh at High Pavement. Sandstone basements in new garden; 1876 spire; 1870s Italianate and curiously bare 1770 Shire Hall (columned centre). Opposite, cast-iron balcony; tall 1833 pedimented and pilastered windows over sturdy Doric columns (14). Facing superb cruciform St Mary's, good Georgian houses – one with linked Venetian windows at front (plus lunettes), two more at back. Downhill past more exposed sandstone cellars to 1823 neo-Tudor almshouses (15).

Past E end of St Mary's, to explore exciting townscape (16) of 4 or 5-storey redbrick 1850s/60s lace warehouses; walk at least along Broadway (double bend picked out architecturally) to pilastered former C18 theatre (17), and round block with best (1855) warehouse (18). Then two C18 houses (19): railings; People's Hall (even quoins, Gibbs doorway, good staircase); Georgian topshops (20); Victorian architect's house (21); pedimented warehouse (22). Back to Market Place down fine late C19 redbrick and stone Victoria Street.

West central area (Map II)

First sally N to good late C19 public buildings: stucco 1865 Theatre Royal (1) with Corinthian columns; 1888 Guildhall (2) since map; Gothic 1881 university buildings (3) – before university moved out in 1928 to Lenton. (To N, up Mansfield Road, early C19 redbrick houses and terraces (4) with classical doorways. Nice Italianate (5) and pedimented/pilastered (6) stucco 1850s villas. Castellated 1867 Gothic school with tower (7). More mid C19 houses: Italianate villas (8), Gothic (9), redbrick rows (10) uphill.)

Across IRR into good mid C19 area at Regent Street (11), with Dutch and Renaissance gables. Down to centre of circus, new 'Rep', and red tower of 1909 Albert Hall. Out past Pugin's fine 1840s black stone Gothic RC cathedral with central spire (12), past chunky new College House (13), up to 1830s stucco Canning Terrace (14) with tower over cemetery entrance.

Then along Derby Road: on right redbrick Georgian, 1900s Baroque stone GPO, redbrick Gothic church, up Wellington Square past Italianate villas to Georgian industrial terrace (15); on left stucco villas and Italianate terrace (centre rebuilt); ending with stucco Italianate terraces both sides (16). To S stucco pedimented and pilastered villas of Western Terrace (17) – at an entrance

to The Park, whose redbrick villas were built after 1856.

One can return towards the castle across The Park: to the central circuses and fine villas, such as splendidly lavish Gothic redbrick (18), redbrick and stone neo-Jacobean 'Lace Market' (19); explore extraordinary sandstone tunnel which ramps up from (20) to emerge, unofficially, in carpark of (13); and climb up steps between hospital and stucco villas with cast-iron balconies at back (21). Or one can return to (16), to follow stucco Italianate and classical villas, above (20) to (21) – along the sandstone ridge the whole way.

Leicester

Medieval town (Map I)

Roman (with important Roman remains), a centre of Danelaw, Leicester was later a thriving medieval town. The line of its wall (no remains) is defined by extramural streets from (1) past site of North Gate (2) to (3); s past East Gate (4) to (5); w past South Gate (6), past castle area to West Gate (7); the river formed the Western boundary. Since map, river Soar navigation has been straightened for a mile s of (7), with attractive late Victorian bridges and 'boulevards' either side, and the delightfully intricate street network shown within the walls disrupted first by the Great Central Railway, basically following the river N – S, with its station (1892) in new street (8), and by a destructive Inner Ring Road through (6) past (21). Nonetheless Leicester has much worth seeking out, amid appalling mid c20 development.

Start at Roman Forum (9) and St Nicholas. sw past two Georgian houses (redbrick with good door, stucco pilastered) to late c19 cast-iron bridge amid IRR (7). (Similar bridge further w (10); to N early c19 factory with cupola (11) next to canal.) Into gardens (original outer bailey) to delightful castle area: splendid St Mary de Castro with sculptural 1890s factory tower on left (12), through timberframe gateway next to rusticated gatepiers, to green (inner bailey) and 1695 court facade concealing c12 great hall with timberframe roof. Past redbrick cottages (nice pair) in front of castle mound, through second gateway into second outer bailey added in c14 – the 'new work' (Newark). Coming out again SE, medieval hospital to w with c14 remains; next to polytechnic, fine c18 house (13) with quoined central windows; E to c16 chantry house with buttresses next to c17 gabled facade with good interiors (museum), tunnelling to c15 Newark gateway amid IRR, s of (6).

Along extramural Millstone Lane, marking s limit of walled town, with Georgian houses (pair with recessed centre) both sides (14).

Leicester I OS 6″ 1888   **149**

Then classical frontages from splendid 1792 Assembly Rooms (15) with huge tripartite windows, anti-clockwise round Georgian houses (horrid fascias) facing Market Place; cast-iron arcade, stucco recesses on corner, Victorian group, Doric shopfront columns, whitebrick flanking alley, to giant recessed arch facing c16 Tuscan column, 1st-floor bow windows on corner (16); in the centre, statue and modern covered stalls masking splendid mid c19 bridge/ staircase up to Italianate Corn Exchange.

Past island (good shopfronts) to fine Friar Lane: early c19 terrace with round 1st-floor windows, opposite group with segmental windows, starting with 1750s mansion (brick with stone dressings, rusticated pilasters, elaborate pedimented centre); to pair with nice door surrounds (17). N up mid c18 New Street (pedimented row, 3-storey bay windows flanking columned doorway) to St Martin's with redbrick terrace (keystones) and Georgian house with segmental porch (18) – plus two others, facing E end of churchyard. Past St Martin's (now cathedral) to Guildhall Lane: to E nice c18 group – good shopfront; to W splendid medieval Guildhall – with courtyard, superb interiors (c14 roof); and, across street, pilastered house (costume museum) with elaborate centre, c16 rear (19).

If keen, one can seek out: mutilated c17 Grammar School (20) with Georgian house beyond (fine fanlight): across IRR (21), Georgian houses near All Saints (22); along streets with nice historic names to Perpendicular St Margaret's tower (3). To N, park with site of abbey, plus ruins of c17 house beyond (23). S, via delightful 1707 chapel with strange 1830s overhanging timber warehouses behind (24), to Victorian classical bank facing (4).

Nineteenth-century Leicester (Map II)
Start at spiky 1868 clocktower (1) at city centre, next to 1894 ceramic front of Thomas Cook building. These introduce the later Victorian/Edwardian Leicester we are now to explore – basically redbrick wih dressings, plus attractive often pilastered warehouses and factories, some of which have been passed already. Through delightful 3-storey 1891 arcade (2); across Market Place to (3); S down commercial street past (4) noting varied styles, materials and amazing details of banks (usually on corners), culminating in roofscape of Grand Hotel (5). If keen, to NE: fine stuccoed chapel front (6) with honeysuckle frieze; two best warehouses splayed on corners (7) and (8) with Art Nouveau one opposite; to Georgian row (9) with good doors (fanlights, double centre under curve).

Past red Gothic bank corner tower (4) into Town Hall Square – all round late Victorian, plus third fine chapel facade (pediment, round windows). Out to three fine early c19 classical stucco buildings (10): curved with frieze on columns, square with Doric

pilasters, pilastered with fluted Ionic columns 'in antis'. These introduce delightful pedestrian *New Walk* (11) laid out in 1785: trees, cast-iron street lamps and railings painted black and gold, with attractive Regency and early Victorian buildings, as also in streets to S.

Italianate greybrick terrace (12), stucco with pedimented 1st-floor windows, villas with bow windows, stucco terrace with pilasters every bay, Italianate greybrick again – facing square. Back to New Walk: fine stucco villas – good porch, pilastered with recessed centre (ironwork); nice redbrick, stucco with trelliswork (13), opposite columned portico of Museum. Over new road along railway, to greybrick pilastered terrace with recessed doorways (good fanlights) – facing square (statue) as is 1+5+3+5+1 Italianate terrace; past oval garden becomes nice late Victorian to end at park (14). (To S, 1912 De Montfort Hall (15); Granby Halls (16); and the University which incorporates an 1837 classical building (17), intended for another purpose.)

Back along New Walk beyond (13) to square: stucco round Museum past its back portico, past pilasters to little row (18); then redbrick terrace with round windows (19); pair with advanced centre and recessed doorways (20); along buttressed wall of prison past its stone castellated front, to late C18 pair with giant recesses (21). Back and uphill to interesting stucco: terrace (22) with ornamented pilasters, recesses, bands, window surrounds; similar villas; to end with more square-cut terrace, opposite splendid pedimented redbrick crescent (delicate ironwork in centre).

Derby

A centre of Danelaw (hence 'gate' in its street names), an important medieval (though never defended) and Georgian county town, with a disruptive Inner Ring Road (which destroyed St Alkmunds' and Georgian houses round it) and a river frontage which is drearily 'municipal', linked to a much better new shopping centre.

Start at Market Place (1): N side chunky new Assembly Rooms (facade of old C18 one at Crich Tramway museum); S side, between Georgian redbrick (2-storey bow windows), 1841 guildhall with tower – under which to spacious Market Hall with iron and glass roof; E side good classical bank, C18 redbrick. S past pedimented Georgian with Venetian window (1) facing Victorian redbrick street; to another good Victorian classical bank, opposite stone corner (Ionic columns) leading to pilastered stucco terrace (built in 1838 as Royal Hotel); past fine stone Post Office (2) to Victorian streets in three directions. Then fine Georgian (stone surrounds) and c17 gabled with crosswindows (3), opposite library and c18 iron gates. Back to (2); down stone pilastered Victorian curve; through arcade (4); up good Sadlergate (pedestrian) with c17 brick (crosswindows) and timberframe Old Bell to Georgian with elaborate window surrounds facing Market Place.

Then N past nice Victorian (neo-Gothic and pilastered), Georgian redbrick with keystones, gabled timberframe to splendid Perpendicular tower of Gibbs' spacious 1720s All Saints (5) – now cathedral. From All Saints: first w past good Georgian brick (one with stone quoins and doorway), between Victorian redbrick with stone details, to c17 pilastered stone County Hall (6) with Ipswich windows, in courtyard; then N past more timberframe and Georgian, over IRR, to 1680 Seven Stars, opposite grand Georgian stone mansion (7). E to fine RC church by Pugin; chapel and c17 house next to c18 bridge; to N, early c19 classical stone houses (8).

Finally from St Werburgh's w of (4), up fine Georgian Friargate (severed by IRR and handsome railway bridge): stucco pilastered, Georgian redbrick, timberframe; fine mixed frontage with four c17 gables, opposite grand redbrick (elaborate centre) with stucco pilasters; IRR (9); Georgian redbrick both sides with nicely varied details (pedimented 1st-floor windowtops, etc.); railway bridge; nice stone (elaborate 1st-floor windowtops again). Opposite is best frontage: pedimented with recessed centre and Venetian doorway; advanced centre; round recesses, 2 Venetian windows, fine doorway and fanlight; stone row with pedimented centre (opposite stucco pair); Georgian redbrick with good fanlights. Off to N, past Gothick church to nice row facing stream (10); s down stucco pilastered street (one stone, two cast-iron porches) to huge Doric columns of facade (11) of former jail. Then more Georgian redbrick (one stone); N to c17 house (12); out to stucco villas (13) – Ionic porch, bow window. (Beyond (14), facing the station, nice 1840s railway redbrick houses with classical stone doorways.)

Coventry

Cathedral area (Map I)

Its medieval street pattern destroyed, Coventry now has only some superb isolated, historic *areas* left, the best round St Michael's ruins (its superb 295ft high medieval spire the highest of three in the city), forecourt of Basil Spence's famous cathedral (1), built 1954-62. To s, Drapers' Hall with Ionic portico, medieval St Mary's Hall (fine interior, c15 stained glass), two overhanging timberframe houses (carved cornerpost), pedimented 1783 county court. To w fine cruciform Holy Trinity (second spire); timberframe amid ruins of

West front of Norman priory; Georgian houses along site of priory church; culminating in Baroque facade behind fine railings facing cathedral.

Map II

Coventry is an unusual combination of historic and c20 growth town. England's 3rd provincial town in 1377 (starting its town wall in 1355), and 4th in 1523 (only finishing its wall in 1537), it went *down* in population between 1861 and 1871, yet increased fourfold from 1901 to 1951 – the time it destroyed its medieval street pattern (many houses were burnt in the famous 1940 German air raid) and built its dreary axial pedestrian precinct (37). Its later architecture is better, new buildings creating a sense of enclosure in station forecourt (1) and between Pool Meadow bus station and cathedral. The line of the city wall (2⅛ miles long, 20 towers, 12 gates) is shown by numbers (2) to (18).

From the cathedral, through old churchyard amid polytechnic, to stretch of walls (7) – (8) beneath Inner Ring Road; past ruins of stone house (19) to Whitefriars gateway (20), under IRR to Whitefriars (21). At (22): lane to medieval Charterhouse; Italianate lodge into cemetery laid out by Paxton in 1840s. Back to 1910s Gothic Council House (23) and two Baroque pilastered houses, one (past good infill) just a facade (24) amid new offices; up High Street with nice pub off (25), to Godiva statue (26) at city centre. s to splendid timberframe hospital (timber buttress details) with courtyard (27); 230ft Greyfriars spire (the third); medieval manor behind new frontage (28). To delightful green (29): Georgian redbrick (pedimented doorways); Regency stucco house with pilasters (next to George Eliot's school); 1863 stucco quadrant.

Back to (26); N to medieval chapel (30); to best stretch of walls (9) to (10) with gates (10, 11). To (12) over IRR to delightful textures, warehouses of canal terminus basins. Back across to tower (13); round bastion (14); Town Wall tavern (15) on its line. Then Georgian cottages (31); splendid group of medieval Bablake School and Bond's Hospital (courtyard), cruciform church (32); to early c19 'topshops' (33); into largely recreated medieval timberframe Spon Street (34) – best house coming from near (19). Under IRR, past new street frontage, to stone bridge with chapel ruins (35), and timberframe cottages (36). w off map to four streets (Duke, Lord, Mount, Craven) s off Spon End, of Chapelfields, a watchmakers' suburb with topshops, laid out in 1846. Back by (37).

OXFORD AND CAMBRIDGE

Oxford and Cambridge are dominated visually by their historic university and college buildings (many delightful quadrangles/courts); in existing guidebooks, these are not included here. But both places were important towns before their universities – with 'halls' for students, then colleges for both teachers and students – began in c12/13. This book emphasises Town rather than Gown.

Cambridge had an important Roman settlement (Castle Hill area) at the crossing of 2 Roman roads, with Saxon settlements here later and to s round St Benet's; Oxford is Saxon in origin. Both had Norman castles inserted in them after the Conquest.

Cambridge had a market place and c1200 defensive King's Ditch round its Eastern edge (river w defences; (7) (3) (10) (2) (15) (22) to river again), outside which developed its famous Stourbridge Fair. Oxford had markets (replaced by the covered market in 1772) for cattle at Carfax (= quatre voies) and in the nearby streets – Cornmarket, Queen (meat), St Aldate's (fish) and pigs in the High, plus horses in Broad Street; and it had a stone c13 townwall. Remaining timberframe houses in both are plastered rather than exposed, many at Oxford having 'Norwich' dormer gables and 'Ipswich' windows. Later Georgian/early c19 suburbs are stonebuilt (some brick after 1820s) – as are all the colleges – at Oxford (like Bath and Cheltenham,) but greybrick at Cambridge (like Norwich), often plus yellow tiles and mansard roofs (Cambridge colleges had used brick before, often in square gatehouse towers).

The greenery of the riverside 'Backs' and delightfully intimate areas round Cambridge's churches contrast with Oxford's more urban character, culminating in 'The High' and the area round the Radcliffe Camera. Both medieval towns attracted monastic houses and priories (plus later, when the universities became established, friars houses) – fine monastic churches were adapted to become Christ Church chapel/the cathedral at Oxford, and Jesus College chapel at Cambridge. College ownership of town centre land has kept major c19/20 industrial development at both to the East; and 1950/60s college developments arrogantly turned their backs on the 'town' (Longwall, Oxford; King Street, Cambridge). More recent infilling is more sensitive, ingeniously remodelling historic town houses into irregular new courtyards, using upper floors over shops as residential accommodation, a model to other historic towns and cities. Perambulations use fullsize 6″ maps (**Cambridge I**, **Oxford II** and **III**); but the book shows central areas doubled to 12″ (without numbers) as **Cambridge II**, **Oxford I**..

Cambridge

Start at Market Hill (1); late C15 Great St Mary's, 1938-9 Guildhall; N side Georgian greybrick (groundfloor segmental windows), 1934 loggia (under college courtyard facing St Michael's); E side 1890s curved stone gable, fine 1688 shell doorway moved above balcony, Georgian brick. Explore delightful street pattern and lanes to main streets to be seen later: SW, round St Edward's, past Gothick ground floor to King's Parade – as also W (C20 timberframe with pargeting, elaborate mid C19 yellowbrick, stucco) alongside St Mary's; N along Georgian yellowbrick Rose Crescent; NW to Holy Trinity, under recesses into Market Passage; W down pedestrian Petty Cury (overhanging timberframe), through new Lion Yard arcade to 1842 St Andrew's and site of Barnwell Gate (2).

Out SE corner and round Guildhall: late C16 timberframe (segmental windows); stripy 1875 Corn Exchange; Georgian brick, overhanging timberframe, pilastered greybrick (triglyph frieze), mid C19 classical bank on corner. Follow good Georgian frontage opposite Saxon St Benet's tower – Georgian brick, stucco (Eagle has iron courtyard balconies) to stone; back past fine timberframe corner group, down Free School Lane, behind Corpus Christi college (founded by two town guilds), along late C19 Cavendish laboratories, early C17 Perse School hall (now Whipple museum), to Georgian house (laurel doorway); past cottages (1450 chimney) alongside St Botolph's to 1831 Pitt Press tower – site of Trumpington Gate (3).

Now former High Street to (5). Trumpington Street: left, Georgian greybrick down Silver Street (three round doorways, good fanlights), 1850s (surrounds, good shopfronts); 'Cats' and Corpus colleges; 1820 stone hotel (balcony) opposite 1866 Gothic corner bank. Then houses of King's Parade, perfect foil to large-scale college opposite: Georgian greybrick, timberframe; passage; 5-storey purple/redbrick (cartouche), pedimented windows; three timberframe *exposed* (brackets, pilaster strips); crosswindows, greybrick, corner redbrick (aprons). Opposite, superb stone university group: Gibbs' 1720s Senate House; 1750s loggia, windows in round recesses; 1730 Tuscan iron railings. Trinity Street (opposite out-of-scale 1870 Caius corner): stucco (pedimented windows), Georgian purple/redbrick, bargeboarded gables, St Michael's, Rose Crescent. Then, left, Georgian red/greybrick corner (4), Venetian windows, Gothick shopfront, 1905 corner. Right (good curve): lively Victorian Gothic corner, Ionic shopfront, double overhanging gabled timberframe, pedimented (cherubs) doorway, Blue Boar (tunnel doorway), 1880s 'Norman Shaw',

Georgian redbrick (keystone masks, quoins, bracketed eaves). Trinity College – Great Gate and Court left, varied 1860s courts to Sidney Street, right; churchyard. St John's Street, opposite college: 1878 Gothic Divinity School; strange Victorian stone columns, yellowbrick with lavish decoration (roundel heads, mosaics), scroll windows, to stucco corner, facing Norman Round Church (5).

Back to (4) to follow original medieval commercial Milne Street, hythes down to the river navigation severed by 1440s King's College: 16 chimneys of Trinity Lane; 1671 Ionic pilastered 'town house' Bishop's Hostel (6); s past Caius, Trinity Hall, Clare, original King's 1440s gateway; superb King's chapel and 1720s Fellow's Building (by Gibbs, who called the chapel 'A Gothick building *but* the finest I ever saw') – facing former wharfs, site of St John Zachary (great lawn); out along Queens Lane to (7).

Across 1959 Silver Street bridge, past fine Georgian houses (old granary, now college, good 1968 infill); c18 stucco; (ahead delightful post-1875 brickwork of Newnham College); left past 1850s Italianate terrace; 1909 malthouse, early c19 watermill (8); NE across meadows – 1926 Fen Causeway bridge (9) – to mill pool (timber gallery on old granary). Then line of King's Ditch. Mill Lane (7), right: corner pub setting off 1966 graduate centre; overhanging timberframe/Georgian redbrick (good doorway). Pembroke Street, beyond (3): Georgian greybrick corner, recessed window, pilasters, cottages. Into late Victorian/Edwardian 'gownscape': 1880s (on map) laboratories (coupled pilasters) facing inventive Pembroke building; 1900s splayed corner facing block with cupola (10).

Back to (3), continuing Trumpington Street 'extramurally', conduits either side: yellowbrick mansion (4 Venetian windows; pedimented porch, window); contrasting churchscape – assertive 1875 spire, lavish c14 Little St Mary's (timberframe cottages, 1883 columned former museum facing churchyard), Wren's cool classical 1664 Pembroke chapel, 1632 Gothic Peterhouse chapel between colonnades. Then 7-bay 1701 redbrick mansion (gatepiers, railings, stone quoins), smaller-scale gabled timberframe, greybrick pair (college courtyard behind), more Baroque 1727 (pink, redbrick in strips, segmental window, aprons, fine doorway) – with huge 1837 museum portico (and green domes) opposite. Follow early c19 greybrick through 1822 Fitzwilliam Street (little balconies) to (11); returning, dramatic glimpse of museum. Then pilastered corner, recessed doorways, neo-Georgian bow shopfront (Gothick glazing); 1864-5 Italianate hospital. Right, 1770s pedimented greybrick villa (Ionic colonnade), terraces – 1850s 3+6+3+6+3 (railings, rooms over porches; varied windowtops) behind trees, 1839-64

6+9+6+9+6 (iron railings). Left, on nice curve, Victorian bargeboards, early c19 yellowbrick (tripartite door, 4 tripartite windows), 1840 iron porch curving up to recessed arch, to mansard roofs facing 1614 Hobson's Conduit (12) moved from Market Hill.

Turning E, more early c19 greybrick (cast-iron verandah/canopy); opposite, giant round arches; to cottagey corner facing cathedral-like 1887-90 RC church (vaulted interior, central tower, fine spire). Right to greybrick villa (elaborate doorway), terrace (13) – made Italianate 1860s. (Off map: right, nice late Victorian area, Botanic Gardens; 1845 loggia of railway station.)

Now N to (5), along second spine: unexpectedly spacious classical Downing College (like US campus); villa (recessed windows, Ionic porch) opposite inventive 1901 police station; Georgian redbrick (14), 1910s Renaissance store, to 1891 bank spire (2). Beyond Holy Trinity, largely early c19 greybrick Sidney Street (and Green Street): right, well-planned 1930s street (N side part of college courtyard), balconies, college; left, redbrick windowtops like Wisbech, Green Street (one redbrick), Italianate round windows, 9-bay, 1860s Trinity courtyards. Good dense final stretch: left, timberframe, 6-bay dated 1791; right Georgian painted brick (keyheads, quoined surrounds), to (5).

Back to Jesus Lane, to do loop E: 8-bay greybrick; 1860s portico; timberframe; widened road past greybrick row to car park; behind railings, early c18 grey/redbrick mansion (pedimented centre, doorway; back Venetian window) – opposite (15). Then delightful early c19 greybrick suburbs: recessed doorways, left 5-bay redbrick, right terrace, pair (5 identical doorways); past 1864 All Saints, opposite Jesus College (medieval nunnery church, cloister), varied with 'negative pilasters' (tall recess strips) to roundabout (16). Facing common: trees, linked 3-bay villas between recessed ends, 2-storey row N; (off map, two cast-iron 'heart' balconies); 1890 iron bridge (17). Back to (16), across 1828-36 square (three pedimented pilastered centres) to coffered round doorways (18). Orchard (one-storey, mansard roofs, pedimented doorways), Earl, Victoria Streets, to emerge at (19): NE side villas; NW side corner house, 3-storey terrace (verandah/canopy), central pair, terrace again, house (recesses) to fine villa (twin pilasters, laurel doorway), facing 1900s hotel green turrets.

Past pilasters to good 1910 college block facing bus station (20). Across gardens (pedimented terrace to E), past (21) into winding King Street: 1880s greybrick – towards (16), 1790 yellow/redbrick almshouses; Georgian brick (pedimented doorway), part timberframe cottages. Domestic 'town' scale then wrecked by new 'gown' backsides. Thankfully to early c19 Malcolm Street; round corner to

pilastered stone 1913 County Hall, Georgian redbrick (door on brackets), 1850s greybrick (scroll door), back to (2).

Back to (5) and NW. Fine 'typical town' C17 plastered timberframe group (elaborate 1st-floor windows), one restored exposed; similar cottages opposite demolished for John's faceless 1930s kitchens. Georgian greybrick Mitre, as along churchyard, past timberframe cottage, to (22). Past church; greybrick corner round, right, to 1st-floor recesses, facing timberframe. More timberframe to tall early C20 timberframe corner on Quayside.

Over Cambridge's original strategic river crossing (now 1823 fan-vaulted cast-iron arch) to more fine C17 timberframe (carved brackets on both overhangs of one) – two large 'Norwich' dormers in irregular new Magdalene courtyard behind. Round superb corner to cottage group in Northampton Street, facing good old and new group (art gallery) next St Peter's; to Georgian yellowbrick, purplebrick, pub, and two mansard-roofed terraces – greybrick, then plastered, facing attractive redbrick 1899 Presbyterian college (23). SE into St John's: past Dutch gable to timberframe Merton Hall, 1200s stone pre-university 'School of Pythagoras' (24); this faces ingeniously twisting 1000ft 1966 Cripps building (superb view from roof), which winds N of 1825-31 New Court ('wedding cake') to river. Out again, N up Pound Hill to late C19 Italianate (25), William the Conqueror's Castle Mound. Down Castle Hill – nice yellowbrick Castle, gaps, to 3+1+3 pilastered terrace, at crossroads gabled timberframe (museum), opposite 1875 St Giles (inside, Norman door, chancel arch). (Nice loop NE up Chesterton Road: Georgian stucco (advanced centre), one-storey mansard row; over river at Jesus Lock (26); across grass to nice greybrick rows (27), back to Round Church.) Plus, of course, the famous river trip, along superb 'Backs' between (26) and (7).

Oxford

Using **Map I**, double-page **Map II** for numbers, start with finest group of public buildings in Britain. Facing 1930s New Bodleian (1), Hawksmoor's sculptural porticoed 1711-5 Clarendon building; Wren's 1663-9 Sheldonian Theatre, tiny 1678-83 Old Ashmolean; 1613-24 Bodleian (5-tier architectural 'frontispiece' in quadrangle, 1483 Divinity School vault); to Gibbs' superb 1737-49 Radcliffe Camera rotunda (Hawksmoor's idea, facing his 1716-34 All Souls' North Quad with LH 'Gothick' library window, 'Venetian' inside); St Mary's fine C14 spire, spacious late C15 interior.

Clockwise along line of walls (plus extras) Line of Oxford's Saxon and medieval townwall is along S side of the Sheldonian.

Explore E past site of Smythgate – 1520s octagonal chapel (now Hertford), under 1913 bridge; left down passage to C17 pub on ditch-line, with glimpse of superb wall stretch in New College grounds; ahead, Georgian houses – stucco, 5-bay redbrick, railings.

Back to (1) down attractive extramural Holywell – gabled and overhanging timberframe, Georgian (many tripartite windows, as delicate ones on corner King's Arms). LHS: infill shop; 1626 bracketed oriels; 1740s set back pedimented music room – delightfully incorporated into Wadham. RHS: 1883-96 corner; Bath Place (to C17 pub again); early C19 ironwork, scroll doorways, 1639 window brackets. LHS: good frontage to bay windows; road (since map) to 1890s Manchester, 1887-9 Mansfield (2). Then late C19 New College ranges – through gate to battlements, wallwalk, round towers of townwall (if possible, explore inside, and round corner). LHS: paired windows; rusticated pilasters; good gabled stone; bracketed oriel; pedimented window (corner). To N early C16 manor (3), now collegiate; (C) rectilinear 1960-4 St Catherine's College.

Then Longwall S: battlemented college wall; right, mixed Georgian, disruptive 1960s infill (townwall behind), balconies, better infill, gabled timberframe; to site of East Gate (4). E along The High; S, past 5-bay pedimented Georgian (tall first floor, rusticated pilasters), 1630s gateway, into meadows to follow round walls (enclosing Merton garden, with corner); W (wall continued into Corpus, then S to include priory); S; W past 1860s range to (5), site of South Gate (jutting out S end of Christ Church facade).

Diversion S. W side of St Aldate's: timberframe gables, delicate doorway, columned porch; spectacular corner timberframe with 7 gables, oriels on figure brackets (dated 1628), elaborate eaves (good infill behind); timberframe (Clark's Row); tripartite windows, C17 stone and timberframe gables. E side: Georgian chequerbrick; 1830s riverside stone warehouse plus crane. 1844 tollhouse; over 1825-7 Folly Bridge; right strange 1849 island house; left (down towpath) 1780s mansion (6) over water (bay, Venetian windows).

Back to (5) to follow wall line W along Brewer Street: right, Pembroke on city wall; left C17 stone, 1892 choir school, 1930s Campion Hall, triglyph doorway, timberframe (bow shopfronts) to site of Littlegate (plaque). S to stucco with trellis porch (7), its overhanging timberframe front on Turn-Again Lane which follow W to timberframe group; N up Roger Bacon Lane, W behind this group (on city wall). Continue W across new shopping centre: along back-end walkway; up steps round lift; across central concourse; out down ramp to Castle Street (8). W along Paradise Street: late C17 doorway; timberframe corner pub; over bridge to (9) – beneath castle to which townwall connected.

Pleasant loop: along river past Georgian red, chequerbrick (stone plaque) to site of medieval town wharf (10); to w, 1851 Midland Station (11), like Crystal Palace; over bridge; along canal towpath to (12); over cast-iron bridge, past railway swing bridge to main river (13); s to 1888 bridge (14); E to tollhouse; s down Mill Street to remains of mill, abbey outbuilding (15); E across railway footbridge, 1960s Oxpens Road (16) to rehabilitated 1866 housing; N (1702 school next to church), E past brewery, back to (9).

Along Tidmarsh Lane (castle mound, late c11 tower, converted c19 maltings); round 1912 pedimented corner. Past Nuffield, founded 1937 on site of canal basin; below its library tower/spire to 1827-9 porticoed canal house (townwall behind, in Bulwark Lane); past castle-like 1840s County Hall (mid c18, c19 prison behind) to entrance of shopping centre (8); opposite, 1819 chapel behind trees, infill. N up good street. Left, gabled timberframe, 1901 school (continuous groundfloor glazing); 1+3+1 1825 pilastered, 1874 church, grand Georgian (all St Peter's College). Right, nice cottage group; plastered groundfloor, stone 1st; through medieval gate remains, along stone range, to Georgian segmental, pedimented doorways (Frewin Hall); lively mid Victorian over c16.

Past 1878 church steeple to pick up townwall again, at stretch with angle (17) behind 1880 High School, next to Georgian chequerbrick (in George Street). Following wall line E again, intramural St Michael's Street: Georgian chequerbrick, c17 shaped gables, heavy Baroque Vanbrugh house, 1870 pediment; opposite, Victorian Gothic Students' Union buildings (set back); left, stucco (bow); rebuilt c17 timberframe corner. St Michael's tower (reputedly part of c11 townwall); fine late c14 exposed timberframe corner (18), c14 stone. Round block with stretch of walls: intramural Ship Street plastered timberframe to Exeter chapel; left, Georgian pair; stucco extramural Broad Street frontage (tripartite windows) opposite Balliol – explore passages to see walls behind. N side Broad Street back to (1): c17 gabled – stucco and stone; nice stucco group with bay windows (one Venetian, four on Blackwells).

From Carfax South and East with The High from Map I
Carfax corners: NW 1900s bank, Tower house (c14 church tower between); SW, SE 1930s classical; NE exuberant 1900s neo-c17, as is 1893-7 Town Hall (19). Follow this down St Aldate's (1880 Gothic GPO opposite) to gabled timberframe. Attractive Pembroke Street W: RHS timberframe, Georgian chequerbrick; LHS overhanging timberframe, c17 stone with two 3-storey bays – into college for s fronts (columned porch, gabled with central jutting-out staircase); stucco both sides, left timberframe (coat-of-arms); N up St Ebbe's. Queen Street E (round-windowed late c 19).

Now the gentle curve of The High, one of the world's great streets. N side: Georgian stone – 5-bay (pedimented window), twin pilasters over fantopped Venetian window, 4-bay, 1(tripartite)+3+7 (pediment)+3+1 1774 market facade; stucco c17/18 corner Mitre (2-storey bays). s side: Victorian exposed timberframe, c18 stucco, c18 stone, overhanging timberframe (exposed at side); pilastered 2-storey bay; four gables (one set back exposed), timberframe 1637 Kemp Hall at back); 1897; c17 curved bay ('Ipswich' 1st-floor, double 2nd, pediment top) plus medieval bargeboards; plastered corner (tripartite windows). Then N side excellent 1706-8 All Saints (spire; now Lincoln Library); stucco row (eared windows); Brasenose 1886-9, 1907-9, timberframe round corner (1900s satyr doorhood). s side 1866 'Middle Pointed' bank; timberframe (pedimented window); stucco (tall paired, then pedimented 1st-floor windows) to 1873-5 yellowbrick street; stucco – tripartite bay windows (c14 'hall' window, cellar behind), pilastered windows, to 3-storey Oriel Street. Then St Mary's (lavish 1637 porch) facing hall, now Oriel (1908-11 building).

Beyond, s side: handsome 1775 stone (arched, alternate pedimented windows); stucco; 3-storey bays above Doric shopfront; University College; timberframe over triglyph shopfront (Doric columns); pilastered windows: Corinthian (heads) pilasters and shopfront, fan Venetian window, cast-iron balcony; Jackson's monumental neo-c17 1876-82 Examination Schools. N side: All Souls, 1704-5 1+4+1 Warden's Lodgings; tree – 'pivot of the High' (Pevsner); stucco, ending with gables (attic oriel brackets); The Queen's; lane (Norman vaulted chancel, crypt of St Peter's, now St Edmund Hall library); mixed stucco (two gables, 1901 neo-Tudor), 1800s stone corner. s side (4): 1900 Eastgate hotel; tripartite windows – 6 fluted, then 4; delightful 3-bay stone (ovals), 2-bay.

Superb Magdalen frontage, tower, opposite 1632-3 gate, 1835 5-bay (Ionic columns); over 1772-82 bridge –1780s 'Adamish' house (20) now St Hilda's. Along early c19 stucco and redbrick St Clement's: 1700 almshouses (pediment, gatepiers); c18 Port Mahon; to delightful London Place behind grass (buildings removed since map) – incised pilasters, Gothick balconies, yellowbrick gabled (since map); to 1828 neo-Norman church (21).

Back to (4), to explore lanes s of The High. Follow Examination Schools round past quad to its building, N side of cobbled Merton Street (past early c19 stucco, two timberframe overhanging stone with gables between); then c18 (channelled ground floor); 1908 mansion; mullioned c17 (exposed timberframe gables, real-tennis court to N); medieval 'Cotswold' stables; c15/17 Beam Hall (7 gables). Then 1884-5, 1960s Corpus – in delightful Magpie Lane:

off, 1816 Gothick almshouses opposite C17 gables; 8-bay stucco terrace; gabled timberframe to The High (doorhead on carved brackets, bracketed oriel, 1588 overhang). Finally, right round Oriel; 2-storey stucco bays (C17 stone, real-tennis court to N), 1870s Gothic corner; past C17 timberframe cottages to C18 corner Bear, back of block (19).

From Carfax North along St Giles (Map II)

Cornmarket E side: 4-bay stucco former Crown (cast-iron balcony, upstairs Elizabethan wall-paintings); delightful Golden Cross yard – 4 exposed timberframe gables ('Ipswich' windows), C16 with oriels, early C19 stuccoed end; 1+3+2+3+1 pilastered stucco terrace; 1915 stone gabled, 3-storey bays, 1900s stone Art Nouveau/Gothic; two churches. Store (22) – 1894 turret, 1913 Gothic, 1894 classical; 1864 'North Oxford' Randolph Hotel.

Past 1841 Martyrs' Memorial, up E side of St Giles. Balliol; St John's; C17 Middleton Hall (balustrade). Under stucco Lamb and Flag 'inland', past mid-C19 stucco terrace, to two High Victorian Gothic masterpieces: Butterfield's 1868-72 polychrome brick Keble; Ruskinian 1855-60 museum (superb stone, iron, glass interior with 'triforium' gallery), 'Abbot's Kitchen, Glastonbury'; to S, 1929 Rhodes House Cotswold rotunda (23). Back to St Giles: Georgian brick; stone (rusticated ground floor, elaborate central window), columned doorway; 1702 pedimented mansion (gatepiers with urns, back shell doorway, domed gardenhouse); tripartite windows; 2-storey bow; late C17 Black Hall (3-storey bay, 'Ipswich' top; columned porch); 3 timberframe gables. To N, 1960s laboratories (24); opposite, road fork, church, C17 gabled parsonage.

North Oxford (Map III)

Follow Banbury Road LHS into North Oxford Victorian Suburb Conservation Area: 1850s Italianate stucco villas; 1879 terracotta school; late Victorian redbrick villas (one behind neo-Georgian), two sophisticated 1880-1 'Queen Anne'. Beyond link to Parks, follow RHS 52-66 (56 statue), in 'characteristic North Oxford' 1860s estate – brick, stone-dressed Gothic villas – best 60, 62 (1), with an 'atmosphere of leafy sobriety' (Pevsner); many have become university departments/offices; 52 and 54 (with 1896 chapel) Wycliffe Hall. Or parts of new colleges (plus many new buildings): St Anne's (5); Lady Margaret Hall (10), past good villas facing Parks; whole block (4, 7), St Hugh's; Wolfson (11), up 1890s Linton Road; St Anthony's (6), core 1866-8, 1891-4 chapel (library).

Delightful Italianate Cheltenham-like 1853-5 Park Town: stucco villas (7, 8, 10 brick and stone); shrubs; 3-storey stone crescents (channelled ground floor, tripartite windows, eared above); to 1855 yellowbrick/rendered terrace (2). To N, roads were developed

1880-1900s, villas tending to neo-Jacobean/'Queen Anne', like St Margaret's to 1883-93 Gothic church (12), or half-timbered/tilehung 'Bedford Park' like 1886-9 Rawlinson Road (13).

Sample Bardwell Road, N to 1903 'Queen Anne' 2 Northmoor Road (3). Down Banbury Road W side: 1830s (4); 1871-6 Canterbury Road; 1830s stucco and stone villas (conservatory), delightful North Parade between – which follow W; S to (5). Woodstock Road N: LHS 1820-50s Walton Manor estate – 2-storey chequerbrick and stucco (as, opposite (6), with Gothick doorways, terrace with rusticated ground floor); RHS, Street's 1860s Gothic church; 'Park Town' set back villa (7), semis opposite. W past late Victorian pillarbox to (8). S along delightful minor 'North Oxford' 1870s Gothic 114-138, 149-164 Kingston Road. Finally 'Walton Manor' chequerbrick. Left at (9), down chequerbrick and stucco Observatory Street, back to (5).

North-West central (Map II)

Back S down Woodstock Road. 1820s 12-bay redbrick terrace (25) – recessed round windows, cast-iron balconies; superb 1774-94 observatory tower plus wings, 'architecturally finest in Europe' (Pevsner), plus link to house (N side Green College; S side accessible within hospital); infirmary – pedimented 1760s centre, 1891-2 classical left, 1864 Gothic chapel; spacious 1870s RC church plus presbytery; 1800s stucco, as opposite towards St Giles church.

W side of St Giles S of (26). 1850s stone, rendered; two more terraces with recessed round windows, continuous balconies – 1850s 9-bay (railings), 8-bay 1820s; between, two C18 5-bay – fine doorway, alternate pedimented windows; Victorian gabled; C16 set back (gables, trellis porch); narrow 4-bay C18 (alternate pedimented windows, 4 later gables); stucco (balcony); dated 1660, big surrounds; 'similar' front – follow redbrick side to pilastered stucco villa; C17 stone, timberframe gabled (2-storey bays); Georgian (tall-columned doorway). Finally 1911-26 Gothic Pusey House (spacious vaulted chapel); 1920s neo-C17 Blackfriars; 1869 stone Gothic house; 1932 extension, to Cockerell's inventive 1841-5 classical/Baroque (giant columns) corner Taylor/Ashmolean.

Finally 1920-50s again. Stone 1828-37 Beaumont Street (pedimented doorways, square fanlights; cast-iron verandah/canopies, balconies) past 1938 Playhouse (27). Walton Street N: RHS 1850s stucco; LHS C17 stone cottages, c1825 brick – to (28), cast ironwork; monumental 1826-30 facade (giant columns); 5-bay stone (29); behind, attractive small-scale 'Jericho' to 1869 church (campanile). Returning S: fine 1836 Grecian church; left past 1960s concrete frames of Somerville (30); through square; Regency stone street (1826 chequerbrick W) back to (27).

Birmingham

'Mayntayned by smiths' in 1538, supplying 15,000 swords to Parliament in the Civil War, Birmingham developed into the chief metal-working town in Britain, in 1835 'an immense workshop, a huge forge, a vast shop...busy people, faces brown with smoke...nothing but the sound of hammers and the whistle of steam escaping from boilers'. A city of 'small masters', key figures were jeweller Matthew Boulton (who formed the famous partnership with James Watt to make steam engines), William Murdock, inventor of gas-lighting, and Joseph Priestley, chemist. 86,000 in 1801, 233,000 in 1851, Birmingham acquired under Joseph Chamberlain a 'civic gospel', in 1890 called 'the best governed city in the world'. Extending boundaries in 1911 (then 842,000), Birmingham overtook Glasgow in 1951 as Britain's 'Second City', both with populations over a million. Becoming more recently (over)dependent on motor-vehicle (and accessories) industries, it expressed its energy in a notorious 'philosophy of redevelopment' and 1950s Inner Ring Road. It is 'capital' of the West Midlands (2½ million), which includes the very different Black Country and important towns such as Dudley, Walsall and Wolverhampton (with a 'big city' feel and a good Georgian and Victorian central area).

Now in 1980s the redevelopment of Birmingham seems no worse than other bigger cities, and there is much of architectural interest: fine Colmore Row central area; late c18/mid c19 Jewellery Quarter to West; the extensive Regency suburb of Edgbaston, South. 1860-1914 marks Birmingham's greatest national importance architecturally – with Ruskinian Gothic villas of J. H. Chamberlain (1831-83, no relation to Jo), plus, with William Martin, as Chamberlain and Martin (C & M), inventively different libraries and schools (most after C's death) of 'characteristic' redbrick and terracotta; varied churches of J. A. Chatwin (1829-1907); in 1900s, fine 'Arts and Crafts' (A & C) houses, the garden suburb (founded by George Cadbury) of Bournville, and the superb Gothic/Art Nouveau churches of W. H. Bidlake (1860-1938).

Between 1″ **Map I** (1834 plus) and **1889-90 6″ Maps II-V** was Birmingham's greatest growth, but **I** shows how **II-V** interrelate: city centre round St Philip's, Jewellery Quarter round St Paul's (maps at angle of mid c18 Colmore Estate grid); E central (**I** before Joseph Chamberlain's post-1878 'improvement', Corporation Street, 'as broad as a Parisian boulevard'); Edgbaston bottom left. **Map I** shows the canals (Birmingham has a greater mileage than Venice, see my *Canals in Towns*) – even 1840s by-pass canal across

(1), under infamous 1960s 'Spaghetti Junction', past (2) to (3). Exciting towpath walk starts at Gas Street basin (4) – off short length of Broad Street between **Maps IV** and **V**: under Broad Street; past centre of English canal system; across straight cast-iron bridge over Telford's twin-towpath 1830s new Main Line; down 1780s flight of 13 locks (on **Map IV**), beneath 500ft 1966 GPO tower; to emerge at Snowhill ringway (5).

Swallowed by city's growth: superb 1618-35 Aston Hall (6) with Chatwin's fine 1880s church (medieval spire); in tube works, Redfern Road, c15-18 Hay Hall (7); a mile beyond (8), c16 timberframe Blakesley Hall (museum); Matthew Boulton's late c18 Soho house (9); early c19 Gothick Metchley Abbey (10). 1601 timberframe farmhouse forms s corner of interesting triangular block (11): E along Stratford Place to crossroads (1883, 1893 C & M grammar school blocks); Ravenhurst Street NW past 1849 Jacobean almshouses (to N, Bradford Street, Georgian 3-bay) to 1840s corner pub; up early c19 Moseley Road curve (opposite park) – Gothick doorway, redbrick and stucco, 2-storey bows.

Expressing city's growth (churches unreliably open) are: J. L. Pearson's superb vaulted 1879-81 St Alban's, Conybere Street (12), next to 1879 Chatwin almshouses (above 1980s mosque!); impressive 1890s St Aidan's, Herbert Road (13); Bidlake's Pearsonesque 1892-3 St Oswald's (14) plus 1899 vicarage behind (Dora Road); fine C & M terracotta schools – 1883 Waverley Road (15), 1885 Stratford Road (16); next door is Bidlake's masterpiece, 1899-1901 St Agatha's (inventive tower; spacious interior), whose fine vicarage, 100 Sampson Road, faces mid c18 Lloyd farmhouse (17). Beyond Bidlake's 'Glaswegian classical' art school (18): attractive 1890-1914 suburb (beyond Moseley parish church); 1790s Moseley Hall (hospital); another mile, in Yew Tree Road, 1879 Gothic 'Highbury', by J. H. Chamberlain for Jo; two miles beyond (19), Bournville. Finally three Bidlake churches NW: apsidal Handsworth New Road 1903 Bishop Latimer (20); and beyond parish church (21), superb (in Oxhill Road) 1907 St Andrew's (interior wall-piers), intricate vaulted 1909-10 cemetery chapel.

City centre (Map II)

Within IRR (includes Great Charles Street, LH edge of map). Start at Archer's sophisticated 1709-25 Baroque St Philip's (now cathedral), extended 1883-4 by Chatwin, chancel interior similar to his 1862-4 bank facing churchyard (1).

First, via 1875-6 classical arcade (2), 1880s Arts and Crafts (3), 1898-1901 terracotta and green faience City Arcade (4), 1878-1900s Corporation Street: down original frontage (threatened) to good corner (5) – facing station approach, 1867-75 palazzo bank; back up

Old Farm
Wilks Green
Grove House
Rectory
21
Hill Top Farm
Birchfield House
New Inn
Heathfield
Bristnels End
3
Crick Farm
Soho Hill
Burton Woo
unt all
Thornhill
T.G.
Soho
ick Hall
Soho Works
Station
9
Spring Grove
20
Cape of Good Hope
5
Summerfield House
Tunnel
State
ten Park Lodge
Rotten Park Reservoir
Monument
4
The Oaks
2
Oak hill House
Speed Knaves End
Botanical Garden
hurst
Edgbaston
Mill
Hill top
Harborne Heath
Mass House
10
Birmingham Canal
19
River Rea
Metchley Abbey
Averys Mill

1900s terracotta lane to (3). Past site of early c18 Old Square (now roundabout) to lively A & C 1890s terracotta (6), 1882 stone classical county court. Ending with lavish display of red terracotta: Aston Webb's 1887-91 Victoria Law Courts (7) – first major use in Birmingham; 1898, 1900-2 blocks beyond, 1903-4 Methodist Hall (tall tower) opposite.

Back to (1), past 1900 Perpendicular corner along Waterloo Street: three good classical corners (1830 portico, fine 1869 with coffered entrance, late c19 with round windows) – on Bennetts Hill, which follow up 1827 stucco 5-bay (recessed), pilastered terrace (shopfronts), opposite late 1860s Italianate; interesting Regency frontage – 'Egyptianate' colonnade, rich 1+3+1 with Soanian pilasters, 6-bay, 1+2+1 (aprons), 13 bays (eared surrounds) on curve. Down past grass (church demolished) to varied late c19 New Street frontage (8): redbrick Venetian Gothic; giant-arched stucco, redbrick and stone; stucco corner (Venetian windows).

Attractive civic area: 1889-91 Renaissance GPO (lively skyline); Hansom's handsome 1830s Roman temple Town Hall (behind, 1900s terracotta facade); lavishly detailed 1874-9 Council House (weak front, dome), better 1881-5 Art Gallery elevation (tower), facing 1880 monument (J. H. Chamberlain for Jo); 1970s 'negative ziggurat' central library, site of 1875 Mason College (9) – forerunner of university. Under 1910s bridge (to Council House extension) to Chamberlain's masterpiece – superb 1881-5 Ruskinian Gothic School of Art (10) – sculptural corner, brilliantly asymmetrical facade, 'Art Nouveau' rose-window.

Delightful professional area since map. Round block (11): 1899 'right old mix-up of styles' (Pevsner); delightful 1899-1904 A & C Cornwall Street frontage (Art Nouveau railings) – opposite buttressed 1893 art school extension; 1897 corner, 1900s linked 1st/groundfloor, gabled (varied windows) – similar across Newhall Street. Along IRR past almost styleless 1897-8 corner (for Guild of Handicraft). Church Street 'inland': 1909 'industrial' giant piers (12); Loire-style corner; delightful A & C – bow windows with Chinese ogee tops, 1+2+1. From pilastered 1891 corner (13) up Edmund Street: right, contrasting 1880s Venetian, 1897 A & C Gothic; left 1895 neo-c17, 1898 linked 2-storey bay windows (groundfloor ironwork), giant arch; unusual 1890-1 'Norman Shaw' Dutch-gabled corner; to city's finest terracotta (14) – Frederick Martin's 1896 Bell Edison corner, 'tremendous combination of shapes, excellent strong detail' (Pevsner). Finally 1883-4 classical block, to Chamberlain's late 1870s Gothic school office, Art School.

Finally, alongside Council House, to best street, Colmore Row. 1904 Baroque corner (clocktower); superb 1900 Eagle building –

bronze doors, strange pilasters, chequerboard 'Anglo-Saxon' top (W. R. Lethaby); stucco Italianate; pedimented 1900s Baroque (sculptural arch); early c19 stucco; red stripey granite 1902 bow between towers; Regency stucco pilastered, 7-bay corner. Then, left: corner rich 1870s Renaissance Union Club, as beyond (Ghiberti, Cellini roundels); late c19 Venetian, columned classical; 1869-89 5-bay, 1+4+1 (1937 pilasters), balancing 5-bay – facing (1).

East central (Map III)

IRR continues from Great Charles Street to (1) – end of **Map I** canal walk; past St Chad's RC cathedral to (2) – flyover link past (3) to Spaghetti Junction; to E, University of Aston (chartered 1966), sports centre incorporating unspoilt 1880s Gothic baths interior (4). IRR then curves past (5), (6) to Horse Fair (7). Nearby, in John Bright Street, 1900s corners (8) to Severn Street plus 1881 'Norman Shaw' hospital (on map).

Loop to points of interest. From St Philip's to redeveloped High Street, 1800s Dale End houses (9) – Venetian windows; follow block round down late c19 Albert Street; right, (facing IRR) Ionic chapel (now RC); under IRR. Across garden, down Fazeley Street: right c18/19 pub (10). Under railway, left up to Philip Hardwick's superb Ionic 1838 terminus (11) to original railway line to London (Euston); down Banbury Street through gateway to delightful 1813 Gun Barrel Proof house (12) with 'trophies'; over canal arm to 1840s purple/redbrick facing (13), good warehouse behind. Down Barn/Milk Street, along 1891 C & M school (14); out to Digbeth (winding main street of c16 Birmingham), across river Rea to Deritend and 1902 'Alfred Bird' block (15) with ship gable, then fine early c16 timberframe Old Crown Inn. Beyond (16), block covered under **Map I**. Returning along Digbeth: 1860s Milk Street corner, 'Bonser' warehouse/tower (17); up to St Martin's parish church (rebuilt Chatwin 1873-5), new Bullring shopping centre (6), open-air market overlooked by delightful 1809 Nelson statue.

Jewellery Quarter (Map IV)

Across centre to Pugin's spacious 'hall-church' 1839-41 St Chad's RC cathedral (screen removed), above IRR roundabout (1). Gun Quarter: Bath Street (early c19 corner pub, stucco); round (2) – 1800s (tripartite, Venetian windows), row, right to 2+1 (tripartite, carriageway)+2 1840s works. Back to (1), over canal, to fine Constitution Hill corners: 1896 'Spanish Romanesque' cupola on narrow triangle, right 1880s Ruskinian – behind, richly arcaded 1911 works (3); lavish 1880s commercial palazzo, similar pub next to eccentric Gothic terrace; opposite, 1910s A & C works (4), 1820s (elaborate central arch). Beyond, 1870 'Gothic' pub (5); Rickman's 1821 Gothick cast ironwork (6), 1841 tomb – church gone).

Now loop round attractive Jewellery Quarter – late c18/early c19 houses converted to workshops, mid c19 housing/workshops, 1860-1910s factories. Round late c18 square: town houses (7); fine galleried 1776-9 church (1823 spire); corner Venetian window/entrance – beyond, industrial museum (8) facing 1880s Assay Office; out past 1980s infill, round 1880s pilasters. Along well-modelled 27-bay 1860s orangebrick factory, right, up past 1860s Italianate – both (9), to 1862-3 polychromatic 'Lombardic' arched Argent Works. Round (10). Good Frederick Street: left, 'Lombardic' to Turkish Baths; right, 1870s, delightful 1860s stucco (bearded keystones). Albion Street: left 1860s corner; houses (later workshops) – 1840s left, symmetrical 1830s right with wings (Soanian pilasters); 1883 dark-brick works; 1909 corner – opposite 1820s/60s pub; (beyond, (11), 1830s stucco pair); left to set back 1913 Manton works; left past 1893 narrow 7-bay gabled, back to 'Lombardic'.

Along 1887 wall (flagpole), left into good Vittoria Street: left, 1850s Gothic 3-bay; 1866 round-windowed (keystones); similar 12-bay, 1895 5-bay; right, 3-bay pilastered, 1840s Italianate; 1879-80 'flatted factory' corner (12). Regent Place: 1860s opposite 1883 gabled Gothic; single-bay 1830s houses. Between good curving corners – left, 1909 (big windows), right 1820s – Regent Street: left, lavish stucco 1860s Italianate.

Then Frederick Street stucco (13) – 1860 Italianate works, 1830s pair (Doric colonnade), pilastered villas; 1903 cast-iron clocktower. (Left, 1840s redbrick corners (14); 1860s 2+5+1+5+2 Birmingham Mint (15); cemeteries with 'catacombs'; rich 1893 Gothic C & M library (16); 1830s/40s stucco (17) – terrace). Back into Vittoria Street: 1860s Gothic, 1911 A & C (13) School of Jewellery; opposite, 1840s redbrick, 1870s 'functional'. To delightful 1860s (linked windows) 4-bay Gothic, 3-bay 'Norman' (18).

Then Vyse Street: 1880s French Gothic (19) – opposite 1960s block; 1850s redbrick/stucco houses (20) – Doric doorways; similar splayed corner left, both sides (21); to 1910s arcaded factory (22). (Further out busy road: late Georgian Key Hill corners (left); fine C & M 1883 Gothic school (23); beyond flyover left, 1840s Richmond Road, Italianate villas; up Hunter's Road to Pugin convent (24), 1840s villas beyond. Back into centre. RHS: 1830s redbrick (set back); 1880s Gothic (linked arches), 6-bay. LHS: 1860s palazzo Pelican works; 1880s corner (opposite, three 6-bay 1906-10 works); chequerboard 'Anglo-Saxon' 1912 Ashford and Son (25). Via 1820s redbrick corners left, right, 1850s 1+7+1 terrace/works (26), back to (7).

Edgbaston (Map V)

Leafy spacious c19 suburb with villas, carefully developed by

Gough and Calthorpe families, with many 'listed' historic buildings (Regency, 1840s-60s Italianate stucco and redbrick – on fringes 1900s A & C). Lies s of Middle Ring Road (MRR) – past (1), 1858 almshouses (2), Five Ways (office centre of Birmingham), (3), (4). **Links to centre 1**. From (7) **Map III** to (3): to N, 1856 synagogue (5); 1826-9 church tower; hospital (1840-1 2+3+2, 1873 Italianate).

2. SW from (9) **Map II**, under IRR, to Five Ways, along Broad Street: 1920s Georgian 'civic area'; mid C19 classical, 1781 brasshouse (Venetian window, 1860s Romanesque ground floor), 1848 bluebrick church – opposite 1870s Venetian Gothic (over canal). Loop to mid C19 industrial streets N: Oozells past 1877 C & M school, then SW; to Sheepcote (6), right along good mid C19 frontage, over canal loop, off map to 1840s horseshoe stables (next to main canal) at road junction; back to Broad Street between 1898 bank, 1814 mansion.

Hagley Road (and to North) N side: 1838 pilastered stucco (7); redbrick pair (Tuscan porches); pilastered stucco terrace, villa; bows (8), Gothick inn; 1850-1 Renaissance Oratory house, 1859-61 school – chunky courtyard to 1903-5 'Roman' domed RC church; delightful Regency semis off road, pilastered row (9). Loop N: brick, stucco terrace/rows; past 1758 folly tower (10) to C & M Gothic chimney (11); roads round (12) – varied stucco villa frontages. Then Hagley Road s side: Regency 154, 162, lavish 1860s Italianate (13). Beyond (14), Regency redbrick pair (end pediments), 202 and 204 tripartite windows; to redbrick Italianate, 1840s set back stucco 214 with twin-columned porch. (Further out, N side: 1850s Italianate 405-9; 1900s A & C 415, 431.)

Returning, loop N: Manor Road; E round Chatwin's lavish 1868 St Augustine's (1876 spire) to 1896 A & C 17 and 19 Rotton Park Road; right, left along York Road, 1860s Italianate (15), mixed 1850s to 1880s asylum (16); back to 1800s redbrick, mansion (17). Finally s side: early C19 stucco (bargeboarded pairs) opposite Oratory; brick villa (18).

Perambulation Start from parish church (19), 1717 manor s. Past villa extended as school (20), down 1850s Italianate (21). To 1830s corner, artisans' 165-77 on Bristol Road. (Further out: 1830s semis 211-21; villas 223 (verandah) to 231 (Gothick); 24 Priory Road Chamberlain 1870s Gothic). Into town, RHS: stucco pairs (Soanian doorways); 1840s stucco, mixed (22), Italianate – opposite Regency villas (set back), stucco pair.

Up (23) to follow nicely varied 1830s stucco villas, pairs – round (24) into fine Wellington Road (good 79-73 opposite), increasing in scale 25-39. LHS: 1840s Italianate 63; down lane to 62 (bows), right to folly (25); superb Grecian pilastered 61, set back 60, 59 with scrolls. RHS grand villas – Grecian 47 – back to (20). Roads zigzagging, Ampton: 1830s 1, 2; 1-3 Arthur; farmhouse conversion (opposite 1840s school); Italianate, Tudor, to 1855 Chamberlain Ruskinian (26). Carpenter: LHS Regency stucco 3-15 (cast-iron porches), 1850s; RHS, Chamberlain Gothic, Italianate; across to 1830s pair (27). Down Italianate Gough Road. Charlotte: 1840s classical (28); w side, larger Italianate to corner, down to (29).

Back NE to smaller-scale 1830s Ryland (terrace with wreaths, cottage orné), up delightful Lee Crescent (pilaster incisions) – facing (30). Along MRR, Elvetham left, mid c19 Yew Tree Road, to stucco pairs (31). Past round cottage orné, to explore N (to MRR), then s, two good roads. *George* N: E side Grecian villa, varied pairs; W side back, 1800s symmetrical 4-7 (4 gone), 3-bay, Italianate. s: W, 22 (Tudor coachhouses); E side returning, mixed villas, pair. *Frederick* N: E side pairs – 1830s, monumental 1840s. s: W side, Italianate pair (Chatwin), nice pairs to villa (set back); E, 1820s 27 and **28**.

Facing Five Ways, 1800s townhouse, 1878 iron clocktower. s of (32), Calthorpe Road villas. LHS 1820s, 1840s 24-26, villa extended as school. RHS 1830s pairs (Soanian pilasters) to superb Greco-Egyptian 35,36 (fine entrance), Chatwin's 1884-5 church (33).

Loop West Highfield's Regency villas, beyond (18) to 1850s Italianate. s, out Harborne Road from (34): LHS 1830s 38, 40; RHS 1850s redbrick Italianate corner 81, nice 83, 1848 Elizabethan 89, then 1830s stucco – opposite 1870s Gothic 66, 1840s/Italianate (35). Round (36): Vicarage stucco (ironwork) 12-3; Chad 6, 15, 1850s whitebrick 16 and 17. (Beyond (37): 1830s estate cottages 22 and 24 Hermitage, 34/34A Westfield; large Italianate 16 Norfolk; A & C 1893 20 Westfield, Grade I 1897 25 Woodbourne, 1899 21 Yateley (38) plus 1900s 15-19; Chamberlain's 1870s (39) Berrow Court.) Westbourne back to (33): Regency 17 (40), 'Norman Shaw' 15, Botanical Gardens (1865 glasshouse, 1871 palmhouse), 1870s Gothic lodges, 1840s 5.

Finally Church Road villas: two LHS c1815 – opposite (33); RHS 1850s 50 (set back), 1830s 45. LHS set back: 1840s Tudor brick (41), 1936, Grecian, Italianate, 1840s stucco – opposite halls of residence, early c19 lodges, back to (19). (Edgbaston Park Road beyond (42): c18 Gothick garden cottage; A & C 1901 Garth House (Bidlake), 1903 Winterbourne; Barry and Pugin's 1833-8 King Edward's Perpendicular – rebuilt as school chapel; University of Birmingham 1935-9 Barber Institute behind 1722 statue, Aston Webb's 1900s redbrick Byzantine Quadrant, Great Hall, 327ft campanile. Roads to w: Pritchatts late c17 6; Somerset 1860s Jacobean 25, A & C 1906 24; Farquhar A & C 1907 15, 17 (43), and 79 by Bidlake.)

Bath

A Roman spa, Norman bishopric (see of Bath and Wells, cathedral later transferred to Wells), medieval walled town – Chaucer's Wife of Bath in cloth-making 'passed hem of Ypres and of Gaunt' – Bath underwent a C18 transformation into the 'Georgian City' (with squares, crescents, terraces rising up steep hills into what is still open country), like Edinburgh New Town, one of the most remarkable planned urban developments in Europe. Almost everyone of note stayed or lived at Bath (which became in a sense 'London spa') – Beau Nash (d 1762), Master of Ceremonies, providing social respectability without dullness, Ralph Allen (d 1764) the famous Bath stone, and architects, John Wood the Elder (d 1754) and Younger (d 1782) a Palladian discipline after the early C18 Baroque, with a later Adamesque phase by Thomas Baldwin (d 1820). Damaged in a 1942 'Baedeker Raid', Bath today is a thriving sub-regional centre (despite the proximity of Bristol) with an un-English residential high density, acquiring a university in 1966.

Map I

Start in pedestrian area at w end (angels) of C16 abbeychurch (site of Norman cathedral nave); above early C19 shopfronts, 1720s Baroque 'centrepiece', fluted Corinthian pilasters. w round baths block, anti-clockwise: 1897 Concert Hall (dome); Baldwin's fine 1790s Pump Room – pedimented Corinthian; through pedimented Ionic colonnade; inventive side (rusticated with roundels, coupled columns, pedimented windows), colonnaded main entrance (King's, Roman Baths); under 1889 bridge; to 'square' s of abbey (since map). Loop from main entrance: Baldwin's colonnaded 1780s street (central pedimented windows) to his curved Cross Bath; s to younger Wood's simpler Hot Bath; E past 1820s classical hospital (1884 w extension), little 1859 and 1829 Tudor (courtyard) almshouses. From abbey w end, delightful alleys N: arch (head); E-W 1825 arcade Corridor (1); E-W (end pediment); to (2).

E of abbey: along 1700s row (1896 bargeboards, shell hoods); s to (3), facing columned porch. Explore round block (4) to w: pedimented doorway, C18 Ionic shopfront: s side gabled C17 Sally Lunn's, even quoins; mid C18; N side fluted Ionic portico (opposite pediment, pilasters); in centre, Allen's rich 1727 Corinthian pedimented facade (4). s through 1740s North Parade Buildings (alternating pediment windowtops, Corinthian doorways) to Abbey Green (5): C17 gabled; rebuilt arch; pub with pedimented ends; 1750s towards abbey.

Finally from baths entrance N. Baldwin's 1790s Union Street – 3+3+6+3+3 (twin, half pilasters); both sides; nice island

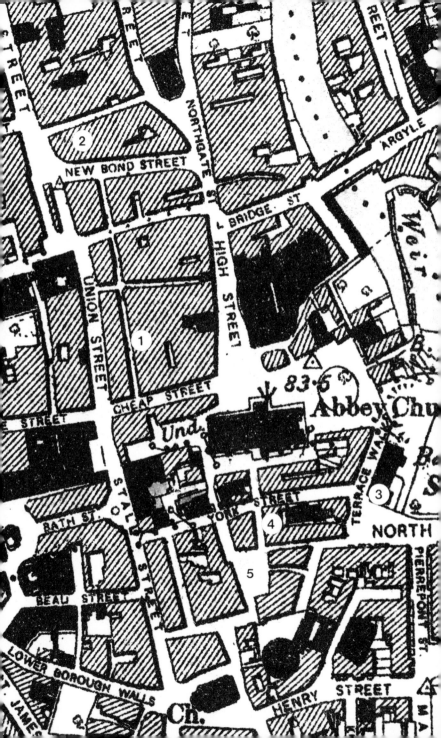

(Venetian windows), left varying windowtops. Finally grand Milsom Street, W of (2): left 3-bay houses with central pedimented windows; right pilastered corner bank; 1904 recessed facade to 1760s Octagon (museum), 6-bay, grand 3+3+5+3+3 (bowed centre, fluted Corinthian pilasters). Off map up to fine classical corner banks, 1875 left, 1845 Corinthian right (facing pedimented George Street terrace). Right, left, up to Assembly Rooms.

Map II

Then along the line of the walls, plus some late c17/early c18 houses outside. N of abbey, in backyard of Town Hall (1), next to 1901 hotel, medieval Water Gate (basement level). Along riverside to 1740s extramural scheme (straight 1st-floor windowtops, central pediments) by Wood the Elder: 3+7+5+7+3 to (2) – garden grotto; Duke Street (pedimented 5-bay opposite pair) to tall 1860s RC church spire; to river (pedimented ends), back past 3+7+9(advanced)+7+3. Under pediment (Tuscan columns), along line of walls (1739 pineapple doorway) to 1844 Ionic chapel (3) – and new shopping area. Past site of South Gate along Lower Borough Walls; SW to 1768 street (4) – pedimented doorways (double, laurels), tripartite windows (1st-floor Venetian). Back to wall line (map triangle); 1570s gables, into St John's Hospital courtyard: early c18 gables, 1727 Wood (the Elder) facade. To site of West Gate (plaque; E, 1720s Baroque 'centrepiece'.

Explore extramurally. W to exuberant 1736 Baroque (5) Kingsmead Square. Round (6): Nash's houses – crude 1720s (rusticated pilasters, volute doorway, bust), second (N) with eagle side doorway; 1720s Beauford Square (triglyph eaves frieze, curved pedimented doorways), 1800s Theatre Royal. E past 1795 chapel into 1700s Trim Street: shell hoods, view under arch, Baroque 'centrepiece'. S (Venetian window) to Upper Boro' Walls: 1860 Jacobean (thin tower); low battlemented town walls, Wood the Elder's Palladian hospital (similar 1850s extension, right).

Back to (1): Baldwin's fine 1775 Guildhall (Banqueting Room), 1890s Baroque Library, Art Gallery (domes, towers), market (octagon). Up Northgate Street to 1830s Early English church. Left to 1700-20 houses: frontage joining church – gabled 1713 Saracen's Head, Baroque centrepiece, 4-storey gabled; three gabled in Green Street (built up 1716) – tall (segmental 1st/2nd-floor windows), nextdoor, 3 gables (7).

Across Milsom Street: (s side) Adamesque 1790s former bazaar (figures), view to arch, Baldwin 1778 3+6+3+6+3 terrace (frieze, pedimented recessed windows) opposite severer 1730s; into (8).

Double-page Map III

First great townscape sequence of Queen Square, Circus, Royal

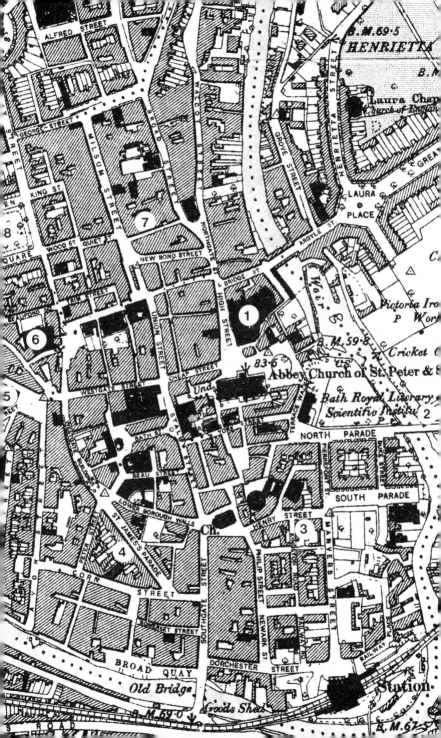

Crescent. Queen Square (1) by John Wood (the Elder): obelisk; w side 7-bay pedimented either side of 1830s 3+3+3 infill replacing original mansion; central pediments other sides; s 3+6+9+6+3, round groundfloor recesses; e side houses (3 5-bay), elaborate doorways; n side, every bay pilastered, alternate pedimented windows. NE, past Wood's surprisingly lavish own 1740 angle house, up 3-bay houses (elaborate No 8), to his superb 1754-8 Circus (2): coupled columns – Tuscan (frieze over) ground floor, Ionic 1st, Corinthian 2nd, balustrade, urns. Out NE, round younger Wood's 1770s Assembly Rooms (colonnade, costume museum) and adjoining streets: n (Venetian windows) to 3-storey bay window; s 9+3+9 terraces (Alfred bust); to raised pavements, taller pedimented 1st-floor windows (3). Back through (2); nice shop-fronts, pedimented doorways, coffin-like Gothick one (4), to younger Wood's masterpiece, 1768-74 Royal Crescent (5) – 114 unfluted Ionic columns (plain ground floor), coupled centre and ends; 1790s houses, 9-bay (6) facade.

n from (4) through 1780 Catharine Place, right, left, across Julian Street (Via Julia), to post-Wood phase. Pedimented tripartite windows up to 1+3+1 mansion (7); smaller Northampton Street. Down angle to 1793 terraces round (8): n, s Corinthian pilastered centre between bows (Venetian); e, w pedimented centre, end tripartite windows. n: 1800s (9) – frieze uphill, balconies; double bowfront villa; 1820s (10) – quoined doorways, scroll windows.

Round columned Doric House; n of (11) to 1730 mansion (moved), 1818-20 3+6+3+6+3 (end bows, pedimented). Down bow/bay windows to Gothick cottage (12). Along hillside from (11): 1793 (13) – strange central broken curved pediment; convex and concave (Ionic centre) 1788-92 crescent (iron 'throws', lamps) to (14). (Loop: 1840s 'crazy tower' (Pevsner); up Regency pairs beyond (15); e along neo-Georgian close; uphill, to Beacon Hill Common; down to (16) past terrace). Down past 3-storey bay windows (17), little terrace with strange incised pattern. (Into 1770s Bath again (18) – Venetian windows). Then 3+28+4+13 (incomplete) grand Corinthian pilastered 1786-92 (19); early C19 Italianate (square porches) below, bows, bays above; 1871 gabled terrace, barge-boarded below; Georgian above, to 4 pilastered pairs (recessed segmental windows) beyond (20). Down Frankley Buildings (pediment); Snow Hill; Brunswick Street (21).

Follow terraces off map along London Road. n side: balconies; round windows centre, ends; pedimented doorways; end, central Venetian windows – facing gardens; (n to 1829-32 Gothick church; Italianate Victoria Place; early C19 Larkhall 'village'); becomes pairs, to grand villas (double bowfronts, bow ironwork). Back s side: 1790 11-bay ends, lavish 'rustic' 6-bay 1800s convex centre; terraces (pediment); chapel linked Venetian windows (22); 1837 porch with bust. Through (23) – pediments both sides, 1845 dispensary, to 1827 cast-iron bridge, Doric lodges.

Along raised pavement (23); 1815 chapel, 1780s church (24). (Left: Venetian windows; classical penitentiary). Back into 1770s: 5-bay, Gibbs windows, Gothick chapel (3), tripartite windows – facing curving Paragon (central pedimented windows), pediment, bow. Finally 1840s pilasters, 1752 school (25), to (26).

Across river Over 1770 'Venetian' bridge into Baldwin's post-1788 ambitious Bathwick: classical shopfronts; loop to 1773 prison (27), Italianate 1860s pairs (28); groundfloor round openings, to pilastered splays (29). Along main axis – strangely random Corinthian pilasters (sometimes halved), pediments opposite streets – to 1796 portico (30), museum. Behind (31); round openings; to tripartite windows (32) – left pedimented, right square. Along (33) – end bowfront, pedimented ends and centre (elaborate 1st-floor windows), frieze; 1810s church; round (34) – central window straight, then pedimented; to (35).

Across gardens to (36), 1800s canal (37). Follow towpath s: through Rennie's tunnels, under canal HQ (38); at (39), sample Clifton-like (40), (41), (42); past converted maltings to (43). Uphill, past pilastered pairs to delightful 1800s (44) – double round doorways (garlands), tripartite 1+4+1 terrace. Gothick chapel (43), to bottom lock (45) – pumphouse. Loop s: 1847 corner, terraces (scrolls), pairs, to (46); half-square (47) – recessed windows; up off map, below varied villas; down left, to delightful 1826 (48) – pedimented, round recessed ends and centre, stream; c18 stonemasons' terrace. (s of (48): good villas, even-graded (horse-drawn railway for stone) Prior Park Road, a mile up to Allen's huge 1740s mansion (1750 Palladian bridge below), impressive mid c19 Corinthian RC church). Into centre: footbridge, tunnel, 1840s Tudor station, 1891 Ionic corners (49).

Loop from classical 1860 station (50). 1800s (51): rusticated ground floor, 9-bay centre, taller first floor. Alongside station to supermarket (into station shed), along riverside walk: terrace with recesses (52); up to grass and Ionic pilastered terrace, 1810 pedimented crescent, regular street (53); 1856 bridge (54). Out to gardens, pilastered lodge (55), view of (5), to entrance (56). Left (Queen Parade Place), two 'Gibbs' bungalows for sedan chair attendants. Right, square porches, to Charlotte Street scroll windows, doorways: 1841 palazzo bank, 1845 Corinthian church facade opposite 1854 Italian Romanesque. Miscellaneous: small-scale mid c19 area (57), redtiled cottages (58); Victorian villas (59); segmental door, medieval chapel, 1761 Gothick cottage, Venetian windows (60) – nice Paradise Street below.

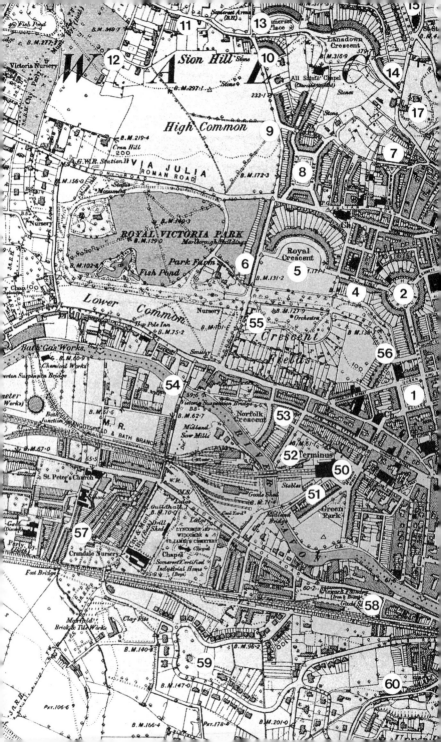

Bristol

Before 1801, England's most consistently important provincial town, Bristol had, before the Second World War, an unrivalled heritage of medieval-early c19 architecture. But it was badly bombed, and badly redeveloped after (aping industrial cities like Birmingham), only recently becoming conservation minded (good infill, schemes for docks). So Bristol (not on 1965 CBA list of Historic Towns) gives a bad initial impression, and has excellent historic *areas* – divided by new roads and 'municipal' gardens, the Frome/harbour being successively covered till 1930s (when a road was driven through across Queen Square). However, extensive (and hilly, with delightful stone-walled paths) Georgian/early c19 Clifton (absorbed in 1835) has the cohesion lacking in Bristol proper, plus superb terraces, crescents, squares and c19 villas.

Maps I and II

Bristol started as a port where the river Frome joined the tidal river Avon, near the Saxon bridge which gave it its name; the Frome descends from (1) on **Map I** to (1) on **Map II** – whence culverted, its medieval course s of (32), (2), to bridge (3), curving round to (4); on the neck of this peninsula (as in Shrewsbury), the Normans established a motte (5) and bailey castle, the first town walls curving round the loop to Bristol bridge. Then to extend the quays, in mid c13, the Frome was diverted s into a trench 2400 ft long, 120 wide, 18 deep, to join the Avon at (7). New walls were built: for Bristol (Gloucestershire) s of the old Frome (c17 King Street and Queen Square developed beyond); for wealthy Redcliffe (Somerset) past (24), (6) to river; Old Market Street had a ditch from (21) past (37), N past (34) to the Frome. Equal to London in 1346 in ships and crews, Bristol was the leading English provincial town in 1334 and the first to become a 'county' (in 1373), with its famous cloth and wine trade (hence 'Bristol Milk'); in 1377 Bristol was second to York, in 1520s to Norwich, in 1662 third to both. Described by Defoe as 'the greatest, the wealthiest city, London excepted', Bristol had an early c18 Golden Age (**Map I** shows its amazing extent in 1830), as the main port for Africa and the Americas (to which John Cabot had ventured in 1497), with the notorious triangular slave trade.

Bristol then lost its pre-eminence in the tobacco trade to Glasgow, as chief West Coast port to the 'wet docks' of Liverpool – both larger (as also Manchester/Salford, Birmingham) in 1801 census. It belatedly built 1804-9 Avon New Cut from (2) to (3) on **Map I**, and made the old Avon and Frome a huge 'floating harbour', topped up by (4). But the port dues were too high, and Brunel's mid c19 efforts were doomed by the narrowness of the Avon gorge, which precluded the larger ships Brunel himself pioneered. So Avonmouth and Portishead docks were developed in 1877 and 1879 respectively, directly on the Severn estuary, and Bristol is more now a Regional Capital, its 1876 college becoming a university in 1909, with the offices of many firms seeking a headquarters outside London.

Architecturally early/mid c18 Bristol (and Hotwells) has characteristic redbrick houses (segmental windowtops or stepped lintels) with even quoins/rusticated pilasters often with shell doorways; then, from 1790s (off Park Street, Portland Square) stone (usually brought by river from Bath) with the rusticated ground floor, pilasters between houses I call 'Clifton'– since frequently used there in subsequent 50 years, plus fine 'Regency' cast ironwork (like Cheltenham), especially 1st-floor balconies/verandahs.

Double page Map II

Map II gives an overall picture of city centre – as does this exploration of *City Docks* (excellent city booklet), from the Arnolfini (7), the end of my exploration of City and Queen Square from **Map III** (some readers may like to do this first). Across 1879 swing bridge, infill offices (housing behind), converted warehouses facing N (8) and s; to w lifeboat and industrial museums (1930s warehouses), 1875 steam crane (9). Stucco corner (10) with 2-storey ironwork, round 1800s basin, 1858 hospital (warehouse ground floor) to c18 Ostrich (11). Past (10) along New Cut: jail (1801, sacked 1831); stucco pediment and 'Egyptian', 1850s Gothic bay windows and porch (12); stucco terrace across river (13); to Brunel's SS Great Britain, launched from dock (14) in 1843, Wapping Wharf (boat trips), N of (12); past little 1840s terrace (15). Onto **Map VIII**: pilastered Avon Crescent, 1880s port workshops (and machinery) behind; early c19 locks, cottages, 1871 Italianate 'Pumphouse'; three huge 1905-19 redbrick (above purple) tobacco warehouses of structural steel and concrete, near 250ft 1965 concrete cantilever swing bridge; through c18 Hotwells (see later). Back onto **Map II** (16), to dockside opposite (14); 7-storey white 1920s tobacco warehouses; to weathervane (17); under 2-storey warehouses since map (now exhibition centre, shops) to lavish 1894 carved gable (18).

Redcliffe Isolated historic buildings in industrial area. From Bristol bridge (4), to 4 timberframe gables (bay windows), Georgian St Thomas, 1828 stone Wool Hall (19) with giant arches; Georgian terrace (20), now in brewery, behind 1865 Venetian and classical Victoria Street frontage; 1899 chapel-like tramway generating station (21) with 'Venetian windows'; mixed Georgian (22), timberframe (big gable of 1636 Shakespeare), c15 Temple church tower (5ft off vertical); stone neo-Gothic station courtyard (23) – left, original Brunel terminus (72ft span 'hammerbeam' roof).

handsome 1852 Jacobean gables and towers. Along line of Port Wall to 1749 house (24) – pedimented school facade moved back later; N to 1883 Italianate warehouse (25). Across Inner Ring Road to superb St Mary Redcliffe, 292ft spire, cruciform with double aisles throughout, vaulted, lavish and unusual N porch. Facing churchyard (26): Georgian terrace (Gibbs doorways), 1784 Gothick, stucco/redbrick corner. Finally nice loop: down Guinea Street to (11) – 1718 Dutch gable (twirly windowtops), domestic Georgian; Ostrich pub; up steps to castellated end of Redcliffe Parade – first 1768 stucco, straight doorways (scrolls), surrounds, then redbrick (27), keystones, broken pedimented doorways.

East Central From medieval centre (28), past grass and ruins of St Mary-le-Port and St Peter's, to historic buildings amid faceless 1950s Broadmead shopping area: (29), past 1701 almshouses to (30); opposite stucco Greyhound, 1825 Ionic arcade (31) – parallel to c18 Wesley's New Room; Quaker Friars (32) – c13 Blackfriars, planning exhibition upstairs (fine roof), 1747 meeting house (segmental surrounds), now Register Office. Across IRR (chasm of 'big city' buildings) to early c18 5-bay facade embalmed in new offices (33). s to Old Market Street, coherent but tatty, being restored/recreated. N side: mixed timberframe (gables), Georgian (alternating pedimented windows) to 1870s pub (34), site of gate. (Still medieval burgage plots to 1829 turreted church (35) along West Street). Returning, s of (34), 1858-83 Tudor almshouses (conical wooden staircase); stucco Georgian, 1706 quoined on columns, to (36) – timberframe, Pie Poudre Court on columns (wooden railings). s to 1884 warehouse (37) facing domestic group – twirly windowtops, pilastered bay windows with frieze. Across IRR to round-arched 1860s brewery (38) – now offices; c13 vaulted castle undercroft (39) amid grass.

City/Exchange and Queen Square (Map III)

Start at Bristol bridge (1) – no longer mid c13 with houses but 1760s, widened 1874. Baldwin Street, rebuilt in 1880s to (2), plus curve to (3), marks line of first town wall; St Nicholas' (historical exhibition) had a gate. Along small-scale High Street frontage to medieval centre (4), 1373 High Cross now at Stourhead.

Down fine Corn Street. 1820 Old Council House (Ionic, Doric columns 'in antis'), 1850s bank palazzo (lavish sculpture), 1930s classical. Left superb frontage: All Saints octagonal tower (two Norman interior bays); pediments either side of John Wood's 1740s Exchange (like his Queen Square, Bath; colonnaded interior roofed later; explore lanes either side to 1740s market, roofed in 1880s); 1900s green dome; 1860s classical (balustrade); 1+3+1 with motifs from Exchange; exuberant tall twin-columned 1864 bank; 1855

corner (tripartite windows). 1880s Renaissance frontage down Small Street to burnt-out GPO, opposite 1870 Gothic Assize Courts/1840s Guildhall (5); pedimented 1810 Commercial Rooms (Soanian dome on caryatids), low Italianate, 1930s Lutyens-like, new corner. Beyond site of gate, 1880s Renaissance corner (and beyond), 1900s octagonal corner. Round St Stephen's fine c15 tower: between 1899 Prudential, 1889 'Norman Shaw' (Ipswich windows); to Quayhead (3), 1884 gable; extramural curve – stucco pilasters, 1875 Italianate, red/yellowbrick, 1904 timberframe (oriels). Back to All Saints (4).

s down lane, to follow intramural curve w: 1867 round-arched, market, giant arches, good shopfront, 1866 Elephant, Georgian brick both sides; 1880s Renaissance (shell windows), 1903 portico (black columns); narrow Leonard Lane to Small Street (explore to (5) past gabled house); round to c14 St John's church/gate (re-set conduit outside); intricate new scheme to site of gate (6).

Past Georgian terrace (shopfronts) to (5) and fine Broad Street. Back to gate: mixed Georgian (5-bay pilastered), 1900 coloured tile Art Nouveau, 1711 gabled timberframe. se to (4): Georgian 5-bay (Gibbs doorway); down court to 1740s Taylors' Hall (pedimented windows), shell doorways; Georgian with Victorian shopfront; 1868 Venetian; Cockerell's inventive Doric 1844 Bank of England, like Liverpool and Manchester; frilly 1-bay 1890s Renaissance, 1905 large bow; 1869 Grand Hotel (top loggia), wing scaled down to 1786 Christ Church (delightful interior).

Then from (1) along Welsh Back to lightship (7), 1869 'Byzantine' granary warehouse, into superb mid c17 King Street, largely gabled overhanging timberframe, plus c19 warehouses: Llandoger Trow with oriels/Ipswich windows; 6-bay early brick; 1652 gabled almshouses (townwall bastion in courtyard); grand Palladian 1740s Coopers' Hall (coved interior now foyer to 1760s Theatre Royal); pilastered pub; 1740 former public library; 1690s almshouses (crosswindows), its courtyard now open to traffic.

Varied group: granary again; gable end; pattern of pedimented windows; early c19, elaborate 1710 Baroque (eared windows, pilaster strips); quoined redbrick. Into 1700s Queen Square, half burnt in 1831 Reform Riots, recent neo-Georgian offices. 1833 'Clifton' to 1837 Custom House (8); past warehouse gable to 1885 'French chateau' port offices (9), 1830s corner. From (10): Redcliffe warehouses – two 1872 redbrick, 1913 cantilevered concrete; c17 pub. Then best 1700s (11) – shell doorways, 2+1+2 (twirly, pedimented windowtops; three orders of pilasters); hideous 1950s; early c18; careful neo-Georgian. w side mixed 1830s 'Clifton' (curved Doric porch; laurels on scroll windowtops), 1700s, to

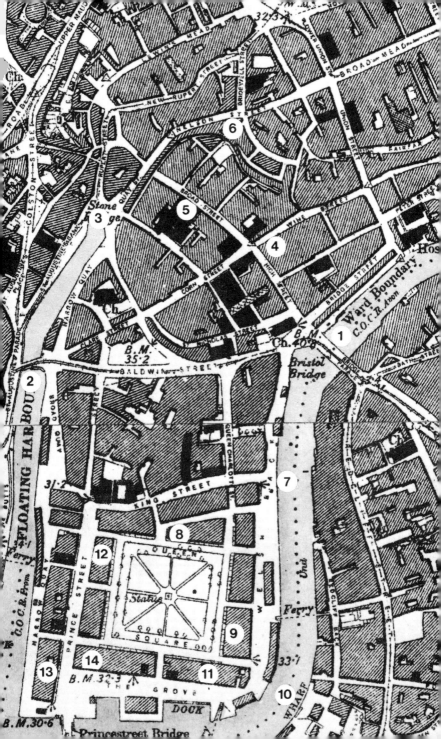

Grecian pilastered terrace (12). Out sw to 1720s Baroque houses (straight, curved pedimented centres); fine 1832 stone warehouse (giant arches), now Arnolfini arts centre (13); opposite, similar conversion, 'warehouse' infill (14).

City Centre to Clifton (Map IV)

To end of harbour (1); mixed small-scale (2); 1867 'Byzantine' Colston Hall facade (3); grand 1839 Corinthian portico (4) of St Mary-on-the-Quay – facing municipal gardens, traffic, bad modern blocks. To (5), noting fine 1788 Lewin's Mead chapel beyond. Up delightful Christmas Steps (paved in 1669): c13 hospital doorway, timberframe houses, as up steps; at top mixed with Georgian, s late c19 almshouses (another conical wooden staircase) with tiny c15 chapel. sw past restored 1600s stone (crosswindows), Georgian stucco to the Red Lodge (6) – museum, lavish 1580s interiors. Down to new housing (7) incorporating c18 stucco, 1790 Gothick church windows.

Past early c18 group to timberframe 1606 Hatchet oriels, facing Entertainment Centre (8). s (early c19 stone warehouse beyond) to unexpected streets built after 1717, windows becoming segmental, rusticated ground floor, grand pedimented. Out to College Green: medieval chapel, two c18 houses; churchyard, 1860s classical Royal Hotel, c18 houses; cathedral (early c14 'hall church'); Norman gateway next to 1906 Tudor/neo-Mackintosh library – Norman gateway arches E of (9); curving 1938-60 Georgian Council House.

Up 1790s stone Park Street; between 1880s Egyptian Mauretania and curved 1823 portico, to Pope/Brunel's grand 1837 Royal Western Hotel (10) – fluted Corinthian terrace above Ionic colonnade. Up Brandon Steep between Gothick house and two bows (Venetian windows), to terrace with round-topped tripartite doorways, 1-bay stucco houses (11). Across park past neo-Georgian (12) along grand 1790s houses: No 7 'Georgian House' museum; irregular colonnade between pilastered ends; St George's 1823 Doric portico; to Gibbs windows/doorway, 1880s shopfront (13). Up, along first stone and cast-iron 'Clifton', to (14); 1898 Cabot Tower (ruins of Civil War fort); into delightful 1800s Berkeley Square – SE side neo-Georgian, 1900s sw corner (eared windows), 3-bay pediment w side. Out, noting Georgian redbrick (keystones, stone pilasters) behind stone, to public group (15): 1871 Ruskinian Gothic (side saddleback tower), Edwardian Baroque Art Gallery and Museum, strategically and appropriately sited 212ft 1925 Gothic university tower/octagon (72ft high entrance hall). Finally 1850s Italianate houses (16), 1820s redbrick, stone pilasters.

North central (Map V)

Start from top of Christmas Steps (1). Up past c18 Rectory (surrounds, Gothick windows) to church (1470s tower), looking onto stucco curve. Along raised pavements, up steep mainly Georgian stucco St Michael's Hill: overhanging gabled timber-frame; redtiled gabled pub, 1691 almshouses (crosswindows, pediment, cupola), Georgian refurbished and infilled, 'Clifton', redbrick, curved pedimented doorway; 'typical', next to 1885 Gothic hospital (2). Sally: up to 1761 mansion opposite 1929 university 'Gothic Keep' (site of 1643 Royal Fort) plus square Ionic pilasters (3); down to 1878 almshouses (4), house with bow. Past new Maternity Hospital to mixed c18 (5); 3 c17 gables plus Gibbs doorway, Grecian pilastered terrace; pediment, 1850s Italianate, 1820s stucco terrace (6). Fine mid c19 villa suburb: w to Whiteladies Road; (7) with recessed centres (ironwork); stucco pairs N down Cotham Hill.

Follow grand Grecian villas past (8) – to s good new intricate whitebrick housing. Through 1840s pilastered stone Clevedon Terrace (9) – some Georgian stucco/redbrick to w, into 1780s hillside development facing SE: stucco and redbrick Kingsdown Parade (10); Freemantle Square (11) – Italianate semis, stucco terraces (round doorways beneath round recesses). Nice 1860s stone suburb N to railway. (Down to busy Stokes Croft – mixed tatty Georgian, 1862 round-arched factory (12), rundown Regency houses (13) in Montpelier). Returning along cobbled Somerset Street: redbrick, curved keystones, stone pilasters; bow, bay windows; to 1781 redbrick (14) with tripartite and Venetian windows. Down lane to 'typical' 1760s King Square: 1½ sides left, doorways Gibbs – and Doric (15); pedimented stone mansion (16). Out to c17 gabled Full Moon (17). (Across traffic circus (replacing square!), through bus station to late c12 St James' (18); between here and (4), huge hospital precinct.)

Along remains of Cumberland Street (Venetian windows) onto double-page **Map II** into redbrick 1766-84 Brunswick Square: Gibbs windows/doorways; 3+12+3; 5+3+5+3+5, pedimented centre; Venetian windows (40). Past 4 Ionic columns of 1835 chapel plus Doric 'in antis' of lodge, into 1790s Portland Square, now stone 'Clifton' (redbrick terrace ends with round Gibbs windows/doorways): two sides 4+6+4+6+4, pilastered centre; 1794 St Paul's (giving name to rundown early c19 stucco area to N towards Montpelier) with Gothick tower. Decayed Georgian: redbrick s to main road, pilastered stucco (41).

Map II: from university tower (42); past 1840s Tudor school (43); to 1792-1815 Bellevue (44) – 'Clifton' E side, stucco w.

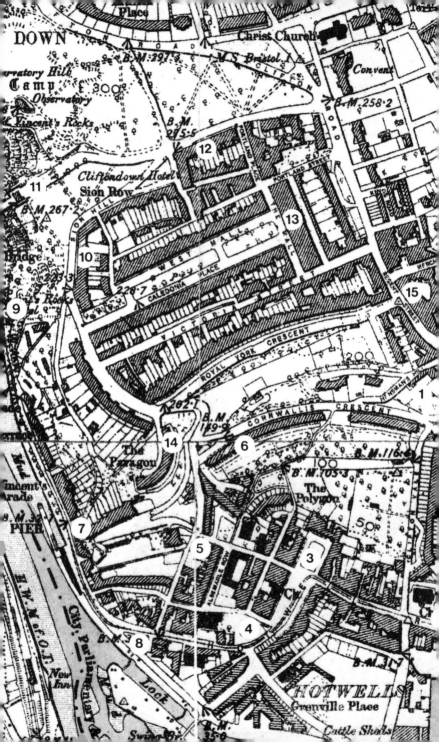

Clifton

Onto **Map VII:** from (1) 1750s pedimented garden front (first of the c18 mansions, then in open country, of the Bristol rich on Clifton Hill); Goldney house (2) Victorianised but c18 orangery, 'canal', Gothick tower, garden house plus bastion, shell grotto – down past c18 corner (3) to 1720s 3-storey bows. Mansions E of (2) – 1711 2+1+2 (segmental windows/porch); and W – 1760s 5-bay (Gibbs doorway/windows), pedimented and pilastered (set back); to rendered, 5-bay 'typical' redbrick, pedimented, 3+5+3 (4); (5).

Map VI: Crescent (1) – 'Clifton' to S (arched basement), N stucco (Ionic doorways); down past 1840s Grecian pedimented 2-bay verandahs; 1830 church (2) to late c17/early c18 spa of Hotwells ('typical' redbrick). Into 1720-50 square (3): red tiles, mansard roofs; pilastered 3-bay, 1+3+1; staircase tower; 1823 tripartite windows. Along nice curve (4 Gibbs doorways), up (4); N, up grand 1760s Albemarle Row (5) – 2 3-bay, 4 5-bay (one pedimented); down, up lane to delightful Clifton Vale – stucco convex curve (Gothick ironwork) below, concave 'Clifton' above (6); down lane S to Gothick chapel, into Hope Square (good infill); past (5), black-and-white corner (3-storey bays, 'pocked' rustication); up to grand stone 1790s terrace, fluted pilasters every bay, end (7) poised above gorge. Down past (5), Freeland Place (balconies), to (8).

Back towards (4). Then down Avon gorge: 3 3-storey bows; nice group; below (7); 'Clifton' (varied ironwork, some Gothick), tiny redbrick 1786 crescent/colonnade. Zigzag up (9) to delightfully varied late c18 houses, best ironwork (10); across Brunel's superb 1834-64 suspension bridge (11), 702ft span, 245ft above high water. Past strange 1860s Italianate terrace (12) – irregular little pediments, ironwork over porches; to 1809 facade (13) – 3-bay bow, advanced, pedimented and pilastered centre, repeated. Along 39 bays (pedimented ends, centre) of 1790s Mall, plus 93 bays 'Clifton' added 1840s; past buttressed and corbelled bay window opposite linked 1790s stucco houses (end bows). Explore S round the Paragon (14): houses 2-bay concave side (curved porches), 3-bay convex, to pedimented, pilastered end; into vale again (6). Finally up steps, along 1810s 'crescent to beat all crescents, over 130 windows long' (Pevsner), to 1870s Italianate street (15), into 1830s 'Clifton' (but straight windowtops, continuous balcony) Saville Place.

Map VII: Back to (2), through churchyard to (6) and elements of Clifton: first stage 1790s rendered (over brick), broken pedimented doorways; 1830s stone, cast-iron 'Clifton' 2+6+8+6+2; mid c19 villas. Left at Grecian villa to 'Clifton' plus triglyph eaves frieze (7); right, 1842 'Sainte Chapelle'; 1840s terrace (8), now with vertical recesses, stone verandah (horrible Students Union opposite). Left at

4+8+4 (triglyph frieze) – before 1930s flats (9); back past inventive 1830s classical villas to unusual tripartite windows, end of (7); behind, 1850s Italianate pairs. Round to (10): Italianate (2+10+2, Venetian bays, round windows); huge pair. 1850s terrace (straight-topped windows) to 1973 RC cathedral (11), superb interior.

Past fine 1840s pilastered villas (12), stucco (like Pittville, Cheltenham) – 4 pairs, pedimented (Ionic columns 'in antis') to Italianate mansion (square towers), bombed Victorian church (13) – new interior (like RC cathedral). Round grounds of Victorian Gothic school (1910 recasting of chapel as octagon), past 1860s tower (14) – church replaced by flats. s, along pilastered 1853 6+6+12+6+6 (15), to Egyptian villa facing (11). w past 1860s red Italianate, Gothic villas; s to sophisticated 1830s (16) – pilastered ends linked by stone verandahs to Ionic centre (balustrades).

Then amazing run of 1830/40s classical villas from (17): bows, Gothick pairs, pilastered bow, twin pilastered pairs (frieze motif);

Bristol VII (Clifton) OS 6″ 1889

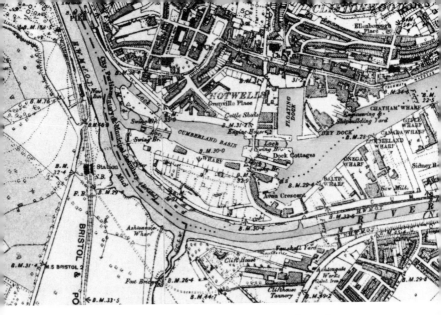

Italianate, neo-Tudor, 'Early English' church; Georgian stucco, 'Clifton' terrace; 8 twin pilasters; 4 linked pairs (colonnades); 2-storey portico (18); pilastered bow; portico; to varied 1860s (19). Past (20), to pedimented 1840s stucco again, into delightful (21): 3+4+4+4+3 (giant arches); 1+1+2+1+1 (tripartite windows). Stucco terrace, Christ Church, 1780s 'Clifton' (22) opposite pedimented mansion, 1760s 5+5 brick pedimented (Gibbs windows). Through arch into (23) – 1850s Italianate terraces (stone, cast-iron roundel balconies); (6); round 1790s 'first stage' to tripartite windows (24).

Map VIII, s of **Map VII,** links to **Map II.**

Map II

Varied Italianate (45), back porches, Georgian stucco (Gothick ironwork); strange 1840s former RC cathedral, early c19 (46) – shell doorways. Out: to 1855 Italianate shopping parade (47); linked 1830s stucco pairs (48) – strange 'negative' pilasters, superb villas; (49) – fine 1841 Victoria Rooms portico, Italianate 1857 Academy. 1840s tripartite NE of 1830s flats (50) and NW (Italianate pairs behind). Round church, stucco terraces (incised Soanian pilasters) to villa (51). Then 1840s terraces off Whiteladies Road: (52); advanced centre/ends (53); just off map, strange alternate advanced, 1 column 'in antis' centre. (Much further: left Apsley, right (hidden) Redland terraces). Finally 1+4+3+4+1 debased pilastered (54), 1830s classical (55), terraces (56).

Bristol VIII (Hotwells, river, docks)   OS 6″   1887   **211**

Brighton and Hove

Doctor Russell's 1750s advocacy of sea water and sea air transformed C17 fishing Brighthelmstone (**Map II** area, St Nicholas parish church on hill outside) into a thriving resort (initially facing inland), the Prince Regent (later George IV) visiting regularly from 1783, his Marine Pavilion spectacularly remodelled 1815-22 by Nash into the 'oriental' Royal Pavilion. 1800s Royal Crescent (first *facing* sea) has Kent/Sussex blueblack mathematical tiles (m-tiles), usually hung on timberframe houses; but stucco 'Regency' Brighton and Brunswick Town (later Hove) is 1810-50, its squares, terraces, crescents overwhelming in extent (like Georgian Bath, Edinburgh New Town), its seafront 2½ miles from Adelaide Crescent to Sussex Square, plus swathes a mile inland. The chief architects were Charles Busby, Amon Wilds (father) and Amon H. (A. H.) Wilds (son) – their 'Ammonite' shell pilaster capitals and round-topped windows 'characteristic', as are bow windows (3 or 4-storey, often shallow 3-bay, pilastered).

Brighton grew from 7,339 in 1801 to over 65,000 in 1851, nearly 100,000 in 1881 (outstanding C19 churches). Now Brighton and Hove (separate boroughs), etc. are over 300,000; 'metropolitan', with royal origins and commuters, 'London-by-the-Sea,' 'capital' of the South Coast, 1961 University of Sussex at edge.

Brighton central (Map I)

From station (1) (1840 front, 1880s trainshed) to beach: Queen's Road (delightful early C19 houses, parallel to W, behind gardens), past Doric porch 'in antis' opposite good 1825 chapel (2) facing garden; 1888 clocktower (3); West Street, past St Paul's 1846-8 octagonal timber tower, first stucco bowfronts (4). Along seafront E: hotels – linked pilastered bay windows (5), corner ironwork, 1826 (Corinthian columns, pilasters), facing 1890s Palace Pier (6).

Continue seafront above aquarium (1872 Gothic interior), 1896 covered walk, past 4-storey 3-bay bows. Inland to 1790-1810 cottages – flint cobbled (usually black), m-tiles, yellowbrick amid stucco. Down Camelford Street. Back W past Ionic shopfront (7), exploring delightfully varied houses: right, facing gardens (8); streets left (9); hidden to right, St James's Place (round recessed doorways); to emerge at Old Steine Gardens (10).

Explore houses E side of continuous valley gardens. To sea: yellowbrick amid stucco; first 'Ammonite' pilasters and window-tops; bow giant arches. Then N: 1st-floor canopies, pedimented doorways, cobbled facing S; Doric porch, round doorways, pebbledash (11); 4-storey bows (grey, redbrick); pilasters, bows, still some cobbled, m-tiles (12); **Barry's fine 1820s St Peter's.**

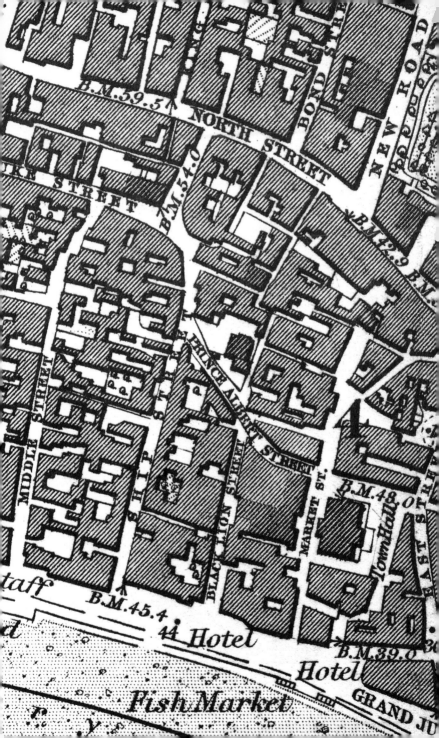

Then yellowbrick bows; Amon Wilds' inventive 1818 villa (segmental arch, tripartite reeded windows, 'Ionic' balcony); 1895 technical college (13); little stucco terrace (triglyph frieze); to A. H. Wilds' delightful 1827 Hanover Crescent (14) behind gardens – bow ends, giant arches, building up to central pedimented 'mansion'; opposite, his strange 1829 (17) – deep Italianate eaves on brackets (laurels at back), occasional pedimented villas set back, behind wooded garden. Past yellowbrick Gothick almshouses (1795 centre, 1859 ends) to St Joseph's RC church (15) – 1880s stone vaulted apse, spacious 1874-5 St Martin's (16).

Returning: in front of, or behind, (17); across market area, to incredible brick Gothic 1872-4 St Bartholomew's (18) – 135ft high interior (tallest in Britain). Back to gardens to follow less interesting W side S: (19) – nice group (cobbled cottages behind), pilasters and bows facing church; (20) m-tiles; W into 1840s 2-storey stucco Pelham Square (21) – start of similar area (Kensington Place Ionic pilasters) SW; yellowbrick bows (22); cobbled both sides (23).

Past George IV statue into (24): domes and minarets of Royal Pavilion; 'Hindoo' North Gate and Lodge (1921 South Gate correctly Indian), 1804-8 yellowbrick Riding School (80ft dome), stables remodelled 1867/8 as Corn Exchange. Out North Gate; along frontage remodelled as Museum and Art Gallery (1873 tiled 'Indian' interior), Library. Along New Road: cobbled wide, redbrick narrow bows; massive Doric portico (25); theatre (rebuilt 1866) colonnade, pilastered yellowbrick terrace; out to hotel porch (26). Down (classical stucco pavilion kitchens, opposite 4 pilasters) to (10) again. Pavilion frontage to N. S: house remodelled 1787 by Adam (information centre, round 'Venetian' windows under pediments); porches; bays, m-tiles, pedimented doorways (27); to grander 1820s hotels – porch, reeded tripartite windows, original facade of one facing (6).

Now explore in detail – use also **Map II** opposite (public buildings dark) – Old Town/Lanes (varied pre-resort Georgian). Through Pool Valley (bus station!) to Ammonite back of hotel (5); inland, round 1830-2 Town Hall (28) – 2-storey porticos, fine staircase; along stucco curve (bows) to Georgian 5-bay redbrick; octagonal Holy Trinity tower (29). Middle Street S: yellowbrick bow opposite stucco; 1874-5 synagogue (lavish interior); redbrick, stucco bows. Ship Street N: 1767 assembly rooms, opposite brick bows; Georgian dressed flint, chequerbrick; delightful lanes W, E (c17 slatehung timberframe); little redbrick terrace behind railings; to cobbled (30), 1979 'historic' Duke's Lane. Use **Map II** for most intricate area to E, slotted-in 1966 Brighton Square (31), 1825 Elim chapel (splayed windows, triglyph frieze).

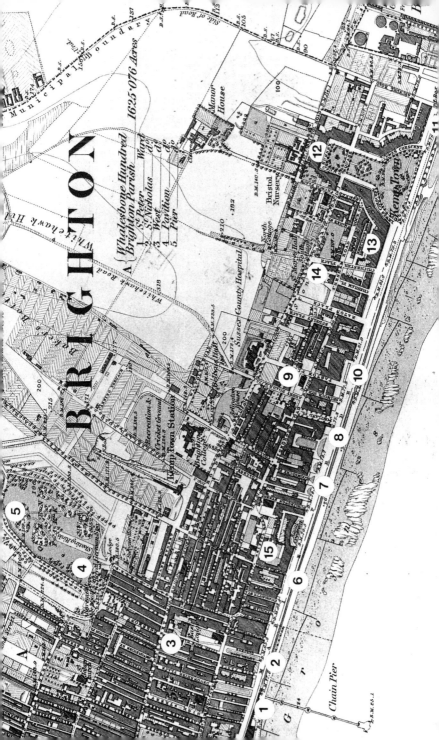

BRIGHTON

Whalesbone Hundred
Brighton Parish 1625·076 Acres

A Ward
1 St Peter
2 St Nicholas
3 West
4 Pavilion
5 Pier

Manor House

Whitehawk Road

Whitehawk Hd

Municipal Boundary

Kemp Town

Sussex County Hospital

Kemp Town Station

Recreation & Cricket Ground

Bristol Nursery

Chain Pier

Brighton east central (Map III)

E from (1) – map shows 1823 chain pier destroyed 1896: left of New
Steine first pilastered bow, right pilastered bows linked by round
arches; Corinthian pilasters (2), 'terrace' and bow. Inland loop from
(2): left, Gothick ground floor, bows; 1879 St Mary's (vaulted
interior); pedimented windows (3). Up Egremont Place (fluted
Ionic pilasters, 1879 classical flint). To Queen's Park, laid out in
1829: Ionic German Spa colonnade (4); beyond (5), loggia (from
villa porch), Corinthian rotunda watertower. S through Devonshire
Place, New Steine, noting varied pilasters (facing S), to (1).

Seafront: in Grafton Street, right, 'Indian' groundfloor windows;
inexorable stucco bows –'giant arch' again, linked fluted Corinthian
(6), six 5-storey *bays*; into delightful 1798-1807 Royal Crescent
(mathematical tiles, bays/canopies/balconies); fluted Ionic pilasters in valleys of bows; colonnade; continuous 1st-floor balconies
linking up Bloomsbury Place (7); nice Marine Square (gardens,
yellowbrick, end colonnade), to first terrace (8) – 3+3+3+3+3,
Corinthian pilastered middle, ends. Small loop: up formal Portland
Place (yellowbrick, pilastered chunks); classical St George's (9),
view to 1828 hospital, 1892 'Indian' mausoleum (pub); back to
straight windowtops (10) – beginning of post-1823 Kemp Town.
Then 3+3+3 round windows, to 1846 pedimented end (varied
windows); 4½-storey 3-bay bows; Corinthian pilastered ends,
'conservatories' over Doric porches; gardens; to 'architectural'
1825-8 Arundel Terrace (11) – 3+9+3+3+3+3+3+9+3, pilasters
every bay, columns picking out ends and middle, facing marina.

Returning, inland up Lewes Crescent (pilastered chunks) to
Sussex Square Doric porches (12); through cobbled and brick mews
(13); bows (14); along Eaton Place scroll windowtops to seafront.
Finally, up past balconies from (7); W into nice mid C19 area; St
John's RC Corinthian columns 'in antis' (15); back to (6).

Brighton west central and Hove (Map IV)

W along seafront: new entertainments (1), Brighton Centre; (2) huge
stucco 1860s Grand, 1888 redbrick/terracotta Metropole. Inland
loop (between hotels): former assembly rooms (pediment, 'Egyptian' columns 'in antis'); beneath towerblock; through Russell
(continuous balcony/verandah, twin pilasters above), Clarence
Square to (3); W (left, Castle Street Ionic facade); S, E, through
Regency Square (pilastered yellowbrick centrepiece, stucco bows,
varied porches), to 1866 West Pier (4). Corinthian pilastered
Cavendish Place to hotel (pedimented windows).

Inland from (5). First A. H. Wilds' pilastered Oriental Place
(symmetrical, pediments, Ammonite pilasters, windowtops), Sill-
wood Place. W, N (Montpelier Road), E to 1820s Gothick, (6) 'Wilds'

own house, Pavilion's baby brother, with dome and Hindoo details' (Pevsner), facing Wilds' Western Terrace (incised square piers).

Direct to Norfolk Square (14), or long loop uphill into delightful leafy residential area: Montpelier Road (more Ammonite capitals, windows) to 1819 (Solomon's) Temple (7) – tapered columns; terrace (continuous balcony), bows, opposite 1843-7 crescent of pedimented and pilastered (Ammonite, Corinthian) villa pairs; to (8) – deep eaves, alternate houses recessed, verandahs. Back, E from (7): St Michael's (fine 1893 interior); right, delightful bow/ verandahs of Montpelier Villas; to Ionic top (9) of smaller-scale Victoria Street; round, E through Powis Square (pedimented central windowtops); 1850 canopies/bays, advanced centre, deep eaves, facing gardens (10); to original parish church (Norman font), 1830 Gothick terrace with central Gothick bay window (11). W, noting twin pilasters (12), villa pairs, pilastered terrace, St Stephen's hall (re-erected 1766 ballroom), Borough Street, to (13). S through (14), and Bedford Square (Ionic pilasters amid bows), to (15).

Along seafront into Hove, past 1864 Norfolk Hotel, curving 1935 flats – unfortunate neighbour to four superb Brunswick terraces: inventive 3+3+6+3+3 (16), fluted Ionic columns at ends, spaced out in centre (pediment), curved round windows between; 3+12+9+12+3, Corinthian pilasters every bay, columns at ends and centre (attic storey); (17) repeat; 30-bay pilastered. Then Decimus Burton's 3+5+3 Italianate pedimented 1833 start (18) of Adelaide Crescent, finished 1850s (pedimented windows), plus 1860s Palmeira Square (tripartite round windows, 'Bayswater').

Along seafront beyond (19). 1850s Avenues scheme, handsome pedimented yellowbrick (corner towers); Grand Avenue leads to Pearson's superb 1890-1 All Saints (cathedral-like interior), huge terracotta and yellowbrick villas of The Drive. Finally terraces again: left, Courtenay (bowfronts, verandahs, facing sea), grass, A. H. Wilds' characteristic (unfinished) 1840s Victoria (inventive centre); right St Catherine's (clustered balcony/verandahs).

Finally inland. Past (20) to (21); 1893 gables (22). E along Western Road (1830s to S, early 1850s to N) to 1855 old town hall (23) – down street, pilastered windows (alternate pediments). Down W frontage of Lansdowne Place: serried bowfronts varied by Ionic colonnade; pilastered 'set-piece' Lansdowne Square (pedimented centre); caryatid porches. Past (17) again; up Brunswick Square's superb 3-bay bows (pilasters alternating with fluted Ionic columns) to straight pilastered N side. E to (24) to explore round former Brunswick Market. Emerge next to its original 1828 approach arch, into 1825-30 Waterloo Street: Corinthian pilasters, Barry's Italianate St Andrew's, down to seafront (16).

Portsmouth

Double-spread Map I: This shows Gosport, entrance to extensive harbour, Portsmouth's unusual island site. A small medieval port, Portsmouth was developed by the Tudors to become, under Charles II, the country's chief naval base. It has been continually fortified: first defences late c14 earth, stone early c15; strengthened by Henry VIII who built Southsea Castle (1); reconstructed on Continental model against gunpowder with late c17 ravelines, etc., with Gosport, plus early c18 Fort Blockhouse (2), 1745 Fort Cumberland (3) at harbour entrances; 1770s remodelling, including Portsea and dockyard; so that late c18 Gosport, Old Portsmouth, Portsea were three separate defended towns, elaborately fortified against land attack, – just before early c19 extramural development of Landport (present city centre) and seaside/residential Southsea.

'Traditional' defences continued up to Palmerston's 1850s scheme, which adapted c18 Fort Monckton (4) plus (1), (2), (3), adding Lumps Fort (5), but included a new outer ring off **Map I** (Fort Brockhurst, a mile NW of (6), open to public), forts along Portsdown hill, Hilsea lines defending island from N – ½ mile N of (7), and four 'islands' in the Solent itself. 1857 6″ **Maps II** and **III** show Old Portsmouth and Portsea just before outer Palmerston forts made their defences redundant, replaced in 1870s by barracks, playing fields, parks, etc. Portsmouth and Gosport are still largely in service occupation, and much of architectural interest cannot be visited (some defences not shown on maps); (5) is accessible, (3) will be, (1) is now fine museum (of defences, etc.).

Gosport (no car connection with Portsmouth) Possible walk: from the Hard (8) – passenger ferry to Portsea – inland along High Street (cohesion destroyed in postwar redevelopment) to four early c19 3-bay brick houses (Georgian columned porch, round doorway; Victorian quoined purplebrick, round windows); N past 1857 barracks verandahs (Georgian North Street houses) to yellowbrick Italianate clocktower, arcade; W to ruined colonnade of 1842 station (9) – once linked to victualling yard (fine 1828 stuccoed entrance down Weevil Lane!); (to NW, 1847 barracks facade (6) – arched recesses, cupola over arch); S along park to 1830s stucco Peel Road, S of (9) – scroll windows, doorways; back to 1889 campanile, SW of (8), of Holy Trinity (delightful 1696 Ionic interior), 1795 purplebrick Governor's house (tripartite windows), and c18 earth, redbrick, water defences; across modern Haslar bridge, impressive mid c18 pedimented naval hospital (1790 terrace behind, 1885 water tower). To SW: three Regency villa pairs (10); W of (11), superb 1826 stucco crescent – colonnade (cast-iron balcony), Ionic ends and centre.

Portsmouth from Map I Portsmouth grew rapidly from 33,226 in 1801 to 188,095 in 1901 – so undeveloped areas on map soon became late c19 terrace housing, while mid c20 growth engulfed a disturbing amount of mainland to N (including market town of Havant). Since map: late c19 extensions to dockyard (12), spoil used to extend Whale Island (13); new urban motorway from (14), E of (13), to continental ferry port (15). Points of interest: entrance lock (16) of 1823 Portsea Canal (not on map), originally to basin near main Portsmouth and Southsea railway station; (17) little 1850s Highland Terrace, behind gardens; (18) St Mary's, island's original parish church, now huge 1887-9 Perpendicular (tower, vaulted chancel). Following seaside gardens E of **Map III**: naval war memorial, Crimean monument (19); pier (20); 1840s stucco pilastered Cumberland house (museum), NW of (5); impressive 1860s Royal Marines courtyard (21) – redbrick (round groundfloor windows in recesses), yellowbrick quoins, stone Italianate (now museum, 2-storey loggia, fine dining room). Campbell Road Conservation Area (22) – trees, 1860s/70s redbrick and stucco villas.

Introduction to Maps II and III

Severely bombed in the War, Portsmouth was drearily redeveloped after, Portsea losing its cohesion, and faceless horizontals disrupting Old Portsmouth's delightful Georgian small scale (with shallow, as opposed to Southampton's semi-circular, bow windows). But post 1970s infill is much better, with conservation areas, pedestrian streets, and a good new urban focus in Guildhall Square.

Portsmouth has four distinct areas worth walking, in this recommended order: Old Portsmouth (**Map III**), worth exploring in detail despite earlier bad infill, with fine vaulted Early English chancels of St Thomas' (two 2-storey bays, plaster vault, now cathedral) and medieval hospital (three one-storey bays, garrison church, ruined nave); Portsea (**Map II**) – isolated groups plus superb dockyard; Landport (**Map II**); Southsea (early c19, remarkable stucco 1837-60 development by Thomas Ellis Owen) with its winding suburban layout, on **Map III**.

Portsea (Map II) Since map, railway extended from (1) via (2) to Harbour station (3) – pedestrian ferries to Gosport, Isle of Wight. From Old Portsmouth (or from (24) down Park Road), follow Burnaby Road past 1687 King James Gate (4), moved from Old Portsmouth, to late Georgian pedimented barracks (5). Down lane to (6) – 1700s rendered 5-bay (recessed centre, pilastered round window over caryatid doorway) between Georgian red and purplebrick; pedimented 1784 school (7) – recessed Venetian window; fine 1754 St George's (central plan), delicately detailed stucco (8) – laurels, 'rustic' quoins; early c19 Ordnance Row; two

Hilsea

7 3

Boundary Post

Highgrove Farm

rth Green illa

67

42

Stubbington F.

Tangier F.

Kingston Cross

P O R T S E A

Copner

Salterns

L a

2

43

Bavins F.

H a r b o

Kingston

18

Portsea Island Union House

16

1

44

Fratton

Milton

3

Cumberland Fort

H 22

Eastnay F.

17

21

Lumps F.

5

20

Victorian stone Italianate (one 1874) on The Hard; to 1708 dockyard main gate (9).

Much of superb dockyard architecture and industrial archaeology inaccessible (cast-iron 1843 fire station, 1717 terrace, 1800s block mills). But visible en route to 1765 HMS Victory (10): right, between 1875-82 boathouses, 1843 one across mast pool; left, late c18 pedimented ranges (colonnades form visitors' route), glimpse to neo-Georgian semaphore tower (incorporating 1778 gate from (14) at base); right, 1,100ft 1770s brick ropery; pedimented 1780s ranges (1840 stone arch) ≟ facing (10); (11) dock with salvaged Tudor 'Mary Rose'. Along Queen Street, isolated Georgian/early Victorian groups, plus: little Georgian redbrick (12) beneath dockyard cupola; Bishop Street group (13) – segmental opening; 1900s stumpy tower facing mid c19 barracks gateway (14), near site of Portsea's 1778 Lion Gate, Unicorn Gate moved from (15) to dockyard entrance (16). Finally, late c19 cathedral (17) – spacious interior; 1900s castle-like barracks front plus campanile (18).

Landport (Map II) Into Commercial Road with 1900s stone Baroque both sides (19). N along pedestrianised stretch (dreary 1950s shops, 1977 fountain) to new road (20), which passes brutalistic 1966 concrete shopping centre to (18); (21) early c19 pedimented school. Past fine 1828 Gothic All Saints (interior vaults: plaster nave, aisles; 1877 chancel stone), beginning of motorway (22). Into delightful little Conservation Area: textures, new buildings N end masking 1970s 'wall' of housing; late Georgian rows (4 identical doorways) yellowbrick, redbrick (Dickens birthplace), with stucco bows between.

Back S to (19); past main station – striking curving glass 1980s office block (23) – under 1980s buildings forming new pedestrian square with impressive classical 1886-90 Guildhall (24) – 240ft tower (top rebuilt); behind, inventive 1900s stone Baroque (corner tower/dome) and polytechnic precinct. Past 1900s corner cupola, redbrick/terracotta gabled 1890s Prudential, 2-storey ironwork of 1884/1900 Theatre Royal, to new road (R); across, 1890s Flemish redbrick and stone Charter House.

Old Portsmouth (Map III) Link N, Cambridge Road to (2): left Burnaby Road and Portsea: right Guildhall and Landport. 1760 Landport Gate (3); 1880s Scots Baronial City Museum (4). High Street from (1): 1850s yellowbrick 5+12+2+4+2+12+5, opposite mixed Georgian, 1+3+1 Italianate ('key' pilasters); Georgian redbrick, refronted timberframe Buckingham house (doorhood), recessed windows. Left at segmental windows, nice 1840s, to frontages (5): stucco, red tiles, bowfront; 5-bay purple/redbrick, fine doorway; smaller with plastered timberframe. Along to Georgian

(6), 1850 Italianate stucco and 3+1+3 purplebrick (balconies) – facing site of 1834 gate (7). To frontages facing (8): 4 late c17 Dutch gables, chequerbrick, stucco (shell doorway), door canopy, mixed brick; NE, redbrick and stucco, bows (Adamish details), bay, pedimented doorways (urns) to round windows opposite stucco Italianate corner. Along churchyard: stucco, Georgian redbrick (tall doorways). St Thomas' church – 1180s chancel, transepts; late c17 Tuscan nave, tower, bell cupola; unfinished 1938-9 'cathedral' nave (9). To S, stucco Dolphin (Doric entrance), Sallyport (4-storey 3-window bays, central pedimented).

Round early c19 corner (rusticated round arches) through Grand Parade (ironwork) to garrison church (10); along c18 stone, water defences to corner (11); back to Square Tower (12) with Charles I bust. Explore Broad Street in detail: site of gate, now **Map II** (4), facing stucco group (bows); along ramparts to 1530s roundtower; through Sally Port to beach. Delightful small-scale Georgian W side, through Bath Square (weatherboarded 1754 bathing house, redtiled boathouse) to purple/redbrick pubs (13). Camber bridge gone.

Southsea (Map III) From Landport, **Map II** (25), follow terraces: Hampshire – some original 1820s houses, opposite 1977 ziggurat polytechnic library (14); Landport, also mixed c19, 2-storey ironwork; Kings (15), 2+3+2 pedimented centre (round recesses); mixed Bellevue (battlemented oriel, 2-storey bows); to 1865 hotel (16). N from (17) into unexpected early c19 inland Southsea. Small-scale Georgian Castle Road: stucco pair, chequerbrick; mixed group (Gothick windows), 4-bay redbrick (set back). Across to minor 1840s terraces (round doorways): redbrick (18) – opposite chequerbrick house (tripartite window); to King Street (pedestrianised, railings, stucco pairs); S past stucco (19). Across, past greybrick pair (pilastered bowfronts) back to (17).

Finally, E into very different 1837-60 'Owen's Southsea': stucco villas (Italianate, some Gothick), terraces (some architecturally 'incorrect'); delightful trees; serpentine layout, evident on map. Excepting main shopping roads (Elm, Palmerston, Osborne), much survives. Perambulation: terrace (channelled ground floor) to 1842 Gothick (20). E: row, terraces (ironwork, square porches – and to N); across to 1870s (21). NW: (22); The Thicket; to (23); opposite, fine set back pair (frieze); 1840s (24) stucco. S: school villas (25); yellowbrick pair; pedestrian (26); 1840s to battlemented (27); to Circle, curving walls (openings), varied 1853-6 pairs (28). N to Osborne Road and terraces: deep eaves facing (29); 1856 pilastered 1+8+1 facing (30); 1845 2+12+4+12+2, tripartite, paired (round, square) windows (31). 1838-40 villas; terrace (pilastered ends); back to (17).

Southampton

Map I shows Southampton's peninsular site between the rivers Itchen and Test. Saxon Hamwih on the Itchen (10) was replaced by Hamtun (giving its name to Hampshire) on the Test (13); then after the Conquest an Anglo-Norman settlement was established to s, round St Michael's, with a motte and bailey castle. Southampton developed into an important medieval port (with its famous double tide), first for trade with Normandy (Winchester was then the English capital), later for armies to France and extensive trade with the Mediterranean, particularly Venice and Genoa, reaching a c15 peak when it acquired county status. The town was defended (Norman earth, c13 stone) on N and E sides; a retaliatory raid by the French in 1338 caused houses along the quays' W and S sides to be incorporated in a new stretch, the finest townwalls in Britain. In Tudor times Southampton declined, with a late c18/early c19 phase as a spa and seaside resort – usually stucco, with characteristic deep semi-circular (usually pilastered) 1st-floor bow windows.

The arrival of the railway in 1840 triggered off continuous development to make Southampton Britain's foremost passenger port, White Star Line moving from Liverpool in 1907, Cunard in 1921. At first new docks were constructed on the tip (Inner 1851 (27) now filled in), culminating in 1911 Ocean Dock, embarkation point of the 'Mauretania', 'Queen Mary', 'Queen Elizabeth', and now 'Queen Elizabeth II'. Then after 1927, Western Docks were created out of the mudlands of 'West Bay', Southampton's 1930s prosperity being expressed in its fine Civic Centre. Badly bombed in the Second World War, drearily rebuilt before and after (especially around and N of Bargate), post-1970 buildings are better, with good 1980s infill housing within the walled town. Now the port chiefly handles containers; and Southampton is as much a regional capital, with a university (college 1902, chartered 1952) in N suburbs.

There are two elements to explore: the superb medieval townwalls plus the area within – despite welcome new infill, much of it is less a 'historic area' than an open-air museum/archaeological site (many medieval vaulted basements, some under new buildings); and the Regency spa/seaside 1820s/40 areas to E and N, often facing or near the city's many attractive open spaces.

Double-spread Map I

First E of walled town into a Regency resort area, which became less desirable late c19 commercial. From yellowbrick 1840 2-storey bow (1) to 1847 old Custom House (2). N past huge 1872 'French Renaissance' hotel; fine 1839 Italianate station (arcade); stucco pilastered terrace (3). W past 7 characteristic bows, bay windows with cast-iron balconies, becoming Victorian (pedimented windows) to pub with bow (4). Back to (2) via balconies, nice curve of bows, along pilastered terrace (5). Follow late c19 commercial frontage (6): crude Italianate stucco, handsome 1899 classical, 1893 Dutch gable, yellowbrick classical; opposite, pilastered corner (behind, strange 1840s Gothic railway warehouses), tripartite windows, 1835-40 classical lettered Canute Castle Hotel, to fine 1977 concrete bridge (7) – central clearance 100ft wide by 80 high.

NW to the shopping centre: stuccoed corner pub, 1853 pilastered Royal Albert (8); under bridge approaches; footbridge (9); to St Mary's – main medieval parish (though extramural), fine 1914 spire, rebuilt 1950s interior, plus c18 house (10), 1850s classical workhouse. Across new road; note, round gardens, 1829 gas-lighting column (11), redbrick group (12) – varied bows, columned porches. To pedestrian shopping street and 1830s stucco terraces (windows – round groundfloor, 1st-floor scroll): incised Soanian pilasters, pediment, ironwork (13); 3-bay houses, Doric porches (14).

Link North to Map III In Ogle Road, (13), mid c19 stone Italianate; 1870 red terracotta Prudential (15) facing Palmerston monument; 1929-39 Civic Centre (16) with 182ft tower; new office area (17) near station; St Peter's 1846 'Sompting' tower, c14 conduit (18); up lane NE onto **Map III**.

Link South to Map II To impressive mainly c13 Bargate (19), 'opened out' since map, most important of 7 gates in c13-15 townwalls (1¼ miles, 25-30ft high, 29 towers, facing sea W and S, plus a ditch or moat to N and E). 14-storey 1963 Castle House (flats) marks the mound (20) of the Norman castle, (21) curving c14 arched bailey wall facing carpark. Of 5 medieval parishes within the walls, St John's church disappeared in c18; All Saints (22), St Lawrence (23) since map. A new Inner Ring Road enters the walled area from E through (24), to curve N from (25) as Castle Way, past St Michael's, E of (20) and (21), through walls (26), past Portland Terrace (14).

The walled town (Map II)

From Bargate, E under shops to stretch of townwall, c18 house, corner tower (1). Down High Street: 1840s with pilaster strips (pedimented windows, garlands) amid dead neo-Georgian, opposite 1900s Renaissance, Baroque (cupolas) banks. (E to wall remains (2) near site of East Gate). Best frontage: 1928 classical Lloyds; infill; early c19 Star hotel (shell window over carriageway, balcony); neo-Georgian (site of St Lawrence's); late c18 extension, pedimented redbrick Dolphin hotel (Venetian window, huge 2-storey bows, timberframe in yard); 1850s Italianate; c14/19 Holy

T BAY

A Bar Gate
B.M.

Above Bar Chapel

HANOVER BUILDINGS

Monu 20.4

45.3

ABOVE BAR

HANOVER ST.

1

2

B.M.14.8

ALBION

Castle

35.97

Lansdowne Hill

STREET

HIGH STREET

B.M.11.6
Bath

West Quay
West Gate

30.3

Michaels Church

BRIDGE ST.   ST. BERNA

3

4

5

West

Baths

Bugle Hall
B.M.20.3

Site of Town Wall
B.M.15.3

6

Royal
Pier

Dolphins

Pontoon

Town Pier

Well

Oyster
Beds

Hard

7

24.5

20.3

14.9

Rood church ruins and tower – opposite fine 1867 classical corner bank (facing mid c19 warehouse). Then Red Lion (3) – bogus timberframe front, genuine solar interior; 1894 redbrick and terracotta GPO opposite similar Gothic (stone oriels), Italianate ('Austrian' roofline).

E along Inner Ring Road into markets area to pick up townwall (4), and follow it round to Bargate. S to superb early c15 square spur (over sluice to Eastern ditch), gate (museum); through gate to almshouses, rebuilt 1861, 1190s chapel interior; outside past stucco warehouse to LHS of Water Gate, 1860s Italianate, 6-storey redbrick 1866 warehouses. Behind, ruins of c12 house, medieval basements facing (5). Round to (6): superb c14 Wool House (museum); 1846 stucco Italianate former Yacht Club (shell windowtops, colonnade); 1890s Royal Pier and rotunda – only place where water still near walls. Slender 1913 tower; along walls rampart walk to c17 timberframe, Georgian redbrick, new infill. Out c14 West Gate to battlemented early c19 stucco inn. Then c14 stretch incorporating stone walls of earlier merchants' houses, 'arcade' of 19 arches providing rampart walk (explore inside, along c12 house ruins, to Tudor House museum). Equally impressive beyond (Victorian terrace behind), with rounded towers and corner (7); E past 1960 breach to Bargate.

Across carpark; to top of Catchcold tower; curving castle bailey wall; down 'forty steps'. Back round outside of superb W stretch of walls to (6). Dive inland between Yacht Club and Wool House, to explore Bugle Street N to castle area. Left, early c19 stucco pair, infill, Georgian redbrick (good doorway), infill. Right stucco, modern offices, 1958 housing – forming courtyard round site of St John's with early c16 overhanging gabled Duke of Wellington; go through it to mixed medieval 'Norman House' (vault), vaults under new block facing IRR to N; to s, in French Street (as opposed to English, now High Street), tall 1903 warehouse (Art Nouveau panels), shell of c13 Weigh House.

Back to Duke of Wellington and superb 'historic street'. Right early c19 stucco, c19 brick RC church. Left, c18 with large 1st-floor bay window, two 2-storey square bays, 4-storey redbrick with keystones (pedimented doorway); c17/early c18 (string courses, Dutch gable); stucco (tripartite windows, arched recesses above); grand early c19 pedimented (lunette) yellowbrick (Doric key-pattern porch); infill, stucco (doorhood); to superb exposed timberframe (3 overhangs, 4 gables) c15 Tudor House museum (contemporary interiors, access through garden to c12 house ruins and townwall).

Tudor House facade forms W side of market place of Anglo-

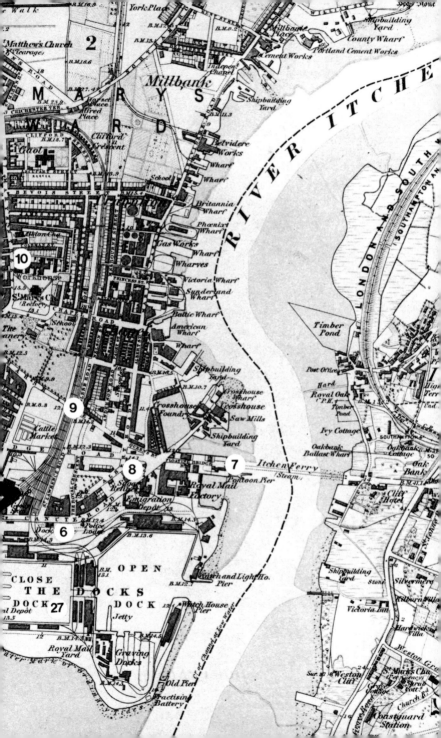

Norman town; E side St Michael's (Norman central tower, 1732 spire, 1170 font); s side corner Georgian bay windows, 1870 school, exposed timberframe (little oriel); N side early C19 Gothick three-arched redbrick. N, past new infill, house over C14 vaulted undercroft (Simnel Street), Castle House towerblock; to late C18 redbrick (good doorway, early C19 railings), facing fine 1851 Italianate yellowbrick County Court (quoins, arched centre).

North central (Map III)

Into 1770s Polygon layout (1) – 1840s yellowbrick (verandah), little pilastered terrace (segmental, tripartite windows). Past stucco/ redbrick (2) – ironwork, porches. Across gardens to Watts memorial, Cenotaph (3), (4). Returning W: polygonal 1852 church tower; yellowbrick (5 characteristic bows); columned porch; redbrick tripartite windows. Into remains of square: carpark, bus station (5) but 3 stucco villas (pilastered bows).

From (5), N into delightful Regency area. Facing pub with good porch: stucco terraces to left (s pilastered, N laurel-topped windows); good mixed frontage (columned porch, pilastered bay windows, bow with balconies over); nice brick Canton Street between; to yellowbrick and stucco bows (6), shell windowtops.

Explore superb stucco 1830s Carlton Crescent. N side: good infill, pilastered corner; advanced centre; 3-storey bow, ironwork; 4 pilastered villas; 4 massive porch columns; to bow (7). N into yellowbrick 1840s courtyard of Ordnance Survey (where maps in this book were prepared) – coat-of-arms gate, 1866 advanced centre, fantopped windows. Back to (6) s side: rows – pilastered (balconies), 4 bows, leading to minor stucco, giant arches (8); 3-storey bow; 3+3+3+1 terrace (pilastered ends, rusticated ground floor, round openings); yellowbrick infill; terrace (pilasters between houses, straight windowtops). Round varied 1830s villa pairs (scroll groundfloor windows, pedimented recessed centres): 2+3+2 splayed; 2+3+2; 1+2+3+2+1; 2+3+2; to yellowbrick, twin pilastered, shell windowtops of OS corner (9).

Across to Cranbury Place: N side trees, damaged yellowbrick terrace – pilastered ends, centre (pedimented porch, urns); s 3+1+2+1+3, balconies, tripartite, fantopped windows. To stucco villa (fluted Corinthian pilasters 'in antis'), little terrace (advanced centre) – opposite Ionic pilastered yellowbrick, pilastered stucco with 2-storey bows (10). (1840s stucco houses (11) with surrounds, quoins, porches on columns). N of (9) trees, bushes, 1850s-70 yellowbrick villas – nice cast ironwork (12) – extend to the Common, with C18 Cowherds Inn (13).

Plymouth

Superbly situated between rivers Tamar and Plym and their many inlets, present city developed from a medieval walled town on Sutton Pool (Barbican area), not called Plymouth till 1439, and a naval dockyard established in 1691 at Devonport, with a third town, Stonehouse, developing on promontory between. High mid c19 growth resulted in large areas of attractive stucco terraces, still with classical details, many with linked round groundfloor openings.

In 1888 Plymouth and Devonport became separate county boroughs, merging in 1914, becoming a 'city' in 1928. Plymouth is largely a military town – army and marines as well as navy – with much attractive c18 and c19 simple well-proportioned stone classical 'military' architecture, most inaccessible to the public, such as the c17 Citadel, not even shown on Map II. My exploration deals with outlying townships from **Map I** – which shows the Citadel and dockyard fortified against land attack, before, as at Portsmouth, an outer ring of post-1860 Palmerston forts was built (off map to N; best seen N of present A38 by-pass). It then concentrates on the Old Town (from **Map II**) – s of main shopping centre (between (1) and (19), bombed in 1941 and rebuilt to a dreary axial design which destroyed original street pattern).

The Hoe and Millbay areas (Map I)

Find Smeaton's re-erected 1756 Eddystone lighthouse. Loop to explore attractive early c19 stucco 'seaside development': curious 1836 Esplanade w of (1), incorporating three blocks with Corinthian columns and urns on top, Italianate beyond; sw to West Hoe terrace (pedimented centre) on coast; inland, past stone warehouses behind Millbay piers; lavish stone Gothic 1865 Duke of Cornwall and Italianate stucco Continental hotels (2). E to fine crescent (on map) – incised Soanian details, segmental windows and recesses, LH end giant round arches; to s, Regency villas (incised details). s past Italianate Lockyer Street villas (curious central tripartite windows); back to (1). Much of early c19 stucco development was by John Foulston (1772-1842), who laid out Union Street w, with a circus (some remains) N of (2), to Stonehouse and Devonport (largely his 1820s/30s design).

Stonehouse (Map I)

sw of Union Street, stucco pedimented terraces of Emma Place (3) with incised pilasters. s past impressive marine barracks, along main street (stucco terraces with good doorways and fanlights); to slate-hung houses and pilastered corner (4). Right, to grand gateway of Royal William Victualling Yard, 1826-35 by Rennie, impressive with colonnades (inaccessible, view from Devonport).

N of Union Street: nice stucco terraces (Adelaide Street and Clarence Place); 1761 naval hospital with huge courtyard (5) – pediments, colonnade, cupola; Foulston's Wyndham Square (6), framed by bay windows, three-bay sections alternately advanced and pedimented round St Peter's (1880s plus 1906 tower with green copper roof). Across Mill Bridge to impressive 1797 military hospital (7) with colonnade (now school).

Devonport (Map I)

Across bridge to explore from centre (8) of Foulston's planned town – 1760 former chapel, pilastered terrace, 1840s 'palazzo'. W up Ker Street to strange 1823 'Egyptian' style (former library), Town Hall Doric portico, Doric column; S past Italianate stucco to 1795 Government House with pavilions (9). To N, similar Cumberland Road, NW to 1852 market tower (since 1960 in dockyard). Past C18 church (behind, 1850s pedimented barracks centre with tower) to (10). W to main entrance (11) of dockyard (extended since map): 1720s gun wharf by Vanbrugh; C18 roperies 1,200ft long, huge timber 'slips' to house rigged sailing ships; access difficult.

Numerous stucco houses of mid C19 suburbs to N can be sampled: across stucco Albert Street to columned porches of Haddington Road (12); verandahs, ironwork at Albemarle Villas (13), with slatehung Waterloo Road to E; Italianate Nelson Villas to N (off Trafalgar Road!); Foulston's crescent of Penlee Gardens (14). Similar houses along Regency by-pass North Road N of (6); to S 1858 Gothic RC cathedral (E of St Peter's); new roadworks near North Road railway station (15); classical Portland Villas with trees (16); to North Devon Place (17).

To N attractive later Victorian suburb of Mannamead (18): stucco terraces with verandahs (College Avenue); stone neo-Jacobean with battlements (Western College Road); pedimented villas (Seymour Road); further out the villas change from Italianate stucco to brown stone. Back past (17) into town: nice Bedford Terrace to left; 1907 stone Museum and Library (19). Out to E, 45-bay pedimented terrace on left (20).

Plymouth Old Town/Barbican area (Map II)

None of medieval stone townwalls and gates of Sutton (later Plymouth) survive. Wall ran from c15 castle, sw of (9), to Hoe Gate (10); w to edge of map; n to (12), (13) – sites of gates (now shopping area); e to (2), s to original East Gate, n of (7). In 1590s, walls were extended to include Bretonside, with new gates at (14), just e of (15).

Start at spacious medieval St Andrew's (1). To n, rebuilt centre has destroyed street plan on map; w, splendid stone 1870s Gothic Guildhall with huge windows, irregular tower (to s stone house dated 1798); e, pilastered corner leading to over-restored 1450s house in High Street. To s, c15 stone Prysten House, good chunky new magistrates courts, cobbled area, splendid c16 timberframe and stone Merchant's House (museum). Mid c17 Gothic Charles church (2) is now impressive ruin on roundabout.

e past stucco terrace (3) to explore in detail superb bohemian Barbican area – cobbled streets, stone Georgian warehouses, boats, many historic houses. First Southside Street to Fish Market (4): remains of medieval Blackfriars in brewery; opposite, curving warehouse (sculptural round openings), later Georgian redbrick and stucco; several timberframe; crude pilasters, huge segmental windows; late Victorian and mixed Georgian, to Italianate curving corner, facing timberframe island house. Along water's edge to The Parade at end of basin: fine stone warehouses both sides; stone 1590 old custom house (good doorways) facing 1810 Custom House (round windows over rusticated arcade); inland to Georgian houses (mansard roofs), mural on warehouse.

Return to fine warehouse frontage behind Custom House (Woolster Street), opposite good infill housing (5). Along water's edge to warehouses (6), (7); to n, Mayflower house (c18 slatehung), on Bretonside. Back s, w up fine Looe Street frontage: Georgian stucco (good shopfronts), three timberframe (one gabled overhanging, two with oriel windows on brackets); to good Georgian (8) with tripartite windows (Arts Centre). s to The Parade, (4), irregular islands and warehouses (9) facing West Pier (plaques).

Finally attractive curving New Street ('new' in 1581): splendid overhanging timberframe, warehouses up lanes both sides; two stucco houses (timber doorways), overhanging timberframe (timber shopfront), stucco above rubble ground floor – opposite new zigzag infill flats. Street narrows at fine gabled warehouses both sides (good Georgian house in Friars' Lane). Emerge at (10), back at early c19 stucco terraces facing the Hoe; n unexpected little Hoe Gardens terrace (11) to chapel. s, lavish 1670 citadel gateway (C).

Cities and Cathedrals

Since many British towns are called cities because, before 1830, they had bishops and cathedrals (a cathedral is the seat of a bishop, from the Latin *cathedra*) and Britain's medieval cathedrals are one of the country's major tourist attractions, the explorer of the cities in this book might expect to find splendid medieval cathedrals amongst the many other historic buildings of interest. But in fact most of the great English cathedrals – Canterbury (archbishopric), Chichester, Chester, Durham, Ely, Exeter, Gloucester, Hereford, Lichfield, Lincoln, Peterborough, St Alban's, Salisbury, Southwell, Wells, Winchester, Worcester, plus the less important ones of Carlisle, Ripon, Rochester – are in 'cities' covered in *Historic Towns*, because they are relatively small towns.

The visitor to the cities in this book is much more likely to encounter cathedrals that look like medieval parish churches, or that are Victorian Gothic rather than medieval, or were built in a modern style in the 1960s and 70s. And many of the cities have two or more 'cathedrals' of different religious denominations: Manchester/Salford and ten others each having two; London has four; Glasgow and Aberdeen, in a sense (see later) three. The table on page 245 tries to clarify this situation with regard to the cities covered in this book, giving also the date they acquired city status (in some cases linked with new Anglican bishoprics, as has already been mentioned), and the dates they acquired self-government by becoming County Boroughs (or a County of a City, in Scotland).

'p.r.' in the table indicates the nine large towns that were called cities in 1830 by 'prescriptive right', but even these do not all have proper medieval cathedrals to seek out. York (an archbishopric, where the cathedral is called 'the Minster') and Norwich certainly do, as do Glasgow and, to a lesser extent, Old Aberdeen (now in the City of Aberdeen) and Llandaff (now in the City of Cardiff). But Edinburgh did not have a medieval cathedral. Bath and Coventry were only called 'city' because their Benedictine abbey churches *shared* the seat of the bishopric (with the cathedrals of Wells and Lichfield respectively); these two cities lost their cathedrals when Henry VIII dissolved the monasteries in 1541-2. Architecturally the abbey church at Bath survives (patched up after unwisely embarking on rebuilding in 1499) but not that at Coventry. At the time of the Dissolution two former monastic churches at Bristol and Oxford were converted to make new cathedrals, though Bristol was to lose the diocese back to Gloucester again between 1836 and 1897. The former Augustinian abbey church at Bristol is a small but exquisite fourteenth-century 'hall church' choir plus a similar nineteenth-century nave; and the former nunnery church at Oxford, also the chapel of Christchurch College, lost its nave for the college's 'Tom Quad'. London (not in this book) has Wren's inventive Baroque late seventeenth-century rebuilding of St Paul's cathedral, and the priory church (nineteenth-century nave) which became Southwark cathedral in 1905.

All the medieval cathedral and abbey churches just mentioned were built, of course, when Britain was part of the Roman Catholic church. The complications start when the Reformation led to the break-up of Christianity in Britain into various branches of the Protestant faith. In England, Henry VIII simply transformed the established Roman Catholic church with bishops under the Pope, into an established Church of England with bishops under the King – the doctrinal differences coming later. But Scotland, after considerable strife, ended up with an established Presbyterian Church of Scotland that does not have bishops. As a result, in England the medieval cathedral churches are in the care of the Protestant Church of England and are still the seats of 'Anglican' bishops. So also they are in Wales, where the Anglican Church *in* Wales is so called because it was 'dis-established' in 1920. In Scotland, however, the medieval cathedral churches are technically 'kirks' of the Church of Scotland and are not functionally 'cathedrals' today at all.

Roman Catholics, having originally had all the cathedral churches, became a persecuted minority and were not allowed to have churches, let alone bishops and cathedrals, until after Catholic Emancipation in 1829. Excluded from the traditional Anglican cathedral cities like Lichfield, Worcester, Oxford (and Cambridge), they then set up new bishoprics in the up-and-coming manufacturing towns that were to gain city status and which form the bulk of this book, starting in England in 1850 with Westminster (London, metropolitan), Birmingham, Liverpool and Salford (not Manchester, since an Anglican bishopric had just been established there in 1847); and in Scotland in 1878. Their cathedrals are often converted early nineteenth-century 'RC chapels', but the 1840s St Chad's at Birmingham and St Barnabas at Nottingham are quite 'cathedral-like', designed by Pugin with this status in mind, as is St John's at Norwich, and as his 1840s St George's at Southwark in London eventually became when rebuilt after damage in the Second World War.

In Scotland not only the Roman Catholics but the later Episcopal Church of Scotland lost the medieval cathedrals (the Episcopal Church is part of the Anglican Communion, linked with the Church of England). They had to build new nineteenth-century cathedrals

The cities in this book and their cathedrals

	made city	made county borough	'Anglican' cathedral	Roman Catholic cathedral
ENGLAND			*Church of England*	
Bath	p.r.	1888	—	—
Bristol	p.r.	1888	1542, medieval	Clifton, 1850, new
Coventry	p.r.	1888	1918, p.c.; new	—
Norwich	p.r.	1888	medieval	1976
Oxford	p.r.	1890	1542, medieval	—
York	p.r.	1888	medieval	—
Manchester	1853	1888	1847, p.c.	—
with **Salford**	1926	1888	—	1850
Liverpool	1880	1888	1880, new	1850, new
with **Birkenhead**	—	1888	—	—
Newcastle-upon-Tyne	1882	1888	1882, p.c.	1850
Wakefield	1888	1915	1888, p.c.	—
Birmingham	1889	1888	1905, p.c.	1850
Leeds	1893	1888	—	1878
Sheffield	1893	1888	1914, p.c.	1980
Bradford	1897	1888	1920, p.c.	—
Kingston-upon-Hull	1897	1888	—	—
Nottingham	1897	1888	—	1850
Leicester	1919	1888	1926, p.c.	—
Portsmouth	1926	1888	1927, hybrid	1882
Plymouth	1928	1888	—	1850
Cambridge	1951	—	—	—
Southampton	1964	1888	—	—
Derby	1977	1888	1927, p.c.	—
Brighton	—	1888	—	—
with **Hove**	—	—	—	—
WALES			*Church in Wales*	
Cardiff	1905	1888	Llandaff, medieval	1916
Swansea	1969	1888	—	—

	made city	made county of city	Episcopal C. of S.	*former cathedrals now C. of S. kirks*	Roman Catholic cathedral
SCOTLAND					
Aberdeen	p.r.	1900	1914	Old Aberdeen, medieval	1878
Edinburgh	p.r.	1894	1879	—	1878
Glasgow	p.r.	1894	1884	medieval	1878
Dundee	1889	1894	1865	—	1886

NOTE: p.r. – towns called 'city' in 1830 'by prescriptive right'
p.c. – cathedrals that were previously parish churches

(designed by Gilbert Scott) in Edinburgh, Glasgow and Dundee (the dates in the table are those of their consecration) and adapted an 1817 church to become a cathedral in 1914 at Aberdeen. So all four Scottish cities in this book have RC and Episcopal nineteenth-century Gothic cathedrals, and Glasgow and Aberdeen in a sense have three cathedrals – 'in a sense' because the third is the historic medieval cathedral church that is no longer the seat of a bishop but a 'kirk' of the Church of Scotland.

The Roman Catholics were so successful in the up-and-coming Victorian manufacturing towns, particularly with Irish immigrants, that the Church of England belatedly established a new set of Anglican bishoprics in major towns (often the same towns that now had Roman Catholic bishoprics) at the same time as or *after* the towns acquired 'city' status by Royal Warrant. Since these were usually based on Anglican medieval parish churches (which had nearly all been enlarged or extended since 1800), they are architecturally a third category, the 'parish-church cathedral', 'p.c.' in the table. They are very different from both the great medieval cathedrals in the cathedral cities and the Victorian Gothic RC cathedrals – cathedrals that architecturally do not look like cathedrals (i.e. no arcade, triforium, clerestory) but like parish churches. So in Scotland medieval cathedrals have become parish churches (kirks), in England medieval parish churches have sometimes become cathedrals.

Cities with these parish-church cathedrals acquired cathedrals because they were 'cities' in the worldly sense; they are not 'cities' because they have cathedrals. Because these buildings are architecturally parish churches rather than cathedral churches, I baulk at describing them as 'the cathedral', since I do not want visitors to expect a great medieval cathedral like Lichfield and then fail to appreciate the considerable merits of Thomas Archer's superb Baroque St Philip's in Birmingham or James Gibbs' spacious 1720s All Saints (with early sixteenth-century tower) in Derby because they were built as parish churches and look like parish churches.

These are the two parish-church cathedrals in my list that are post-medieval; the others should be thought of as fine medieval parish churches that reflected the importance of, say, medieval Bradford or Leicester, before these towns grew to be cities. There are only five English medieval parish churches over 20,000 square feet in area: St Botolph's, Boston; St Nicholas, Great Yarmouth (both towns in *Historic Towns*); the great fourteenth-century brick Holy Trinity at Kingston-upon-Hull; St Michael's at Coventry; and St Nicholas at Newcastle-upon-Tyne. The last two became parish-church cathedrals. Had cathedrals been needed at Hull or Nottingham, Holy Trinity, Hull, might well have become one, or another great cruciform medieval parish church, St Mary's at Nottingham, but nearby Southwell Minster was made a cathedral instead.

The mid fifteenth-century crown-spire of St Nicholas at Newcastle reminds one of the 1495 central crown-spire of the 'High Kirk of St Giles' in Edinburgh, one of an impressive number of large, usually cruciform, Scottish 'burgh kirks', which unfortunately usually became split into several churches after the Reformation (and were sometimes rebuilt); the largest was at Aberdeen; the famous steeple is the only medieval part surviving at Dundee. St Giles is the only one of the three restored to its medieval interior unity and is often inaccurately described as 'St Giles' cathedral' – it was only the seat of a bishop for brief unhappy periods in the seventeenth century.

Visitors may well mistake for a cathedral the lavish cruciform stone-vaulted St Mary Redcliffe at Bristol, described by Queen Elizabeth as 'the fairest, goodliest, and most famous parish church in England', endowed largely by two wealthy Bristol merchants, William Canynge the elder and younger, at the time Bristol became the first English town to attain county status (in 1373).

Back to cathedrals and my list. There are 38 'cathedrals' marked, found in 24 of the cities. Only seven have medieval cathedral churches – two being Scottish kirks; eight have parish-church cathedrals (two eighteenth-century, six medieval); and Portsmouth has a strange hybrid – a small but cathedral-like vaulted late twelfth-century priory choir, 1680s plaster extensions as a parish church, unconvincing 1930s nave as a cathedral. So 22, the majority, of the cathedrals encountered when exploring these cities are nineteenth- or twentieth-century churches, not medieval.

Some of these churches are impressive and 'cathedral-like'; for instance 1873-79 St Mary's Episcopal cathedral at Edinburgh by the famous English church architect Gilbert Scott is, in my opinion, the most impressive Victorian Gothic cathedral in Britain – its three spires reminiscent of Pearson's late Victorian cathedral at Truro. (Bentley in his great 1890s Roman Catholic Metropolitan cathedral at Westminster in London deliberately chose a Byzantine style to avoid comparison with Westminster Abbey.) Gilbert Scott's sons, George Gilbert and John Oldrid Scott, designed the amazing stone-vaulted 1884-1910 Roman Catholic St John's at Norwich 275 ft long and 80 ft high, only recently given the cathedral status it so fully deserves; and his grandson, Giles Gilbert Scott, designed the huge twentieth-century Gothic Anglican cathedral at Liverpool, only finished in 1978, the largest cathedral in area in Britain, with 104,275 square feet compared with Wren's St Paul's in London at 87,400, and the largest medieval cathedral, York Minster, 60,952 (figures from *Blue Guide England*). The Roman Catholics also built a brand new twentieth-century central planned cathedral in Liverpool (Gibberd's 1960s concrete 'Mersey Funnel') on Lutyens extraordinary 1930s Byzantine/classical crypt; and at Clifton, Bristol, they replaced a timber shed of 1848 (on a different site) with a more sophisticated central plan cathedral, designed by the Percy Thomas Partnership and consecrated in 1973.

This chapter is summed up by the example of Coventry: like Nottingham earlier, 'typical' of the cities in this book in its population of 300,000 and its combination of medieval and nineteenth/twentieth-century elements. Coventry had first a medieval priory church which shared the seat of the bishopric with Lichfield – the diocese of Coventry and Lichfield – which made Coventry a 'city' by prescriptive right. The priory church was dissolved in the 1540s and destroyed. Coventry then acquired a parish-church cathedral in 1918, the huge medieval St Michael's, which was burnt out in the famous air-raid of 1940. This was replaced by Basil Spence's 1954-62 cathedral – 'modern' in its concrete, zigzag windows with stained glass (plus Piper's superb curved baptistery window) and Graham Sutherland's huge green tapestry, but 'traditional' in its basilica plan with slender columns supporting merely the 'vaulted' canopy and in sharp contrast to the new RC cathedrals at Liverpool and Clifton. All three of Coventry's cathedrals are encountered when one visits the area today: for the ruins of medieval St Michael's form an impressive forecourt (which emphasises its area of over 20,000 square feet) to Basil Spence's cathedral which, being sited north-south rather than the usual east-west, means that the present altar, under the tapestry, is, as a nice piece of cyclical history, on the site of the altar of the great Norman Benedictine priory church (marked today by the Georgian Priory Row) that formed Coventry's *first* cathedral.

Further notes on the maps
First edition OS 1" maps

The first edition OS 1" maps reproduced in the book are as follows:

SCOTLAND

Sheet	30	Lanarkshire	**Glasgow I**	published 1866
	48	Perth ⎱	**Dundee I**	1870/
	49	Arbroath ⎰		1862
	77	Aberdeenshire	**Aberdeen I**	1872

ENGLAND AND WALES 34.03 series with additions

Sheet	11	Hampshire	**Portsmouth I**	1810+
	23/24	(published together) Devonshire	**Plymouth I**	1809+
	35	Gloucestershire	**Bristol I**	1830+
	36	Glamorganshire	**Cardiff II** (top half)	1833+
	62	Warwickshire	**Birmingham I**	1834+
	79	Lancashire	**Liverpool and Birkenhead I**	1840+
	82	Yorkshire	**Sheffield III**	1840+
	88/89	Lancashire	**Manchester and Salford I**	both 1843+
	88	Lancashire	**Manchester and Salford III**	1843+
	93	Yorkshire	**Leeds I**	1858

(Two 1" sheets are used for Dundee, 48 Perth on the left, 49 Arbroath on the right; the two used for Manchester and Salford are similarly side by side, 88 being the sheet on the left.)

Continued

First edition OS 6" maps

Most of the maps come from only one 6" sheet (publication date given first, followed by the survey date in brackets):

SCOTLAND

Aberdeenshire 75	**Aberdeen**	1869 (1865–67)
Edinburghshire 2	**Edinburgh**	1855 (1852)
Forfarshire 54	**Dundee**	1865 (1860–62)
Lanarkshire 6	**Glasgow**	1865 (1858)

ENGLAND AND WALES

Cheshire 13	**Birkenhead**	1882 (1872–75)
Devonshire 123	**Plymouth**	1867 (1856)
Glamorganshire 24	**Swansea**	1884 (1876–79)
Hampshire 65	**Southampton**	1871 (1866–69)
83	**Portsmouth**	1857 (1856)
Lancashire 104	**Manchester and Salford**	1848 (1845)
Norfolk 63SE	**Norwich**	1887 (1880–83)
Northumberland 97	**Newcastle-upon-Tyne**	1864 (1858)
Nottinghamshire 42NW	**Nottingham**	1885 (1880–81)
Somerset 14NW	**Bath**	1887 (1883–85)
Sussex 66	**Brighton and Hove**	1880 (1873–75)
Warwickshire 21SE	**Coventry**	1888 (1887)
Yorkshire 174	**York**	1853 (1846–50)
216	**Bradford**	1852 (1847–50)
218	**Leeds**	1852 (1846–47)
240	**Kingston-upon-Hull**	1856 (1853)
248	**Wakefield**	1854 (1849–51)
294	**Sheffield**	1855 (1850–51)

Four cities need two 6" sheets, one above the other:

Cambridgeshire 40SW	**Cambridge**	1888 (1886)
47NW	(city centre)	1888 (1886)
Glamorganshire 43	**Cardiff** (city centre)	1886 (1875–81)
47	(Bute Town)	1885 (1878–79)
Lancashire 106	**Liverpool** (city centre)	1851 (1845–49)
113		1850 (1846–48)
Oxfordshire 33	**Oxford** (city centre)	1887 (1876)
39		1886 (1876–78)

Two cities use two 6″ sheets, side by side:

Derbyshire 49SE 50SW   **Derby** 1887 (1880-82)/1890 (1880-82)

Leicestershire 31SE 31SW **Leicester** 1888 (1884-85)/1888 (1885)

Two cities, most awkwardly, use four map sheets, one pair above the other:

Gloucestershire for **Bristol**

71SE	1889(1880-83)	72SW	1889(1881-83)
75NE	1887(1881-83)	76NW	1887(1881-84)

Warwickshire for **Birmingham**

13NE	1890(1886-88)	14NW	1889(1887-88)
13SE	1890(1882-87)	14SW	1890(1887-88)

For a map buff who wants to find out which maps use particular OS sheet(s) – not uniquely defined by the date of publication given in the caption – 1″ maps, Bristol I and Birmingham I, give the general picture and double-page 6″ maps, Bristol II and Birmingham V (Edgbaston), include all four sheets (Warwickshire 14NW ,covering Birmingham city centre, Gloucestershire 71SE Bristol Clifton).

Acknowledgements

As with my earlier book, *Historic Towns*, Nikolaus Pevsner's marvellous Buildings of England series has again proved invaluable. I should like to thank the planning departments of all the cities in the book (and of some former County Boroughs which were finally excluded). They provided information on Conservation Areas, and listed buildings – and many commented on early typescripts. I should particularly like to mention Menna Gerrard and Kenneth Lightfoot of Swansea, and Mr. E. Davies of Cardiff; Mr. J. A. Souter of Aberdeen and Mr. P. J. Marshall of Dundee; Stuart Eydmann of Edinburgh and Mrs G. McLaren of Glasgow – detailed information on Welsh and Scottish cities being of special importance because they were not covered by Pevsner. And also: Elizabeth Irving of Newcastle, Christopher Hughes of Bradford, Mr. B. Wilson of Manchester, Mr. G. Lane and Mr Nierop-Reading of Norwich, Mr. R. Craig of Nottingham, Shirley Harris of Leicester, Mrs Oviatt-Ham and Mr N. Hellawell of Cambridge, John Ashdown of Oxford, Mr Wark of Southampton, Mr K.D. Fines and Roger Dowty of Brighton, Michael Ray of Hove.

Finally, I am most grateful to Anne Watts of A & C Black as a most patient editor, and to Paul White for his constant encouragement and enthusiasm for the maps – on which he inserted the numbers with amazing dexterity and historical sensitivity.

Index